TRANSITION AND TRADITION
IN MORAL THEOLOGY

Other Books by Charles E. Curran

Christian Morality Today

A New Look at Christian Morality

Contemporary Problems in Moral Theology

Catholic Moral Theology in Dialogue

The Crisis in Priestly Ministry

Politics, Medicine and Christian Ethics: A Dialogue with Paul
    Ramsey

New Perspectives in Moral Theology

Ongoing Revision in Moral Theology

Themes in Fundamental Moral Theology

Issues in Sexual and Medical Ethics

Dissent in and for the Church (Charles E. Curran et al.)

The Responsibility of Dissent: The Church and Academic Freedom
    (John F. Hunt and Terrence R. Connelly with Charles E. Curran
    et al.)

Absolutes in Moral Theology? (editor)

Contraception: Authority and Dissent (editor)

Transition and Tradition
in Moral Theology

CHARLES E. CURRAN

UNIVERSITY OF NOTRE DAME PRESS
NOTRE DAME - LONDON

Library of Congress Cataloging in Publication Data

Curran, Charles E 1934–
    Transition and tradition in moral theology.

    Includes index.
    1. Christian ethics—Catholic authors—Addresses,
essays, lectures.   2. Social ethics—Addresses, essays,
lectures.   3. Medical ethics—Addresses, essays,
lectures.   I. Title.
BJ1249.C843   241'.04'2   78-20877
ISBN 0-268-01837-5

On July 30, 1968, after having studied the papal encyclical *Humanae vitae*, I acted as spokesperson for a group of theologians in issuing a statement recognizing that in theory and in practice Roman Catholics could dissent from the specific conclusion of the encyclical condemning artificial contraception. Over 600 persons with competency in the sacred sciences eventually signed this statement. The declarations and actions of the twenty signers from The Catholic University of America were examined by a board of inquiry which deliberated for the greater part of the academic year. On April 1, 1969, the final report of the inquiry committee found that "the commentary made by the subject professors in their July 30, 1968, statement is adequately supported by theological scholarship, and their actions in composing, issuing and disseminating this statement did not violate the professors' commitments to the University or to the academic or theological communities."

This book is gratefully dedicated to

my colleagues, the subject professors at
The Catholic University of America

our legal counsel,
John F. Hunt, Jr., and Terrence R. Connelly
of the firm of Cravath, Swaine and Moore of New York City

our academic counsel, Robert K. Webb

all those who supported or signed our statement
especially those unjustly accused of disloyalty

Contents

Acknowledgments   ix

Introduction   xi

PART ONE: GENERAL MORAL THEOLOGY

1. An Overview and Appraisal of Contemporary
   Moral Theology   3

2. Moral Theology in the Light of Reactions to
   Humanae vitae   29

3. Moral Theology, Psychiatry and Homosexuality   59

PART TWO: SOCIAL ETHICS

4. American Catholic Social Ethics, 1880–1965   83

5. Social Ethics: Future Agenda for Theology
   and the Church   117

6. The Right to Health Care and Distributive
   Justice   139

PART THREE: MEDICAL ETHICS

7. Roman Catholic Medical Ethics   173

8. Abortion: Ethical Aspects   207

9. Abortion: Legal and Public Funding Aspects   230

   Index   251

Acknowledgments

I want to thank all those who have encouraged and helped my research. At this time I am particularly grateful to the librarians of The Catholic University of America, especially Carolyn T. Lee, head of the Theology Library, and her associates Shirley Pototsky and David Gilson, as well as Nellie Lee Powell, head of the Nursing Library; also to Johann Klodzen, administrative assistant of the Department of Theology, to Patricia Whitlow for typing the manuscript and to Mary Maher, S.S.N.D., for preparing the index. I also appreciate the encouragement and assistance of the administration and staff of the University of Notre Dame Press, especially that of John Ehmann.

Many of these studies were first presented in various symposia and lectures sponsored by academic institutions. In particular, Chapter Two was originally prepared as the Aquinas Lecture at the College of Great Falls in Great Falls, Montana; Chapters Six and Nine were originally composed for a symposium "Health Care Delivery: What's Needed? What's Fair?" sponsored by the School of Religion of the University of Iowa.

I appreciatively acknowledge the permission of the following publications and publishers for permission to include in this book studies which first appeared in their publications: Academia Alfonsiana, Rome, for "An Overview and Appraisal of Contemporary Moral Theology," which originally appeared in *In libertatem vocati estis: miscellanea Bernard Häring*, ed.

H. Boelaars and R. Tremblay; *Hospital Progress* 59 (July 1978), for the first part of "Moral Theology in the Light of Reactions to *Humanae vitae*"; *Commonweal* 105 (July 7, 1978), for the second part of "Moral Theology in the Light of Reactions to *Humanae vitae*"; *The Bulletin of the National Guild of Catholic Psychiatrists* 24 (1978), for "Moral Theology, Psychiatry and Homosexuality"; Fordham University Press, for "American Catholic Social Ethics, 1880–1965," which was published in *Thought* 52 (1977); Seabury Press, for "Social Ethics: Future Agenda for Theology and the Church," which appeared in *Toward Vatican III: The Work That Needs to Be Done*, ed. David Tracy with Hans Küng and Johann B. Metz; "Roman Catholic Medical Ethics" and "Abortion: Ethical Aspects" are reproduced by permission of The Free Press, a Division of Macmillan Publishing Co., Inc., and The Kennedy Institute of Ethics, Georgetown University; they were originally published in *Encyclopedia of Bioethics*, Warren T. Reich, Editor in Chief; copyright © 1978 by Georgetown University, Washington, D.C.

Introduction

"Transition" aptly describes what has been occurring in contemporary Roman Catholic moral theology. Since the time of the Second Vatican Council the Roman Catholic Church has been experiencing many changes. Perhaps nowhere have these changes been felt more keenly than in the area of moral theology. Different approaches are present throughout Catholic life and theology, but questions of moral theology often have greater existential impact on the life of the church.

One might properly describe the changes that have taken place in the last few years in moral theology as drastic. On the level of methodology gone is the perennial philosophy which served as the basis for moral theology until a few years ago. Now within Catholic moral theology there exist many different methodological approaches. On the level of content questions and specific issues one sees a diversity or pluralism that contrasts sharply with the image of the pre-Vatican II church. On the level of response to hierarchical church teaching on moral issues there is talk of the possibility of dissent at times rather than the absolute insistence on obedience.

"Tradition" has often been linked with Catholic theology. The Catholic faith position has insisted on the place of both scripture and tradition. Catholic theology has viewed its faith and life in continuity with the community of believers who have lived through the centuries. In the theological enterprise tradition has been most significant. The church continues to venerate and study the theological geniuses of the past. The historical roots of our theology are constantly being explored from the patristic times through the Middle Ages and the Reformation era down to the present.

Can the acceptance of transition be reconciled with the insistence on tradition? This question constitutes the underlying theme of this book. The studies stand on their own as independent essays on significant methodological and substantive questions in contemporary moral theology. Without attempting to impose a false unity on these different studies, one can find in all these pages an attempt to grapple with the problem of transition and tradition.

There can be no doubt that transition characterizes much of what is found in these chapters. The differences between these studies and the manuals of moral theology which were used until the time of the Second Vatican Council in the mid-1960s are startling. There are those who have seen so much transition in my approach to moral theology that they claim I have abandoned the Catholic tradition. My ethical methodology differs considerably from that proposed in the manuals. Specific questions are answered in ways even opposed to the answers given in the past. My vision of the church recognizes a degree of pluralism and of differences on specific moral questions which was totally unheard of a few years ago. No attempts are made to gloss over differences with the past teaching. I insist that the papal teaching condemning artificial contraception for married couples is wrong. The chapters on medical ethics and homosexuality indicate many concrete solutions which differ from past Catholic approaches and from the official teaching of the hierarchical magisterium.

Despite the obvious emphasis on transition these pages also give great importance to tradition. To my knowledge nowhere else does there appear a history of medical ethics. Chapter Eight, presenting a long historical overview of this topic, does not in any way pretend to be a full history or a final word, but rather constitutes a significant beginning which calls for much greater development. Even though my own response to specific questions in many areas such as homosexuality and abortion laws disagrees with some older solutions, these chapters at least show the need to know and be familiar with the tradition. Chapter Four also has important historical significance as it represents a first attempt to study, compare and contrast different approaches to social ethics in the history of the American Catholic experience. Chapter Six attempts to use the traditional category of distributive justice in discussing the very contemporary question of the individual's right to health care. Readers will probably be surprised to see how often the Catholic theological tradition is referred to in these pages and how much emphasis is given to the historical aspect of questions.

Aspects of both transition and tradition appear throughout this book. Are these two aspects merely juxtaposed and existing uncomfortably in what might be called a loose pluralism which is so weak that it has room for everything? The underlying theme of the book is much different. There is no incompatibility between transition and tradition properly understood. Yes, there will always be tensions and even disagreements, but the proper understanding of tradition should include the reality of transition. Tradition must be an ongoing, living reality—something more than merely a dead letter or fossil remain from the past. Tradition from the theological perspective refers to the ways in which the Christian community throughout its history has lived and thought about itself. This ongoing history of the Christian community both in thought and in action has not only a past but also a present and a future. Tradition must always be a living tradition.

Roman Catholic theology today cannot simply jettison its theological and ethical traditions which have been so much a part of our historical existence. At the same time Catholic theology must avoid the ahistorical fallacy of uncritically accepting and repeating what was said and done in the past. A true understanding of tradition recognizes both its importance and limitations. Historicity reminds us of both continuity and discontinuity with the past. The challenge for Roman Catholic theology is to recognize this historicity and be true both to its historical development and to the signs of the times.

This book is written from such a perspective. Although

there are many disagreements and differences with aspects of Catholic moral theology as it has been presented in the past, on a deeper level there is a conscious attempt to work out of the Catholic tradition and to modify the tradition in the light of contemporary realities and the eschatological pull of the future. Transition and tradition, rather than being opposed, can and should be unified in the concept of a living tradition. Living tradition will be willing to recognize continuity and discontinuity, truth and error and strengths and weaknesses in the past. The studies presented in this book attempt to illustrate the meaning of doing Catholic theological ethics within the framework of a living tradition aware of the past, in dialogue with the present, and hoping in the future.

TRANSITION AND TRADITION
IN MORAL THEOLOGY

PART ONE

General Moral Theology

1: An Overview and Appraisal of Contemporary Moral Theology

Change and aggiornamento have characterized Catholic life and thought in the last fifteen years. It could be argued with conviction that change has been felt in the area of moral theology more than in any other theological area. The theoretical aspects of moral theology have opened up many new horizons, but changes in moral theology have above all reflected and affected the way in which Catholic people live their lives.

The first part of this chapter will briefly and systematically summarize the changes that have occurred in moral theology. The second section will try to show that these changes in general are in conformity with the best understanding of the Roman Catholic theological tradition. The third section will point out some of the continuing questions and challenges that face moral theology now and in the future.

I. New Developments in Moral Theology

Perhaps the most basic change in moral theology has been the orientation of the discipline itself. The manuals of moral theology which were generally used before the Second Vatican Council focused primarily on training confessors for the sacrament of penance with an emphasis on what constitutes sin and the difference between mortal and venial sin. Such a moral theology became separated from the other aspects of theology—especially scriptural, systematic and spiritual theology—and was characterized by minimalism, legalism, extrinsicism and juridicism. The Tübingen school of moral theology and the Thomistic renewal in the twentieth century reacted against such an approach, but Bernard Häring's *The Law of Christ* together with his other prolific writings and lectures has had the most influence in changing the orientation of moral theology.[1] This section will frequently use Häring's contributions to illustrate the changes which have occurred in moral theology.

Moral theology has also tried to overcome the older dichotomy between the supernatural and the natural, the gospel and daily life, and the church and the world. All these dichotomies basically come from the same two-layer view of the world no longer accepted by most contemporary Catholic moral theologians. The natural order as such does not exist and never has existed. There is only one history. The gospel and God's loving gift must be related to the personal, political, social and economic circumstances in which we live.[2] There will continue to be discussions about the exact relationship between evangelization and humanization, but theology can never again accept such a two-layer version of reality. I have proposed a stance for moral theology based on the fivefold Christian mysteries of creation, sin, incarnation, redemption and resurrection destiny to avoid both the danger of a two-layer view and the opposite danger of collapsing the eschaton and thereby immediately identifying all reality with the kingdom of God. One must overcome the dichotomy but recognize that limitation and sin still characterize our present human existence, and the fullness of the eschaton will always be beyond us.

Perhaps the most basic question in systematic moral theology concerns the model chosen as the paradigm of the Christian life. Philosophical and theological ethics have traditionally talked about the deontological and the teleological models, which base ethics on moral duties and final causes, but lately a third model of relationality-responsibility has emerged.[3] Although the Thomistic teaching was teleological (the first discussion in the *Summa* of Aquinas concerns the ultimate end, and moral theology then considers the means by which this end is attained), Catholic moral theology and catechesis were heavily deontological. The framework of our teaching was the ten commandments. Law became the primary model for moral theology and Christian life. It is interesting as an example to see the contrast in the developing moral theology of Bernard Häring. In his major systematic work, appearing early in the 1950s, he insisted on an ethics of responsibility based on the Christian's response to the gracious gift of God in Christ Jesus. The biblical foundation for such an approach rested on the primacy of God's love and the covenant relationship between God and God's people.[4] However, the book itself was entitled *The Law of Christ.* The deontological model still was present in the very title of the work, although the law was now understood as the law of the spirit giving life in Christ Jesus. In later works the deontological language changes to a relationality-responsibility formula for moral theology and the Christian life.[5]

Emphasis on the person and interiority should characterize Catholic moral theology. To its credit a Thomistic approach insisted on the importance of the virtues as modifying the subject.[6] Contemporary theology, perhaps because it has been overly concerned about the question of situation ethics, sometimes fails to give enough importance to the subject and the dispositions which should characterize the subject. From his earliest writings Bernard Häring insisted on the importance of the biblical concept of conversion. In response to the gracious gift of the kingdom the Christian must change one's heart and believe in the good news. An insistence on continual conversion as the law of the Christian life illustrates the dynamic aspect of the Christian life. Through growth in the virtues one shares more deeply in the Christian life.[7]

This approach to moral theology insists on the universal call of all Christians to perfection and thus overcomes the minimalism of an extrinsicist and legalistic approach to moral theology. No longer can one admit the existence of two classes of citizens in the kingdom of God. The older distinction between spiritual theology and moral theology can no longer exist.[8]

Moral theology today is intimately connected with both sacred scripture and the liturgy. A scripturally based moral theology lays the foundation for overcoming the dichotomy between the gospel and daily life and for the insistence that all Christians are called to be perfect even as our heavenly Father is perfect (Mt. 5:48). Questions are being raised today about the methodological problem or the proper use of the scriptures in moral theology. Such questions arise in the light of both the importance and the limitations of the scriptures. The scriptures themselves are historically and culturally conditioned so that one cannot go immediately from the scripture to present circumstances. In addition, eschatological overtones affect much of the New Testament considerations of the Christian life. It is essential that there be some hermeneutic or methodology by which one employs scriptural insights in developing a systematic moral theology.[9]

Newer approaches to moral theology recognize the importance of the liturgy. The manuals of moral theology presented the sacraments in terms of obligations to fulfill in administering and receiving these "channels of God's grace." The Christian life consists in our response to God's gracious gift, so that we human beings are primarily worshippers. If the sacraments truly symbolize and make present the gift of God's love and our response, then they take on an important aspect for the living out of the Christian life and for our reflection on Christian existence.[10]

Other significant changes have occurred in moral theology's understanding of anthropology. The personal aspect receives more importance than in the manuals of moral theology which stress nature rather than person. The danger of identifying the natural with the physical and the biological has been recognized. Häring, for example, was one of the first to point out that masturbation for seminal analysis or artificial insemination did not participate and share in the moral malice of masturbation as such.[11]

Both scriptural and contemporary philosophical insights

point to a more historical understanding of human existence. A more historically conscious moral methodology realizes the need for a more inductive approach in moral theology. Bernard Häring constantly emphasized the *kairos* as the appointed time that called for a fitting response.[12] In addition, Häring has recognized the importance of reading the signs of the times.[13] However, in this endeavor one must employ the data of the other human sciences that can reveal to us the proper meaning of the signs of the times. Here Häring has used sociological insights and findings in his attempt to understand better the meaning of the human.[14]

All these changes in Catholic moral theology have resulted in a pluralism of moral theologies today. No longer is there a monolithic Catholic moral theology based on a perennial philosophy. Today there exist a variety and multiplicity of methodologies with different philosophical underpinnings.

All these changes in orientation and methodology have had a bearing on different approaches to particular questions. Catholic theologians have argued for different positions on such questions as contraception, sterilization, the beginning of human life, the possibility of remarriage after divorce. Especially in the area of sexual and medical questions and of absolute norms in moral theology contemporary moral theologians have argued for a change in some of the past moral teachings of the Catholic Church. In this area the most striking development has been the emergence of dissent within the Roman Catholic theological community from the teachings of the hierarchial magisterium on specific moral issues. The question of dissent came to the fore in reaction to the papal encyclical *Humanae vitae* in 1968 condemning artificial contraception.[15] Chapter Two will consider these questions in detail.

II. Justification of the Developments

The second section will attempt to justify as legitimate these developments which have occurred within contemporary

Roman Catholic moral theology. Obviously it would be impossible to attempt a justification of all these different developments. It is necessary to limit the following considerations to
the general direction of the changes in contemporary Catholic
moral theology, especially in comparison with the teaching and
approach of the manuals of moral theology. In general, I
maintain that the Catholic theological tradition properly understood serves as a basis for the type of changes which has
occurred. These changes are not aberrations but rather are in
keeping with the best of the Catholic theological tradition,
even though they might seem to be at times different from and
even in contradiction with the moral theology found in the
manuals used before the Second Vatican Council.

Catholic moral theology has always insisted on the reality of
mediation; in fact, mediation characterizes much of the
Catholic self-understanding in all areas. Catholic theology sees
the church as mediating the presence of the risen Lord in our
midst. While other Christians might insist on immediate
relationships with God, Catholic theology sees the relationship
with God and Jesus in and through the Spirit and the church as
the visible reality which makes present the mystery of God's
love. God comes to us and we go to God in and through the
church. The whole sacramental system of the Roman Catholic
Church rests on this principle. Catholic insistence on Mary and
the saints likewise illustrates the principle of mediation, since
these people shared more fully in the mystery of God's life and
responded more fervently to the call. The danger which was
not always avoided in the past consisted in absolutizing the
medium and failing to recognize that it was a means to another
reality. The church readily became identified with the kingdom rather than being understood as a sacrament or a sign of
the kingdom. Exaggeration in devotion to Mary and the saints
also absolutized what was to be only a mediation and participation in the mystery of Jesus. However, these abuses do not take
away from the importance of the reality of mediation itself.

This same principle of mediation serves as the basis for
Catholic theology's characteristic acceptance of analogy and
reasoning from the creature to the creator. Catholic thought

insisted that the goodness and beauty of the creator can be seen in creation. An older apologetics went so far as to claim that one could prove the existence of God on the basis of the beauty, order and goodness of creation. Here again in my judgment the claim to prove the existence of God from reason alone went too far, but the underlying theological understanding is correct. There is an analogy between human existence and divine. The God of creation is the God of redemption who is also made known to us in the work of creation. Today theologians often see this analogy in other terms than that of natural creation, but the acceptance of analogy remains basic to the Catholic theological tradition.

Catholic moral theology exemplifies the same basic acceptance of mediation. The natural law according to the Thomistic understanding is the participation of the eternal law in the rational creature.[16] How do we know what God wants us to do? Ordinarily the Catholic tradition does not appeal immediately to the will of God, the reason of God or the word of God. Human reason is able to discover the order that God has put into the world. The natural, the human and reason are all mediations. Catholic moral theology has insisted that to discover what it is that God is asking of us, we ordinarily appeal, not directly and immediately to God, but rather to human nature and human reason.

As a result Catholic approaches to ethics have insisted that ethical wisdom and knowledge are to be found not only in the scriptures but also in natural law, not only in faith but also in reason. It is the one God who both redeemed and created and does not contradict himself. So firm is this understanding that Catholic thought boldly proclaimed that faith and reason can never contradict one another.[17] One can only admire the courageous vision that would make such a strong assertion.

The early church recognized this aspect. Bernard Häring indicates that the chief preoccupation of Clement of Alexandria was to show the intimate relation between the positive values of pagan philosophy and morality and Christian revelation and morality.[18] This positive approach to reason was behind the church's fostering of education and universities in the Middle Ages. Theologians in the Middle Ages were often people with a great interest in all aspects of science as illustrated in the work of Albert the Great and Roger Bacon.

Thomas Aquinas, the greatest theologian in the Catholic tradition, exemplifies this same approach. The great genius of Aquinas showed itself in his use of Aristotelian philosophy to better understand and explain the mystery of Christian faith. Aquinas was not satisfied with merely repeating what his predecessors had said, but rather he used the new Aristotelian philosophy which had been purified from its poor translations for developing a systematic theological synthesis which will be admired by all subsequent theologians. Thomas Aquinas thus stands as a challenge to all theologians to do in their times and circumstances what he did in his.

However, at times the Catholic theological tradition did not always live up to the basic insight that faith and reason can never contradict one another. In the nineteenth century Catholic life faced new developments in many areas of existence—politics, science, philosophy, scripture and theology.[19] The French Revolution had ushered in a new period of democratic government based on freedom. The cry then arose for a free church in a free state with a call for a separation of church and state. The Roman Catholic Church generally struggled against these new democratic forms of government. Papal teachings opposed the concept of freedom which seemed to deny any aspect of God's law and human beings' obligations to God.[20] The Roman Catholic Church stressed the obligation of the state to worship the one true God in the one true church.

Evolution was being proposed by science, but the Catholic Church often saw this as an attack upon the doctrine of creation by God. In scripture studies German scholars were beginning to apply the tools of historical research to the scriptures themselves. Fruits of this scholarship included, for example, the recognition that the Pentateuch was not written by Moses but rather it contained a compilation of different traditions which were written much later. Again Roman Catholicism saw a threat in these new developments. Later the

Pontifical Biblical Commission was established and served as a means of preventing the use of these critical tools in Catholic biblical scholarship.[21] In the intellectual world a number of scholars headed by Johann Döllinger believed that Catholic theology and philosophy must come abreast of contemporary philosophical developments. In 1863 they scheduled a conference in Munich, but the reaction of Rome was negative to that particular development and to the thesis behind it.[22] Later the whole question of modernism surfaced some of these same concerns.

In general, one can characterize the reaction of the Catholic Church to developments in the nineteenth century as negative. The best illustration of this can be found in the Syllabus of Errors, a collection of eighty propositions culled from previously condemned statements and issued by Pope Pius IX in 1864.[23] These newer viewpoints were often rejected in the name of the past and in what had existed in an earlier period. The Middle Ages was looked upon as a golden period which unfortunately began to crumble with the Protestant revolution and the attacks of the Enlightenment. In the realm of philosophy and theology modern developments were condemned, and the teaching of the past was instilled. It was only in the nineteenth century that Thomas Aquinas was made the patron of Catholic theology and philosophy.[24] As expressed in the Code of Canon Law, Catholic theology and philosophy is to be taught *"ad Angelici Doctoris rationem, principia et doctrinam"* (1366). Thus in the nineteenth century philosophy and theology were further cut off from the current thought patterns of the day. Catholic philosophy and theology were identified with scholasticism and especially with the teaching of Thomas Aquinas.

The good features of the Catholic reaction to what was happening in the nineteenth century must in fairness be pointed out. Not everything that occurred in the nineteenth century was good. The liberalism of the time often rested on a poor concept of individualistic freedom which exalted the individual and forgot about the individual's important relationships with God, neighbor and the world.[25] In the economic sphere this one-sided individualism supported a *laissez faire* capitalism which the popes strongly condemned by reminding all about the rights of the workers and the obligation of owners and employers. The Thomistic renewal brought about by Pope Leo XIII accomplished many good things as exemplified in the area of social ethics and the papal social encyclicals beginning with *Rerum novarum* and continuing to the present day.

But there were very significant negative aspects in the official reaction of the church to developments in the nineteenth century in general and especially in regard to the official imposition of Thomism as *the* Catholic philosophy and theology. There can be no doubt in the light of the historical circumstances that the official imposition of Thomism was an attempt to prevent any dialogue with the contemporary world and its thought patterns. Catholic theology and philosophy became even more entrenched in an intellectual ghetto during the twentieth century. The Second Vatican Council called for dialogue with the modern world, but before that time dialogue was anathema. If a continual dialogue had been taking place since the nineteenth century, there would have been no need for the Second Vatican Council, or at least its work would have been less dramatic. The horrendous irony is that in the nineteenth century and for the first part of the twentieth century Thomas Aquinas was used to prevent dialogue with the modern world, whereas his great theological genius was to explain and understand the Christian message in dialogue with the thought patterns of his own day.

The era of the Second Vatican Council differs considerably from the previous one hundred years because we are now called to dialogue with other Christians and non-Christians and with the modern world. Moral theology like all theology and life in the church has undergone very significant changes in the past few years as a result of this more open environment. And these changes seem all the greater because before then an unwillingness to dialogue prevented any kind of change from occurring. Yet at times in the last decade some theologians have not been critical enough of the contemporary ethos and of developments in science and technology. Human limitation and sinfulness will always affect reality. Dialogue calls for an honest and critical relationship and not merely an uncritical acceptance of whatever exists.

The previous era had not followed out that very significant principle of Catholic theology that faith and reason can never contradict one another. However, such an understanding of the importance and significance of human reason, even though at times it can be partially lost, is so engrained in the Catholic theological tradition that it cannot be forgotten for long. With this self-understanding Catholic theology possesses a methodology which can and should serve as a basis for self-criticism and continual development. In this way one cannot definitively prove that all the contemporary developments in Catholic moral theology are true, but one can and should see them as very healthy signs of the ongoing search of faith and reason to understand how the Christian is called to respond to God's gift in Jesus Christ in the light of the scriptures, the historical tradition and the signs of the times.[26]

There is a second significant characteristic of Catholic theology which also helps to explain and to a certain extent justify the trend of recent developments in moral theology. Catholic theology has perennially emphasized that the scriptures alone are not sufficient. The Catholic theological outlook has recognized that scripture and tradition are necessary.[27] There is an obvious connection between the insistence, on the one hand, of faith and reason and, on the other hand, of scripture and tradition. In my judgment both these couplets point to the Catholic insistence on mediation which was mentioned earlier.

The insistence on both scripture and tradition recognizes that one must always understand the gospel message in the light of the times and circumstances in which one lives. Such a recognition at the very minimum acknowledges the hermeneutic problem that one cannot go directly from the scriptures to the contemporary situation. This understanding also calls for a continual growth both in the life and in the theology of the church which unfortunately was forgotten about in the period before the Second Vatican Council.

One of the significant periods in the life of the church

occurred in the fourth and fifth centuries in the controversies about the Trinity and Christology. Here discussions centered on the most important aspects of the Christian faith—what do we mean by God and who is Jesus Christ? Gradually the church accepted the understanding that in God there are three persons and in Jesus Christ there are two natures and one person. It is important to recognize the significance of such a development. The scriptures themselves did not know the meaning of the terms nature and person. The early church learned of these terms from the contemporary philosophical world. But the early church clearly saw the need to understand and express the Christian message in the thought patterns of its own day. The insistence on scripture and tradition truly takes seriously the principle of mediation which theologically finds its deepest expression in the incarnation. The experience of the first centuries called the church to move beyond the language and understanding of the scriptures. Some objected to using these terms derived from Greek philosophy in our understanding of God precisely because they were not biblical. It is important to note the development that here occurred on such central issues of faith.

The Catholic insistence on the sacraments again illustrates both the significance of mediation and the importance of tradition in the life of the church. For the greater part of its existence the Catholic Church did not recognize the existence of seven sacraments. It was only in the twelfth century that marriage was finally accepted as a sacrament of the church.[28] Here again we can note the developments in our understanding of the faith because of the recognition of tradition.

An acceptance of tradition shows the need to understand the gospel in the light of the circumstances of the times as well as in a continuity with the gospel message and historical development. However, this means that theology can never merely repeat what has been said in the past as if that were the last word on the subject. Even in the matter of Christology, for example, one cannot say that the early councils have uttered the last word on the subject. Today we have a different understanding of nature and of person. Since Jesus is truly a human being, some contemporary theologians argue that Jesus had to be a human person.[29] Continual discussions of these questions are necessary for the life of the church and of theology.

The Catholic insistence on scripture and tradition again calls for a theology which is attempting to understand the gospel message and make it incarnate in the historical and cultural ethos of the present-day reality. This furnishes another significant reason for recognizing that in general the current ferment in Catholic moral theology is totally in keeping with the best of the Catholic theological tradition. The Catholic acceptance of mediation with the importance of both faith and reason and scripture and tradition gives some important backing to the general shape of the changes that are now happening in Roman Catholic moral theology, even though one cannot prove conclusively the truth of all these developments on these bases.

III. Multiple Relationships of Moral Theology

The third section of this study will view the present situation of moral theology primarily in terms of the multiple relationships in which moral theology is involved. Some of the tensions and problems of moral theology will be discussed in the hope of shedding light on possible future developments.

First, it is necessary to understand the description of moral theology and its different aspects. The manuals of moral theology define their subject as the theological science about deliberate human acts and often add that such acts are then seen in relationship to the norms of actions existing in the supernatural order and to the ultimate end which is to be attained through these acts and through the means of salvation.[30] There are some elements of this definition which should be corrected in the light of the comments made in the first part of this chapter. Perhaps a simpler description of moral theology on which most people could agree is: the reflective, systematic study of Christian life and action.

Implicit in these descriptions are three very important relationships for moral theology which help to understand the nature of the discipline but also cause inherent tensions for moral theology. Moral theology is related to the church, to reason or to the academy and to life and action. First, moral theology as a systematic reflection on Christian life and existence must be seen in relationship to the church. It is self-evident that theology is related to the church, for the church makes present the mystery and the life of the risen Lord in our midst. Theology is intimately connected with faith and the understanding of faith. Moral theology is directly related to Christian life and action which has its center in the church.

Second, moral theology is related to reason, science or the academic. By definition it is a systematic reflection. Scholasticism discussed the exact way in which theology itself might be considered a science. Theology thus appeals to reason and has a place in the academy beside all other rational and scientific endeavors, even though it presupposes faith.

Third, moral theology is connected with and interested in action and life. How should Christians and others act? This question has always been with us but now is posed with a greater urgency in the light of the changing conditions under which we live. But there are many influences other than moral theology which affect life and actions. How are all these to be related?

These three important aspects of moral theology and especially their mutual relationships and resulting tensions raise some of the most significant methodological questions for moral theology now and in the future.

The relationship of moral theology to the church has been most significant in influencing and shaping the discipline itself. The *Institutiones theologiae moralis,* which came into existence in the seventeenth century and continued as the basis of manuals of moral theology until the Second Vatican Council, responded to the pastoral need of training confessors for the sacrament of penance. The very discipline of moral theology was shaped by the concrete pastoral requirements of the church. Today the change in orientation of moral theology also comes from recognizing the narrowness of the earlier approach which truly prevented the discipline from being a systematic reflection on the whole of the Christian life.

Catholic moral theologians have exercised a very significant role in instructing Catholics about which acts were good and which were evil and to be avoided. The outcome of the controversy over probabilism in the seventeenth and eighteenth centuries was the conclusion that five or six recognized theologians would constitute a probable opinion that could be followed in practice.[31] The practical questions facing many directors of souls, confessors, and the faithful themselves were often solved by recourse to the opinions of theologians. On a pastoral level this function was carried out in question-and-answer columns written by moral theologians. Practically all the journals in major languages for priests always had such regular features. In addition, in more popular Catholic publications there often appeared a "question-box" column which similarly gave answers to problems of conscience. No one can deny the intimate connection of moral theology with the life of the church.

However, until a decade or so ago the role of moral theology was seen, perhaps even primarily, in terms of defending and explaining the teaching of the hierarchical magisterium. Only in the last decade has the possibility of dissent arisen. Many Roman Catholic moral theologians no longer see their function primarily as defenders and interpreters of the teaching of the hierarchical magisterium. Dissent from the teaching of the hierarchical magisterium has appeared in the area of contraception and now exists on many other specific questions. This factual situation must be admitted by all. Appraisals of the validity or the healthiness of such a situation differ. Elsewhere I have recognized the existence of such pluralism in the church on specific moral issues and acknowledged it as something good;[32] others disagree.[33] It is obvious that at present there are significantly different opinions about what is the role or function of the moral theologian. The next chapter will discuss the question of dissent in greater detail.

Another problem today concerns the split between the

methodology adopted by many Catholic moral theologians as summarized above in the first part and the methodology still being employed by the documents of the hierarchical magisterium. This difference highlighted the "lively debate" over the encyclical *Humanae vitae* in 1968. Moreover, the documents of the hierarchical magisterium often still use this same moral methodology as illustrated in the Declaration on Sexual Ethics of the Congregation for the Teaching of the Faith issued in December 1975.[34] Here, too, I am willing to recognize the need for a pluralism of theological and ethical methodologies, but there exists a definite chasm between the way many moral theologians do moral theology and the approach employed in the official teaching of the hierarchical magisterium. Again, one can only hope that in time there will be a greater rapprochement, even though a pluralism of methodologies will continue to be present in Catholic moral theology.

Roman Catholicism has always taken theology and theologians very seriously. This is intimately connected with the importance that the Catholic theological tradition has given to the role of reason. Even in condemning certain theological positions or theologians the church shows the importance of the theological enterprise. The Catholic Church in my judgment takes its theologians much more seriously than the Protestant churches do. Very often in the United States one has the impression that the work of Protestant ethicists is often ignored or overlooked by their own churches. This is not true of the Catholic Church, because even if there are differences with contemporary theologians, the hierarchical church cannot overlook the work that is being done by these theologians. On the popular level Catholic theologians in general and moral theologians in particular are constantly in demand to speak to adult education groups, religious educators, parish groups and others.

The very fact that Catholicism takes its theologians so seriously can result in the friction that has existed in the past and very often exists today between the hierarchical magisterium and the theologians. There are some who seem to argue that such friction should not exist. From my perspective there will always be the need for some tension between theologians and the hierarchical leaders of the church. If there was no tension, this would be a sign that the theological enterprise was not taken seriously. But I agree that in the process there should be an overall working together for the good of the church and a mutual respect for the rights of all.

One obvious sign of the times is the condemnation of some theologians and the dismissal of theologians from their teaching functions. Here, too, one can see the tension between two aspects of the role of moral theology—the relationship to the church and the relationship to the academic world. Although the church has fostered universities in the pursuit of truth, theology and the university have always known the tensions of coexistence. I believe that theology should retain its place in the university together with all the other disciplines, but in order to do so it must enjoy the same autonomy and academic freedom as all other university disciplines. Yes, theologians will make mistakes. The hierarchical teaching office at times should address itself to possible theological errors. But ultimate judgments about the competency of theologians as university teachers should be made by peers and not by the members of the episcopacy as such.[35] This problem becomes even more acute in theologates which are not protected by the same academic safeguards as universities. Here, too, I believe the ultimate judgments about theological competency and ability to teach should be made by theologians and not by bishops, but the bishops do have their significant pastoral role. Needless to say, these tensions will continue to exist in the future. In the present situation the theologian can best serve the church by striving to be as good a theologian as possible.

There is no doubt that the moral theologian has exercised a most significant pastoral role in the life of the church in the past. However, in my judgment the significance of this role will probably decrease in the future. One of the main reasons for this is the fact that most human moral decisions are no longer made primarily on the basis of whether or not there is a law. Even under the old manuals of moral theology the vast majority of human decisions were made, not on the basis of a universal law, but rather on the basis of values and prudential human judgments. The theologian will always have a role to play in the area of moral life and moral decision making, but the shift in moral theology and in the Christian life will augur for a lesser role for the theologian.

The consideration of the church-related aspect of moral theology indicates that it is impossible to consider one of these relationships apart from the others—thereby to show the tensions within which moral theology must operate. However, for the sake of convenience one can still group the problems under the three different relationships mentioned above. Attention will now concentrate on moral theology as a reflective discipline and the needs of systematic moral theology as such.

The close relationship between moral theology and the life of the church has both helped and hindered the systematic development of moral theology as an academic discipline. Intimate contact with and service to the life of the church have made moral theology take a special interest in the practical problems that arise in daily life. The Catholic theological tradition was willing to submit the problems of daily life to careful rational analysis to determine whether they were right or wrong. Protestant ethics has traditionally not given that much importance to individual acts. Contemporary philosophical ethics, especially in an American setting until a few years ago, did not discuss particular ethical questions but was more concerned with linguistic and metaethical concerns. Recently there has been a great interest developed in biomedical ethics, but Catholic moral theology has a long history of concern for these problems.[36] The Catholic tradition on such questions as the ordinary and extraordinary means of conserving life has made a great contribution to contemporary discussions of this question. Even today there is a danger that discussions of medical ethics will concentrate on the more esoteric types of problems rather than on the ordinary problems faced by the doctor and the patient.[37] The concentration on the practical problems that arise in daily life marks a very significant strength of the discipline of Catholic moral theology, influenced heavily by its relationship to the daily life of the people of the church.

Catholic moral theology today desparately needs more in-depth, systematic treatments trying to propose a general methodology for the discipline. There are many reasons explaining why this is a missing aspect in moral theology today. Concern with the practical problems that have been discussed within the life of the church in the last ten years has taken most of the time and energy of Roman Catholic moral theologians. These questions have covered the gamut from contraception, sterilization and abortion to social change, nonviolence and nuclear weapons. Discussion of these particular questions has obviously been important, but as a result more systematic treatises have not been developed.

There is another important factor contributing to the lack of systematic approaches in moral theology. Until a few years ago moral theology was a monolithic discipline in which there was only one basic methodology. Today the situation has greatly changed. The pluralism of moral theologies is evident, but there has not been enough time to develop truly systematic approaches to moral theology. Different theologians employing different philosophical bases have proposed some new approaches, but by necessity these are incipient and limited. The need for truly systematic presentations of moral theology remains the greatest challenge for contemporary Catholic moral theologians.

The magnitude of the task of constructing any systematic theology also makes it very difficult. There are a tremendous number of questions that have to be settled by anyone trying to propose such a systematic study. The many recent developments as mentioned in the first section of this paper indicate how difficult it is to understand, put together and synthesize all the aspects of the discipline. The moral theologian must be familiar not only with all the elements in one's own discipline but also with aspects of other disciplines such as scripture, biblical theology, systematic theology, philosophy and many of the human sciences. The vastness of the field makes it all the more difficult to construct a truly systematic approach to moral theology.

A systematic moral theology must above all bring together the many elements that should enter into moral theology, but in such a way that both the personal and the social dimensions of action and life are properly accounted for. Recent developments in systematic theology, on the one hand, and in ethics, on the other, indicate the need for an explanation that does justice to both the personal and the social aspects of human and Christian existence. Political theology and liberation theology have both pointed out the privatized character of much of contemporary Roman Catholic theology. The same charge could be made against Catholic moral theology. A relational model for understanding the Christian life furnishes, in my judgment, the best starting point, for here the moral self is seen in terms of the multiple relationships with God, neighbor, self, the structures of society and the world. There is need for a pluralism of such methodological and systematic approaches. Thus the greatest challenge for the discipline of moral theology today calls for much work to be done in this area.

The discipline of moral theology must also have room for different specialties. Medical ethics, for example, has flourished in the Roman Catholic tradition, and today many philosophers and other theologians give much attention to this discipline. However, there are other areas that also call for renewed interest today, such as political and economic ethics. Here questions arise about the use of the sciences in moral theology. Moral theology needs to be familiar with disciplines such as economics and political theory and have a methodological way of incorporating the data of these sciences into its own. The complexity of these other disciplines only makes the problem for the moral theologian more acute, but the need for such specialization in moral theology continues to exist.

Moral theology reflects systematically on Christian life and action. It is obviously interested in action, or what today is often called praxis.[38] The Christian believer and member of the church is quite concerned about how Christians in the church should act. This problem has come to the fore recently in many discussions over liberation theology. The question naturally arises about the exact relationship between moral theology as a systematic reflection and action.

An integral person strives for continuity between reflection and action. The truth is to be done. In the last few years the academic world has witnessed an intensified interest in the positive relationship between thought and action. University students throughout the world rebelled against thought which was not related to the world in which they lived.

On the other hand, systematic reflection on Christian life and existence is not the only way or even the most effective way of influencing action and commitment to particular involvements. There are many other realities that can have an even greater influence on life and action. In the context of the church, liturgy can and should bring about Christian participation in the living out of the gospel. Scripture reading, either alone or in groups, can and should greatly affect how we act here and now. Meditation likewise can strengthen our commitment to specific causes. But none of these constitutes moral theology as such.

Perhaps the question can be posed in a slightly different way: Are moral theologians the best living Christians in the world? Such a question is quite crass and would need important theological nuances to be properly understood, but the question in its bald form still serves the purpose. Most people (especially honest moral theologians) would admit that moral theologians are not the best living Christians in the world. We know that many people who have never studied moral theology magnificently bear witness to the gospel in their daily lives, whereas we who study moral theology know how far short we fall in living out the gospel, and even in making good decisions.

Some light might be shed on the problem by posing an analogous question. Without in any way disparaging or categorizing a group or profession we can ask if psychiatrists are the most mature and emotionally balanced people in the world. Again, most people would answer in the negative.

There are many people who have never read Freud who are very mature and well-balanced, perhaps even more so than those who have spent a lifetime studying human behavior and emotional maturity. But still psychiatrists can and do offer great help to neurotics, psychotics and others suffering from emotional disturbances.

In many ways the functions of the psychiatrist and of the moral theologian are analogous. The psychiatrist studies systematically, reflectively and thematically the question of human maturity and emotional behavior. Psychiatry in this sense is a second-order discipline which operates on the systematic and reflective level of thinking and discourse. On this level, one tries to systematize and thematize all those elements which are present in daily life and experience. However, what the psychiatrist does in this way, every human being must do in a nonsystematic and nonthematic way. Many individuals are very well-balanced even though they have never systematically reflected on human behavior or why they are emotionally mature.

So too is the case in moral theology. Moral theology involves second-order discourse, since by definition it reflects systematically and thematically on the Christian life. Moral theology is very important, in fact essential, for Christian life and existence. It is precisely through such explicit systematic reflection that an important critical tool is brought to bear on our life and action. But moral theology is not the only or even the most important influence on good action. What distinguishes moral theology is its reflective, systematic and thematic character; that is, the fact that it is second-order discourse as distinguished from other realities that influence life and actions. Although such a discipline is very important for a critical evaluation of Christian life and action, many people live Christian lives without ever engaging in moral theology. There are also many other realities operating on the first level of discourse which also greatly affect Christian life and actions — reading, preaching, hearing and celebrating the Word are all examples of what can effectively move people to action, as well as the witness and good example of others. People can and do live good lives and make good ethical decisions without ever having studied moral theology.

Moral theologians striving to be committed believers experience a tension between the reflective character of their discipline and the urgency of particular Christian actions and involvement. As integral human beings and Christians, moral theologians might at times operate in other capacities and try to affect action by their example, personal involvement, preaching, and similar witness. But such actions, strictly speaking, do not constitute moral theology. One must recognize that there are many gifts and functions in the church in the service of the gospel. Moral theology is a very specific function, but there are many others, which also contribute to living out the gospel.

This final section has attempted to discuss moral theology as it exists presently and give some indications of its future development. In the process of this discussion moral theology has been considered in terms of its three important relationships—with the church, with reason and systematic thinking and with action and life. This completes the overview and appraisal of contemporary moral theology proposed in this opening chapter.

NOTES

1. Bernard Häring, *Das Gesetz Christi* (Freiburg im Breisgau: Erich Wewel Verlag, 1954). Note the many subsequent editions and translations. English translation: *The Law of Christ,* 3 vols. (Westminster, Md.: Newman Press, 1961, 1963, 1966). For a brief historical survey of moral theology see *The Law of Christ* 1:3–33. As an illustration of the Thomistic approach critical of the manuals see Th. Deman, "Probabilisme," *Dictionnaire de théologie catholique* 13, part I, col. 417–619.

2. Such an approach was incorporated into the Pastoral Constitution on the Church in the Modern World of the Second Vatican Council. For Häring's contribution to that document see Viktor Schurr, *Bernard Häring* (Rome: Marietti, 1971), pp. 81ff.

3. H. Richard Niebuhr, *The Responsible Self* (New York: Harper and Row, 1963), pp. 47–68.

4. Albert R. Jonsen, *Responsibility in Modern Religious Ethics* (Washington: Corpus Books, 1968), pp. 86–107.

5. E.g., Bernard Häring, *The Christian Existentialist* (New York: New York University Press, 1968); *Morality Is for Persons* (New York: Farrar, Straus and Giroux, 1971).

6. George P. Klubertanz, *Habits and Virtues* (New York: Appleton-Century-Crofts, 1965).

7. Häring, *Law of Christ* I, pp. 387–562; idem, "Conversion," in Ph. Delhaye et al., *Pastoral Treatment of Sin* (New York: Desclée, 1968), pp. 87–176.

8. Häring, *Law of Christ* I, pp. 306ff.; idem, "The Universal Call to Holiness," *Homiletic and Pastoral Review* 66 (1965–66): 107–114.

9. For Häring's approach to this question see Bernard Häring, "The Normative Value of the Sermon on the Mount," *Catholic Biblical Quarterly* 29 (1967): 265–385. For a more popular treatment see Häring, *La morale del Discorso della montagna* (Alba: Edizioni Paoline, 1967). For a recent survey of the literature from an ecumenical perspective, including the authors' own approach, see Bruce C. Birch and Larry L. Rasmussen, *Bible and Ethics in the Christian Life* (Minneapolis: Augsburg, 1976).

10. Bernard Häring, *Christ in einer neuven Welt* (Freiburg im Breisgau: Erich Wewel Verlag, 1961); English translation: *Christian Renewal in a Changing World* (New York: Desclée, 1964), pp. 263ff. Also Bernard Häring, *Gabe und Auftrag der Sakramente* (Salzburg: Otto Müller Verlag, 1962); English translation: *A Sacramental Spirituality* (New York: Sheed and Ward, 1965).

11. Bernard Häring, *Medical Ethics* (Notre Dame, Indiana: Fides Publishers, 1973), pp. 42–64; 91–94.

12. Bernard Häring, "La theologie morale et la sociologie pastorale dans la perspective de l'histoire du salut: la notion biblique de 'kairos'," *Sciences Ecclésiastiques* 16 (1964): 209–224.

13. Bernard Häring, *Die gegenwärtige Heilsstunde* (Freiburg im Breisgau: Erich Wewel Verlag, 1964); English translation (partial): *This Time of Salvation* (New York: Herder and Herder, 1966).

14. Bernard Häring, *Macht und Ohmacht der Religion* (Salzburg: Otto Müller Verlag, 1956); idem, *Ehe in dieser Zeit* (Salzburg: Otto Müller Verlag, 1960); English translation: *Marriage in the Modern World* (Westminster, Md.: Newman Press, 1966).

15. Häring addressed himself to the encyclical *Humanae vitae* in a number of his works: "The Encyclical Crisis," *Commonweal* 88 (September 6, 1968): 388–94; *Krise um "Humanae vitae"* (Bergen-Enkheim: Verlag Kaffke, 1968); "The Inseparability of the Unitive-Procreative Functions of the Marital Act," in *Contraception: Authority and Dissent*, ed. C. E. Curran (New York: Herder and Herder, 1969), pp.

176–193; Bernard Häring and Karl Rahner, *Riflessioni sull' enciclica 'Humanae vitae',"* (Roma: Edizioni Paoline, 1968). See also Schurr, *Bernard Häring*, pp. 98–104.

16. *Summa theologiae*, Ia IIae, q. 91, a. 2.

17. Vatican Council I, 3rd session, Dogmatic Constitution "Dei Filius," Cap. 4 "De fide et ratione," in *Enchiridion symbolorum definitionum et declarationum de rebus fidei et morum*, ed. H. Denzinger, A. Schönmetzer, 32nd ed. (Barcelona: Herder, 1963), n. 3017. Hereafter referred to as *DS*. See also Fifth Lateran Council, *DS*, n. 1441.

18. Häring, *Law of Christ* I, p. 7.

19. For an acclaimed history of the time see Roger Aubert, *Le pontificat de Pie IX* (Paris: Bloud & Gay, 1952).

20. See the important encyclicals of Leo XIII, especially *Libertas praestantissimum, Acta Sanctae Sedis* 20 (1887): 593–613; *Immortale Dei, Acta Sanctae Sedis* 18 (1885): 161–180. English translations and commentary can be found in *The Church Speaks to the Modern World: The Social Teachings of Leo XIII*, ed. Etienne Gilson (Garden City, New York: Doubleday Image Books, 1954).

21. Jean Levie, *The Bible, Word of God in Words of Men* (New York: P. J. Kenedy and Sons, 1961), pp. 7–76.

22. Mark Schoof, *A Survey of Catholic Theology 1880–1970* (New York: Paulist Press, 1970), pp. 39ff.; Aubert, *Le pontificat*, pp. 193–211; *DS*, nn. 2875–2880.

23. Etienne Borne, "Le problème majeur du Syllabus: vérité et liberté," *Recherches et Debats* 50 (1965): 26–42; M.-D. Chenu, "Pour une lecture théologique du Syllabus," *Recherches et Debats* 50 (1965): 43–51; Aubert, *Le pontificat*, pp. 224–261; *DS*, nn. 2901–2980.

24. Leo XIII in his encyclical letter *Aeterni patris* of August 4, 1879, *Acta Sanctae Sedis* 12 (1879): 97–115, prescribed the restoration in Catholic schools of Christian philosophy in the spirit of St. Thomas Aquinas. For subsequent papal directives on following the philosophy and theology of St. Thomas see Pius X, *Doctoris angelici (motu proprio), Acta Apostolicae Sedis* 6 (1914): 384ff.; Pius XI, *Officiorum omnium* (encyclical letter), *AAS* 14 (1922): 449ff.; Pius XI, *Studiorum ducem* (encyclical letter), *AAS* 15 (1923): 323ff.; various allocutions of Pius XII, *AAS* 31 (1939): 246ff.; 38 (1946): 387ff.; 45 (1953): 684ff.

25. John Courtney Murray, "Leo XIII on Church and State," *Theological Studies* 14 (1953): 1–30.

26. Very significant for the present development is the new climate of freedom in theology. See Schoof, *A Survey of Catholic Theology*, pp. 157–227.

27. For a summary of the debates about the relationship between scripture and tradition at the Second Vatican Council and in recent Catholic theology see Joseph Ratzinger, "Dogmatic Constitution on

Divine Revelation," in *Commentary on the Documents of Vatican II,* ed. Herbert Vorgrimler (New York: Herder and Herder, 1968), III, pp. 155ff, 183ff.

28. Pierre Adnès, *Le mariage* (Tournai: Desclée, 1963), pp. 89–94, 140.

29. Donald P. Gray, "The Divine and the Human in Jesus Christ," *Proceedings of the Catholic Theological Society of America* 31 (1976): 21–39.

30. E.g., Marcellinus Zalba, *Theologiae moralis summa* (Madrid: Biblioteca de Autores Cristianos, 1952), I, pp. 3ff.

31. Ibid., p. 306.

32. Charles E. Curran, "Moral Theology: The Present State of the Discipline," *Theological Studies* 34 (1973): 446–467; idem, "Pluralism in Catholic Moral Theology," *Chicago Studies* 14 (1975): 310–334. See also Charles E. Curran et al., *Dissent in and for the Church* (New York: Sheed and Ward, 1969).

33. For a position opposed to my view see Thomas Dubay, "The State of Moral Theology: A Critical Appraisal," *Theological Studies* 35 (1974): 482–506; idem, "Pluralism and Authenticity in Moral Theology," *Homiletic and Pastoral Review* 77 (1977): 10–22.

34. *Acta Apostolicae Sedis* 68 (1976): 77–96.

35. John F. Hunt et al., *The Responsibility of Dissent: The Church and Academic Freedom* (New York: Sheed and Ward, 1969).

36. In addition to Häring's *Medical Ethics* note his *The Ethics of Manipulation: Issues in Medicine, Behavior Control and Genetics* (New York: Seabury, 1976).

37. Charles B. Moore, "This Is Medical Ethics?" *The Hastings Center Report* 4, n. 5 (November 1974): 1–3.

38. For an overview of recent discussions about praxis see Matthew L. Lamb, "The Theory-Praxis Relationship in Contemporary Christian Theologies," in *Proceedings of the Catholic Theological Society of America* 31 (1976): 149–178.

2: Moral Theology in the Light of Reactions to *Humanae vitae*

On July 25, 1968, Pope Paul VI officially issued the encyclical *Humanae vitae* in which he upheld the teaching that artificial contraception is always wrong. The Pope himself has referred to "the lively debate" set off by this encyclical.[1] The ensuing years in the life of the Roman Catholic Church have witnessed great agitation over this teaching.

From the very beginning there have been mixed reactions to the papal encyclical. Many national and regional conferences of bishops totally supported the teaching; some bishops' conferences seemed to hedge, while a third but smaller group significantly modified the teaching even to the point of accepting in theory and in practice the possibility of a person remaining a loyal Catholic and dissenting from the teaching on artificial contraception.[2] Theological reaction was quick and strong. In the United States over six hundred persons with certified competency in the sacred sciences signed a statement of dissent from the ban on artificial contraception.[3] In the ensuing decade it is safe to say that the majority of Roman Catholic theologians have disagreed with the papal conclusions on artificial contraception for married couples. However, other theologians have strongly supported the papal teaching.[4]

Many Catholic people seem to have rejected the official teaching in their behavior. According to the studies of the National Opinion Research Center, in 1963 45 percent of American Catholics approved artificial contraception for married couples, whereas in 1974 83 percent of American Catholics approved of artificial contraception.[5] Andrew Greeley and his associates have concluded that the issuance of the encyclical "seems to have been the occasion for massive apostasy and for a notable decline in religious devotion and belief."[6] Greeley attributes the great decline in Catholic practice in the United States in the decade 1963–1973 to the encyclical.[7]

The issuance of *Humanae vitae* has brought to the fore two significant questions: the methodology employed in moral theology and the teaching function of the church in moral matters. In the years since the encyclical these two subjects have generated much discussion. This chapter will reflect on these two very important questions as they were raised by the encyclical of Pope Paul VI and discussed by theologians.

I. Methodology in Moral Theology

This first part will be limited to the methodological question that has received most of the attention in moral theology — the question of absolute norms that are always obliging. It is necessary to insist that this is not the only, or even the primary, methodological question in moral theology, which must also consider the attitudes, dispositions, virtues, values, goals and decision making of the Christian. One further introductory note is necessary. It is impossible for theologians to address this question from a neutral perspective, since those who have been writing about the encyclical have already taken a position. I acted as spokesperson and leader of the American Catholic theologians who signed the statement of dissent. I have not changed my mind. This chapter attempts to evaluate what has occurred in moral theology after the encyclical, but I must honestly admit my own previous opinions and positions.

Physicalism in the Encyclical

What is the primary reason for rejecting the papal teaching condemning all artificial contraception for married couples?

The primary objection of most dissenting theologians centers on the papal insistence that the biological structure of the marital act is normative, and human beings must always respect its God-given finality and structure. This approach has been called physicalism.

Dissenters point to indications of physicalism in the encyclical itself. Direct interruption of the generative process already begun is to be absolutely excluded. Similarly excluded is every action which either in anticipation of the conjugal act or in its accomplishment or in the development of its natural consequences proposes either as an end or as a means to render procreation impossible (par. 14).[8] The condemnation of contraception is based on the intimate structure of the conjugal act (par. 12). The encyclical insists on respecting the laws of the generative process (par. 13). The divine plan and law are written into the act of marital love. Rhythm or natural family planning is acceptable because it involves a legitimate use of the natural disposition and does not impede the development of natural processes (par. 16).

Defenders of the condemnation of artificial contraception deny that it is a question of physicalism. The condemnation of artificial contraception is not based merely on the inviolability of the physical or biological structure of the act. Even before the encyclical Germain Grisez maintained that interference in the marital act involves more than just interfering with the biological structure of the act.[9] Dietrich von Hildebrand insists that there is a deep connection between the biological nature and the person. Physical processes should be the expression of spiritual attitudes. Not everything that is connected with biological conditions is itself biological. There is involved here not only a biological nature but an eminently personal value. It is not a merely factual or exclusively biological connection but rather a great and sublime mystery that God has entrusted the generation of the human being to the intimate union of man and wife who love each other in wedded love and who, becoming two in one flesh, participate in the very creative act of God. The active, artificial isolation of this marital act from the possible generation of a human being constitutes a sin of irreverence toward God.[10]

What is the personal value or meaning which is expressed in the physical structure of the act? I think there is no moral value or meaning preserved here but only the physical and biological structure itself. One way to prove this assertion is to note the development which has occurred in the Catholic understanding of the meaning of human sexuality. An older opinion going back to patristic times maintained that marital relations without a positive intention of procreation were wrong. The procreative intention justified marital intercourse. Much later it was accepted that the procreative intention could be missing and marital relations would not be wrong. In 1951 Pope Pius XII officially acknowledged the morality of the rhythm system.[11] One could have marital relations and positively intend not to procreate. Marital relations with the expressed intention not to procreate are morally acceptable.[12] The value of procreation can intentionally be excluded from the particular act, but the physical structure cannot be interfered with. Human experience and reflection indicate that contraceptive marital relations can be an act of love. As a result, it seems there is no moral value or meaning which is expressed in the biological structure of the act. For these and other reasons the moral methodology of the encyclical has been rejected on the basis of its physicalism—identifying the human moral act with the physical structure of the act.

Physicalism in Moral Theology

In the ensuing decade it has become evident to many Catholic moral theologians that the problem of physicalism exists in other questions and not merely in the issue of contraception alone. However, a word of caution is in order. The physical or biological structure of the act is not necessarily identical with the moral aspect, but sometimes the physical and moral cannot be separated. The best example is the human person. The human person and the physical life of the human person cannot be separated—at least in this world. There is no human person apart from the physical reality of the person. The test for the death of a human person, whether it is the lack of heartbeat, or of breathing or of brain waves, is based on physical criteria. In attacking the problem of physicalism one must avoid the extreme of giving no importance to the physical or of denying that at times the physical and the moral are the same. In the last fifteen years and especially in the decade since *Humanae vitae* many Catholic moral theologians have begun to question a number of previously held, official Catholic moral teachings. It is impossible to discuss all these questions in depth. Our purpose is more limited — to gain intelligibility and understanding. Why are these teachings being discussed and questioned by some today? The problem areas are primarily those in which the human moral act is equated with the physical structure of the act.

First, there are questions concerning human reproduction. The official Catholic teaching insists that the marital act cannot be interfered with. Contraception, sterilization and artificial insemination, even with the husband's seed, are wrong. It should be noted that sterilization and contraception involve the same basic moral issue. According to the technical definition, contraception involves interference in the sexual act, whereas sterilization involves interference in the sexual faculty. The pill, which is often referred to as a contraceptive, is in ethical terminology a temporary sterilization because it affects the sexual faculty by preventing ovulation. Logically, if one cannot interfere with the sexual act, then one cannot interfere with the sexual faculty. If contraception is morally acceptable, so is sterilization, although a more serious reason is required if the sterilization is permanent.

Pope Pius XII condemned artificial insemination even with the husband's seed, because the end of having a child does not justify a bad means.[13] The physical act of depositing male semen in the vagina of the female is always required. Some have wrongly accused the official Catholic teaching of being pronatalist at all cost. This is not true, since the end of procreation cannot justify doing away with the physical act of marital intercourse. Today many Roman Catholic moral theologains accept the morality of artificial insemination with the husband's seed.[14] In fact, I hold that artificial insemination

with donor semen (AID) is not always wrong. It is not absolutely necessary that the seed be biologically the husband's
seed, although there are significant moral values in the fact
that the child is the fruit of the flesh of the parents. It is easy to
recognize that those proposing different opinions do not
accept the fact that one cannot interfere with the sexual act or
the sexual faculty.

A second area of contemporary debate is the principle of
double effect which has been used in moral theology to judge
the morality of actions involving more than one effect. Of
crucial importance here is the condition requiring that the
good effect not be produced by means of the evil effect. The
evil effect must be equally immediate causally with the good
effect. The physical causality and structure of the act determine whether an effect is direct or not. In the area of abortion
it is a direct and therefore morally wrong abortion to expel the
fetus in order to save the life of the mother threatened by the
pregnancy. The two best-known illustrations of indirect abortion are the removal of the cancerous uterus and the case of the
ectopic pregnancy. Both these cases illustrate the fact that the
physical structure and causality of the act are determinative. In
the case of the cancerous uterus the act is directed at the uterus
and the fetus is not directly attacked. In the case of the ectopic
pregnancy it would be wrong for the doctor to remove
immediately and directly the ectopic pregnancy itself, but the
doctor can licitly remove the infected and dangerous tube
which happens to contain a fetus. Many contemporary
Catholic moral theologians reject or modify the older understanding of direct and indirect. At times there is some significant moral difference between direct and indirect, but the
physical structure and causality of the act cannot always and
necessarily be the determinant of the morality of the act.[15]

Third, abortion has frequently been discussed in the last
decade. There are two fundamental questions involved in the
morality of abortion—when does human life begin and how
does one solve conflict situations involving the fetus. The
principle of double effect for solving conflict situations has

already been mentioned. The issue of when human life begins illustrates aspects of the problem of physicalism. Remember, again, our primary purpose is merely to seek intelligibility and not to give solutions to all these practical problems. Why do many people have difficulty accepting the understanding that truly human life begins at conception? Modern genetics by stressing that the unique genetic package, which is the never-to-be-repeated genotype, becomes present at conception seems to give strong confirming evidence that truly human life exists at the moment of conception. Yet many people in our society do not accept such an approach. Why? Basically they argue that truly human life involves more than the biological and the genetic. Some French Catholic moral theologians have argued that relationship and relationality are necessary elements of being human. The biological and genetic do not constitute the truly human but form only one aspect of it. Truly human life is not present and abortion is allowed if there is no relationship and no acceptance of the fetus by the parents or society.[16] Many other Catholic theologians including myself have argued against such a position. Chapter Eight will develop my own position on the question of when human life begins and will criticize other theories, including the relational understanding of when human life begins.

A fourth area of great discussion in recent years concerns human sexuality. The accepted teaching maintains that the marital act or the actuation of the sexual faculty is wrong if it is not in the context of a marital relationship between husband and wife. On this basis, masturbation, homosexuality, fornication and adultery have strongly been condemned. The physical act outside marriage is always and everywhere wrong. Our teaching allows married persons to share their deepest secrets and most intimate thoughts with someone other than their spouse, but this particular act described in its physical structure is always and everywhere wrong outside marriage. Defenders of the accepted teaching point out that there is much more than the physical involved, for the physical act here incarnates very significant personal and human values. However, our present consideration is merely seeking to understand why questions are being raised today on these issues.[17]

Fifth, there is the matter of euthanasia. Roman Catholic medical ethics has taught that human beings do not have to do everything possible to keep human life in existence. We have an obligation to use ordinary means but not extraordinary means. Extraordinary means are often described as those means which involve excessive pain, expense, or inconvenience or do not offer a reasonable hope of success. In the light of the traditional teaching one can even remove extraordinary means such as a respirator. Catholic teaching, however, has always opposed euthanasia, for human beings do not have full dominion over their lives and consequently cannot directly take life. However, in one sense the Catholic tradition has admitted a right to die at least in terms of a right to refuse treatment and not to use extraordinary means to preserve life. We do have some dominion and power over our living and our dying. Now some theologians have been questioning the absolute condemnation of euthanasia described as an act of positive interference to bring about death. The positive act of commission is always wrong, but omission of something necessary to preserve life under some circumstances is not wrong. Why is the physical act of interfering to cause death always wrong? Many theologians would strongly maintain the difference between commission and omission as well as the absolute prohibition of euthanasia.[18]

One current issue which at first sight does not seem to include the question of physicalism is divorce. Even here, however, one can point to a dimension of the problem that involves the question of physicalism. According to official Catholic teaching a marriage between two baptized persons is perfectly indissoluble only after consummation. Consummation is described in physical terms as one act of sexual intercourse after marriage. In addition, there is a problem analogous to that of physicalism. The older teaching spoke of the bond of marriage as a metaphysical reality coming into existence through the contract of marriage and remaining forever. Today many theologians including myself question the absolute indissolubility of marriage and the existence of a metaphysical bond apart from the relationship of the persons.[19]

The question of physicalism thus appears as the primary and foremost explanation for many of the discussions that have taken place in the last decade in Roman Catholic moral theology. In this light one must honestly admit that the discussions about *Humanae vitae* involve more than just the one issue of artificial contraception. Many of those who supported the conclusion of *Humanae vitae* rightly pointed out that the questioning of the particular teaching on artificial contraception would lead to the denial or at least the questioning of other Catholic moral teachings. Some of those who disagreed with the teaching of *Humanae vitae* emphasized that a change in the teaching on artificial contraception would not lead to a change in other teachings. If one is questioning the methodology and the concept of natural law on which the encyclical is based, it is obvious that a different methodology might lead to different conclusions on other questions. The history of the last decade has indicated that some of the fears expressed by defenders of the encyclical were true.

Premoral Evil

In trying to develop newer and different methodologies to overcome the problem of physicalism different approaches have been taken by theologians. Many contemporary theologians accept a theory of physical evil, premoral evil or ontic evil. In the examples of physicalism mentioned above and in many other actions there exists some evil (called physical, premoral or ontic), but moral evil arises from the act seen in its total concrete reality, including the end and circumstances as well as the object of the act. These positions maintain that for a proportionate reason premoral evil can be justified.[20] I am in basic agreement with what this generic approach to moral theology is trying to do, but I have a number of difficulties with the theory of premoral evil especially as applied to the case of contraception.

If contraception is a premoral evil, the conclusion seems to be that noncontraceptive marital relations constitutes the ideal, but something less than the ideal can be justified for a proportionate reason. In my judgment such a theory still gives too much importance to the physical and fails to realize that the ultimate problem here is one of finitude and not of evil.

The moral judgment furnishes the ultimate and most universal perspective within which a human act is considered. Every other consideration is particular and relative. There are many different aspects under which the human act can be considered—the psychological, the sociological, the pedagogical, the hygenic, the eugenic, the aesthetic, and so on. Nothing is perfect from all these perspectives. The ultimate moral judgment must consider all these relevant and different aspects. A more historically conscious approach examining the entire situation with all its different perspectives would not speak of a moral ideal based on only one particular aspect of the complex reality of the human act.

At the very minimum one would have to admit that there is premoral evil involved in every human act in this world and that premoral evil involves more than merely the physical aspect of the act. What is the ultimate basis of this conflict? The grounding of this problem is in human finitude and not in evil as such. Precisely because of our finitude nothing is perfect from every perspective. As finite creatures in a finite world there will always be an incompleteness and lack of perfection about our actions. The Catholic tradition has rightly distinguished between finitude and evil. They are two different realities. In my perspective the problem involved in contraceptive marital relations stems from human finitude and not from evil.

Conflict situations can ultimately be traced to a number of different sources—finitude, sinfulness or the tension created by eschatology. In this case of contraception the ultimate basis of the conflict is finitude and not evil. In the next chapter I will suggest that in homosexuality the problem arises from evil (but not personal moral evil) and not from finitude. One important

difference is that noncontraceptive intercourse does not constitute a moral ideal or a human ideal, whereas heterosexual
relations do.

Even those who accept the theory of premoral or ontic evil
must recognize that not all the evils are of the same importance. Obviously there is a great difference between the evil of
contraception (if one wants to accept that) and the evil of
killing a human being. At the very minimum the terms
premoral or ontic evil constitute a very broad and generic
category of evil. It is necessary to delve more deeply into what
is the precise evil involved in all these situations if one is to
decide on the basis of proportionate reason whether or not
such an evil can be done. This immediately raises the question
of the values which are involved. Since premoral evil is such an
undifferentiated concept, moral theology should speak more
precisely about the human values and meaning involved.

Values and Norms

Moral norms must be seen in terms of the protection and
promotion of human values and meaning. In this connection I
agree with the methodological approach taken by the authors
of the recently published *Human Sexuality* which was a study
commissioned by the Catholic Theological Society of America.
These authors distinguish several levels of moral evaluation.
On the first level human sexuality is governed by a very generic
principle formulated as creative growth toward integration—
an absolute and universal principle but obviously not specified
in terms of physical behavior. This principle provides an
overall direction for the meaning and moral evaluation of
human sexuality. On the second level this general principle is
spelled out in terms of the values in human sexuality that are
conducive to the creative growth and integration of the human
person. The following values of human sexuality are enumer-
ated as embodying creative growth toward integration—self-
liberation, other-enrichment, honesty, fidelity, social responsibility, service to life and joy.

The third level of moral evaluation consists of more concrete norms, rules, precepts or guidelines which attempt to distill from the experience of the Christian community the most practical and effective way of activating these values. To the extent that they refer to concrete physical actions they oblige *ut in pluribus* and cannot be regarded as absolute and universal moral norms.[21]

Such a methodological approach, as distinguished from the material content, is much superior to the methodological approach found in *Humanae vitae* and recently reiterated in the Declaration on Sexual Ethics issued by the Sacred Congregation for the Doctrine of the Faith on December 29, 1975.[22] This document finds the immutable principles transcending history and culture which govern human sexuality in the finality and structure of the sexual faculty and act. These very specific principles are part of the eternal, objective and universal divine law. Such a methodology can and should be criticized for finding specific, immutable laws in the structure of the sexual act and faculty, and for making these norms the primary and practically the only level of moral evaluation and discourse. Rather, one should first of all discuss the general principles and the values which are present and only then develop laws and norms in terms of safeguarding the values.

Although I am in basic agreement with the methodology proposed by the authors of *Human Sexuality,* I have some criticisms of their approach to sexuality. First, the tragic aspect of human existence must receive more importance and thereby modify the general principle of creative growth toward integration. The tragic aspect of human existence in general and of sexuality in particular is frequently found in human experience and often depicted in literature and in the arts. Christian revelation reminds us of the presence of evil and the paschal mystery. Through death the Christian comes to life. There is an obvious danger in so emphasizing the sinful, the negative and the tragic that human sexuality becomes something evil or very dangerous. Such an approach must be studiously avoided, for human sexuality is basically good, as is all God's creation, even though it will always be somewhat affected by human sinfulness. The fundamental principle of creative growth toward integration must be tempered by the recognition of the paschal mystery. I would stress the striving aspect of the creative growth toward integration and the potential pitfalls more than *Human Sexuality* does. Human integration and sexual human integration are never fully accomplished and are often marked by suffering, problems and difficulties. Likewise, the fragility and danger of exploitation in human sexuality cannot be overlooked even though these can never receive primary significance.

Second, some more importance should be given to the procreative aspect of human sexuality and also its female-male aspect in discussing the values and meaning of human sexuality. There is no doubt that in the past Catholic thinking has exaggerated the procreative dimension of human sexuality, but it must be given some greater importance than found in this recent study. The Christian understanding of human sexuality sees sexuality not only in terms of the individual person but also in terms of the female-male relationship. These are distinguishing aspects of human sexuality which must be considered in discussing the values and meaning of human sexuality. The values proposed in *Human Sexuality* are too general and could apply to many different types of relationships and friendships. The more specific values and meaning of human sexuality must be considered.

Third, the social aspect of human sexuality and of sexual morality deserves greater importance and will influence the role of concrete norms and of rules governing sexuality. The perspective of the authors of *Human Sexuality* is primarily that of the individual. The criteria are those values that are conducive to creative growth and integration of the human person. Such a perspective is somewhat incomplete. Moral theory must also recognize the need to protect certain societal values and realities.

The Christian moral tradition and most other ethical traditions have rightly valued the fundamental importance of the family and have tried to protect, defend and promote the good of the family. Norms governing human sexuality cannot so concentrate on the individual person that they forget the family or the institution of marriage. Today we recognize the problems that are besetting marriage and the family on all sides. However, I remain convinced of the absolute and fundamental importance of the family and of the need to strengthen the family in the midst of our society with its emphasis on competition, technological efficiency and impersonal structures. Moral norms must protect and promote such important and social realities as the institution of marriage and the family.

Ethical theories often recognize that the protection of social values at times more readily calls for norms that do not admit of exceptions. For example, in the midst of a dry summer often it is necessary to make a norm prohibiting all fires in the forest. Undoubtedly some individuals could carefully control and extinguish their fires without any harm being done to the forest. However, the absolute norm is made to protect the forest even though in some individual cases one could prove there is no danger of harm.

Within my perspective of giving more importance to promoting and defending the institution of marriage and the family, I would insist more strongly on a norm prohibiting all adultery. This is necessary to protect the institution of marriage in our society. One might argue that in individual cases the values of human sexuality would not be jeopardized or threatened by adultery. In theory this would always remain a possibility. However, the need to protect a most important social value can and should call for an absolute norm against extramarital sexual relations.

In summary, the methodology employed in *Human Sexuality* marks a significant improvement in the approach to moral questions, but I would modify somewhat the material content proposed on the three levels of moral discourse—the general principle, the values involved and the norms protecting and promoting those values. In my judgment there is no doubt that in the future in moral theology there will be less emphasis on absolute norms when the prohibited action is described in terms of the physical structure of the act. However, one must remember that sometimes absolute norms might be required because of the need to protect important societal values and goods such as marriage and the family.

II. Moral Teaching in the Church

Having considered the methodology of moral theology in the light of the discussion over *Humanae vitae*, the second section of the chapter will now discuss the role of the church as moral teacher with special emphasis on the hierarchical magisterium. *Humanae vitae* is important because for the first time in recent history it has widely been proposed and accepted that one can dissent from authoritative, noninfallible hierarchical teaching and still be a loyal Roman Catholic. From the very first reaction to the encyclical I insisted that the basic teaching condemning all artificial contraception for married couples was wrong and that a Roman Catholic could dissent in theory and practice from such a teaching.

Attempts to Reinterpret Official Teaching

In the recent past the interpretation of hierarchical teaching on the part of Roman Catholic theologians avoided such strong statements. In the nineteenth century, for example, Bishop Dupanloup of Orleans interpreted Pius IX's Syllabus of Errors in a way which ultimately met with papal approval and at the same time blunted the practical impact of the papal teaching. Dupanloup made the distinction between thesis and hypothesis. The pope condemned all these errors in thesis; that is, in what roughly corresponds to the ideal order. But in hypothesis, or what might be called the actual historical order, many things may be tolerated to avoid greater evils.[23]

In the years preceding the Second Vatican Council John Courtney Murray and other theologians developed a very significant historical hermeneutic to explain how in the twentieth century the Roman Catholic Church could accept the separation of church and state even though papal teaching before that time, especially under Pope Leo XIII in the nineteenth century, had strongly condemned the separation of church and state.[24] The doctrinal principles must be distinguished from the contingent historical aspects. Leo XIII condemned the separation of church and state based on a Continental liberalism which maintained there was no room for religion in society. The twentieth-century American scene was different. The First Amendment to the Constitution is not an article of liberalistic belief that professes no room for God, but rather an article of peace according to which people of different religious beliefs can live together in society. The state is only a part of society and not totally identified with it. There is definitely room for religion in society.

The principles enunciated by Pope Leo XIII can and should be separated from the historical circumstances. The doctrinal aspect of Leo's teaching recognizes the distinction between the two societies, the harmony and cooperation between them, and the primacy of the spiritual which calls for the freedom of the church. The liberalistic notion of separation of church and state should have been condemned, but in contemporary democracies the separation of church and state is in accord with Leo's principles. Murray thus explained how it was possible for Roman Catholicism to reject the separation of church and state in the nineteenth century and accept it in the middle of the twentieth century. A critical, historical hermeneutic of past papal teaching proved that the newer understanding did not involve a contradiction of the older teaching. Without such a notion of development it seems safe to say that the Second Vatican Council would never have accepted the newer teaching on religious liberty.

Before 1968 most Roman Catholics calling for a change in the ban on artificial contraception for married couples (myself included) argued on the basis of development in the teaching by employing approaches similar to the one used so effectively by Murray.[25] Recall that the first articles in serious theological journals calling for a change in the teaching on artificial contraception appeared only in 1963.[26] Such a theory of development could be much more easily and readily accepted by the church than a theory which acknowledged that the previous teaching was wrong.

Undoubtedly there is a great deal of truth in the magnificent theory developed by Murray on the question of church and state and perhaps some truth in its application to artificial contraception. However, even in Murray's approach one must admit both continuity and discontinuity in the historical development. At the very least the papal magisterium was wrong in not correcting the teaching once the historical situation had changed or in not recognizing the situations in which it did not apply. One also wonders if Leo would recognize himself in Murray's reconstruction.

A theory of development and continuity faced very great difficulties in attempting to explain a possible change in the teaching on artificial contraception. In 1930 Pope Pius XI sharply condemned artificial contraception in his encyclical *Casti connubii.* In subsequent years Pope Pius XII and Pope John XXIII often reiterated that teaching in less formal and solemn ways. Such a great historical development could hardly have occurred in such a short period of time. At least the later popes were wrong in reiterating the condemnation.

I in no way mean to impugn the integrity and honesty of those (myself included!) who used the theory of historical development to explain how the Catholic Church could change its teaching on artificial contraception. I feel quite sure that this theory was proposed in good faith by its adherents. However, those who argued against the acceptance of artificial contraception in the Roman Catholic Church in the 1960s recognized the more radical nature of the problem. As mentioned in the so-called minority report of the papal commission on birth control, the primary reason for not changing the teaching was the necessity of admitting that the previous teaching had been wrong.[27] One must honestly recognize that "the conservatives" saw much more clearly than "the liberals" of the day that a change in the teaching on artificial contraception had to recognize that the previous teaching was wrong.

Once *Humanae vitae* was issued and the older teaching reaffirmed, those opposed to it could no longer call upon a theory of historical development. However, there were ways in which the encyclical's condemnation of artificial contraception could be interpreted so that one could mitigate its teaching without at the same time accusing the pope of being in error. From my perspective it was imperative then to take the more radical approach. The teaching condemning artificial contraception is wrong; the pope is in error; Catholics in good conscience can dissent in theory and in practice from such a teaching.

In the meantime there have been a significant number of theologians who have tried to nuance the interpretation of *Humanae vitae* in such a way that one can accept the morality of artificial contraception in some circumstances without accusing the encyclical of being totally wrong.[28]

Karl Rahner recognizes that one can dissent from an authoritative, noninfallible papal teaching. However, he suggests that there might be another way to understand the teaching of *Humanae vitae*. The pope is here proposing an ideal norm which cannot always be effectively realized in all its moral obligations in every situation in human life or by every individual or by every social group. It is conceivable at least in principle that only later will the ideal which is now being taught be understood as having the force of moral obligation in actual concrete reality.[29] In this way one can account for both the truth of the teaching and the actual practice of many Roman Catholics.

Another similar conciliating approach sees contraception as involving premoral, physical or ontic evil. Contraception thus always involves evil, but such evil is not always moral evil. For a proportionate reason contraception can be morally good. Here again a way is found to salvage some of the papal teaching. Many theologians have creatively employed this theory of premoral or ontic evil in other problem areas in Roman Catholic ethics.[30]

Dissent and the Hierarchical Magisterium

From the viewpoint of moral theology one could make a case for these and similar approaches. From the perspective of the life of the church such approaches seem to be a way to preserve greater unity and peace in the church in the midst of very difficult times. However, I continue to maintain that such approaches are inadequate and wrong. I do not think that contraception violates an ideal; nor is it helpful to say that contraception always involves evil. As mentioned in the previous section, both of these approaches still give too much importance to the physical aspect of the act and see the physical as normative. From an ecclesiological perspective we must face the more radical question of the existence of papal error and of the possibility of dissent. Even from a pragmatic and practical viewpoint the contemporary Church must address the question of dissent. There are some significant moral truths in *Humanae vitae*. Likewise there has been some development in the teaching of the Catholic Church on procreation and marital relations. But the condemnation of artificial contraception found in *Humanae vitae* is wrong.[31]

The acceptance of the possibility of dissent within the Roman Catholic Church calls for a changed understanding at least in the minds of many Catholics of the role of the hierarchical magisterium. If the hierarchical magisterium can be wrong in noninfallible matters (there has never been an infallible teaching on a *specific* moral question, so it is not necessary here to enter into the debate over infallibility), then it follows that the hierarchical magisterium cannot be the only way in which the church teaches. Historical studies have indicated that the Catholic tradition recognized this reality, but it was not popularly understood or practically acknowledged especially in the context of the authoritarian Catholicism of the twentieth century.[32]

In the last decade many theologians have recognized that the hierarchical magisterium does not constitute the total magisterial activity of the church. Even before *Humanae vitae*

Daniel Maguire perceptively insisted that the word "magisterium" has a plural. There are many *magisteria* in the church—papal and episcopal magisteria, the authentic magisterium of the laity and the magisterium of theologians. Each of these has a creative service in the church.[33]

Theologians have been further investigating the theological and historical aspects of magisteria. Before the nineteenth century, according to Yves Congar, the word magisterium never signified what twentieth-century Catholic theology called the magisterium—that is, the teaching office of the pope and bishops. The word magisterium was applied to the hierarchical teaching office only in the nineteenth century.[34] A recent doctoral dissertation by Michael Place studies the teaching of four significant Italian theologians in the latter part of the eighteenth and early part of the nineteenth centuries about the nature of papal solicitude in matters of faith and morals. He advances the hypothesis that these authors consider noninfallible papal action in matters of faith to be an exercise of papal disciplinary power. If this is true, the response owed to such teaching is not that of absolute obedience. All would agree that the response to disciplinary regulations admits of some exceptions and the possibility of acting in a different manner.[35]

The acceptance of such a general understanding of the hierarchical magisterium involves the recognition that dissent can exist on more than one issue. It is not enough merely to study the historical development of ecclesiology to show that the Catholic tradition acknowledges the possibility of dissent from authoritative, noninfallible papal teaching. One must also raise the question of why such dissent can and should exist. There are two ultimate theological reasons justifying the possibility of dissent.

First, specific moral teachings are not that intimately connected with faith. Catholic theology has recognized there exists a hierarchy of truths and has carefully attempted to distinguish various truths and how they relate to the central core of faith. In responding to *Humanae vitae* the Canadian bishops acknowledged that some Catholics had difficulty in appropriating the teaching condemning artificial birth control. "Since they are not denying any point of divine and Catholic faith nor rejecting the teaching authority of the Church, these Catholics should not be considered, or consider themselves, shut off from the body of the faithful."[36] The statement of the Canadian bishops espouses a general principle which applies to other questions. Specific moral questions do not involve a matter of divine faith. Consequently, Roman Catholics could disagree on other specific teachings and not be cut off from the body of the faithful.

A second reason justifying the possibility of dissent from specific moral teachings rests on epistemological grounds. Particular moral questions by their very nature involve a great degree of specificity. On a more general level one can and should find great certitude, but as one descends to the particular, the individual and the specific, the possibility of differing positions exists. The greater the particularity and specificity, the more difficult it is to claim for one's solution a certitude that excludes the possibility of error. All can agree on the basic virtues or attitudes that should characterize the Christian life, but their practical realization often involves the possibility of legitimate differences. Peace and justice are both very significant Christian attitudes, but for the sake of justice violence sometimes can be acceptable. All can agree on the need to respect human life, but the Catholic tradition recognizes that in the practical question of capital punishment there can be different positions within the Catholic community.

Although I disagree with those who hold a relational criterion as determining the beginning of human life and will reject such an opinion in Chapter Eight, I cannot say that those who hold such an opinion are outside the Church of Jesus Christ. It is interesting to recall that Catholic moral theology in the 1950s recognized that one could not be absolutely certain when death occurs. Pope Pius XII admitted that the traditional definition of death as the complete and final separation of the soul from the body lacks precision. Hence the church looks to doctors, especially the anesthesiologists, to give a clear and precise meaning of death and the moment of death.[37] Catholic moral theologians distinguished between real death and apparent death. Real death might not occur for a number of hours after apparent death, especially when death results from a sudden accident.[38] If one cannot be certain when death occurs, it seems logical that there is also a lack of certitude about the beginning of truly human life.

Ramifications

The discussion has been limited to the possibility of dissent. Whether or not one should dissent from a particular hierarchical teaching rests with a decision of conscience after a thoughtful and prayerful reflection on all the aspects involved. However, the acceptance of the possibility of dissent calls for significant changes in our understanding of the church.

As a very first step the Catholic Church will have to learn to live with a greater pluralism on specific moral issues. In one sense this pluralism is accepted by the hierarchical magisterium in matters of social morality, but it will now become even more evident in questions of personal morality. The unwillingness to admit legitimate dissent in the case of *Humanae vitae* underscores how difficult it will be to allow dissent in other areas.

An important corollary recognizes that the unity of the church should not be grounded on specific moral issues. Unfortunately, especially in the United States, the unity and distinctive characteristics of Roman Catholicism have often been based on such particular moral issues. Before the Second Vatican Council the good Roman Catholic was the one who went to Mass on Sunday, did not eat meat on Friday and did not employ artificial contraception. It will be very difficult to change these long-ingrained attitudes, but such specific areas so removed from the core of faith can never be the place where the unity of the church is to be found.

One who accepts such a view of the hierarchical teaching office, the possibility of dissent and a greater pluralism in the church on specific moral matters must be consistent. Today this consistency is sometimes threatened in the area of social ethics. Both theoretically and practically our ethical concerns in the Catholic Church have too often forgotten about the social aspect of morality. Contemporary political and liberation theologies rightly show the need for church involvement in overcoming all forms of oppression and injustice. Our theology and our church life can no longer remain privatized and divorced from the human struggle for freedom and justice in the world in which we live. However, here too one must admit a pluralism within the church in regard to particular strategies for bringing about social change. In the light of the gospel and of human experience one can find a strong basis for a negative critique of the injustice, oppression, consumerism and exploitation in our modern world. However, it will always be more difficult to find agreement on what should positively be done and on the strategy best suited to bring about change.

There is no doubt that the model of the church proposed here will not be as prophetic as some people in the church think it should be. For many reasons we all want the church to be prophetic, but we must understand this in terms of a broader ecclesiology. There will always be a tension between the prophetic aspect of the community and the freedom of the individual believer. We all occasionally succumb to the temptation of insisting on pluralism or prophecy depending on where we stand on a particular issue.

I still insist that there is a significant prophetic aspect to the church. Here it is necessary to point out the importance of a negative critique as a form of prophecy. From this perspective the whole church must constantly speak out against the evils which are present in our world. In terms of more positive strategies for social change a greater role must be given to smaller groups within the church. I am not a pacifist or a supporter of unilateral nuclear disarmament under the present historical circumstances. However, there must always be room within the church for groups of Christians who are fighting for such causes. There are many things that smaller groups can together work for which the whole church as such cannot adopt. At times the whole church through the hierarchical teaching office should speak out on specific social questions, but with the realization that some Catholics may disagree. Chapter Five will further elaborate on the role of the church in social teaching and social action.

In the past pluralism was recognized in social matters precisely because of the complexity of the questions involved and their distance from the core of faith. These particular questions can never be separated from faith, but we must recognize that faith is here mediated in and through many human realities. Today I am proposing the same reasons exist for the insistence on a greater pluralism even in questions of personal morality. The first part of this chapter has pointed out that current methodological approaches in moral theology stress that specific moral norms must be seen in terms of protecting human meaning and values; norms are not found in the very structure of faculties. Moral theology today recognizes the danger of physicalism, or of identifying the human moral act with the physical structure of the act. Many theologians rightly deny the existence of moral absolutes when the forbidden behavior is defined solely in terms of the physical structure of the act. In this light the official teaching on questions such as contraception, sterilization, abortion, sexuality, euthanasia, divorce and the principle of double effect has been challenged. However, it must be underlined that now it is impossible to discuss all of these specific issues. Likewise, as pointed out above, there are times when the physical aspect of the act is identified with the moral aspect. I merely want to recognize that the possibility of dissent can exist in these areas.

One should not conclude that there is no role for the hierarchical magisterium in the church. However, the way in which the papal and episcopal teaching offices carry out their function must take account of the changed understandings. Above all, the hierarchical magisterium must use all available means to discern the call of the Spirit and to recognize that it must have the courage at times to admit that past teachings were wrong. In the name of the whole church the hierarchical magisterium at times must speak out. However, even after every possible means of discernment is used, the possibility of dissent will always exist in the area of specific moral teachings.

Evaluation of the Present Situation

I have just sketched the ramifications for the church of the acceptance of the possibility of dissent from authoritative hierarchical teaching. How does this theory correspond with the present reality? In practice it seems that the present situation fits the theory described above. However, the hierarchical church itself often does not officially recognize or accept such a situation.

There is no doubt that many people in the Catholic Church today disagree in theory and in practice with hierarchical church teachings on a number of specific moral issues. Various opinion polls report this understanding of the contemporary situation. A modus vivendi seems to have been reached in matters of birth control, divorce and even homosexuality. Although official teaching has not changed on any of these issues, in actuality the church has changed, for many people acting contrary to official teaching fully participate in its life.

This modus vivendi seems to have provided a climate in which diversity exists without threatening the official teaching of the church. Yes, there are many advantages to the present situation; one could argue that it should continue in existence. However, I strongly insist that the present situation should not continue. The hierarchical teaching office cannot have it both ways. The present situation in which the official teaching and the accepted practice are so different cannot continue. I am willing to recognize there will always be gaps between promise and performance in the Christian life for all of us. Likewise, there will always be tension between teaching the way of the Lord and at the same time showing mercy to those who are not able to fully respond to this teaching. However, the hierarchical teaching authority cannot say one thing in theory and tacitly acknowledge another in practice. Although achieving a kind of peace, the present situation also involves some glaring problems and inconsistencies which call for it to be changed.

Sometimes the contradiction between the level of official teaching and the actual practice will surface. Take, for example, the approach of the Roman Catholic Church to the world population conference in Bucharest in 1974. On the basis of official policy the Catholic Church is still opposed to artificial contraception, even though most of its members disagree. The church's hands are thus tied in trying to contribute positively to the problem of population growth.[39]

A vexing problem has arisen for Catholic hospitals. The ethical directives for Catholic hospitals prohibit any direct sterilization. Many Catholics do become sterilized—often with the advice and encouragement of a priest—and continue to be loyal Catholics. However, Catholic hospitals cannot do sterilizations, which for all practical purposes are only female sterilizations, since male vasectomies are done in the doctor's office. A number of Catholic hospitals today feel that their continued existence is placed in jeopardy because of their inability to do direct sterilizations.[40]

Second, the continuance of the present situation ultimately damages the credibility of the church and of the hierarchical teaching office. Greeley attributes the decline in Roman Catholic practice in the United States to the encyclical. My tendency is to interpret the cause of the decline as more complex, but many Catholics have seen the refusal of the hierarchical magisterium to change its teaching on artificial contraception as a sign that the church is not mediating the word and work of Jesus in our time.

Third, at the very least the present situation does not seem to be honest. The bishops clearly recognize what is taking place in practice, but at the same time they continue to reiterate the older teaching. This situation can only continue to harm the church.

Fourth, in the present situation the role of institutional structures and of the hierarchical office is being steadily eroded. Take, for example, the question of remarriage after divorce. Many divorced Catholics decide, often with the advice of a priest, to remarry and to continue celebrating the sacraments of the church. Such a situation is basically good, but there are dangers of harm and injustice to innocent people which call for some official guidelines. There is a proper place and a need for the hierarchical office to regulate procedures in the life of the church, yet today many practices are developing outside and beyond the official structure. Such a situation cannot and should not continue for too long a period of time.

Fifth, in the eyes of many Roman Catholics there must be important institutional changes in the church. Issues such as divorce and remarriage, women priests, and clerical celibacy call for change. In a sense *Humanae vitae* has become symbolic. If the hierarchical church refuses to change here, there will probably be no change on the other issues.

On the question of artificial contraception the pope and bishops must be willing to admit publicly that the previous teaching is wrong. At the very least they need to acknowledge officially the legitimacy of dissent on this question and the ramifications of dissent in the entire life of the church. From my perspective the issuance of *Humanae vitae* was a tragic mistake in the life of the church, but there have been some good effects. The papal encyclical condemning artificial contraception for married couples has occasioned and even promoted a rethinking both of the methodology of moral theology and of the teaching functions and roles in the church.

NOTES

1. Pope Paul used the expression *la vívida discussión* in a speech delivered to the Second General Conference of Latin American Bishops (CELAM) held at Medellín, Colombia, on August 24, 1968. *Acta Apostolicae Sedis* 60 (1968): 649.

2. These three categories are employed by a number of authors. See William H. Shannon, *The Lively Debate: Response to Humanae Vitae* (New York: Sheed and Ward, 1970), pp. 117–146; also Joseph A. Selling, "The Reaction to *Humanae Vitae:* A Study in Special and Fundamental Theology" (S.T.D. dissertation, Catholic University of Louvain, 1977), pp. 1–139.

3. For the historical description and theological defense of this statement see Charles E. Curran et al., *Dissent in and for the Church: Theologians and Humanae Vitae* (New York: Sheed and Ward, 1969).

4. Perhaps the best indication of the number of American theologians who support the teaching of *Humanae vitae* can be found in the

board members and founding members of the newly created Fellowship of Catholic Scholars. One of their chief purposes is to support the teaching of the Catholic magisterium.

5. Andrew M. Greeley, William C. McCready, and Kathleen McCourt, *Catholic Schools in a Declining Church* (Kansas City: Sheed and Ward, 1976), p. 35.

6. Ibid., p. 153.

7. Ibid., pp. 103–154.

8. *Acta Apostolicae Sedis* 60 (1968): 481–503. The English translation of this encyclical and of the other official documents cited in this chapter can be obtained from the Publications Office, United States Catholic Conference, 1312 Massachusetts Ave., N.W., Washington, D.C. 20005. The paragraph numbers to *Humanae vitae* in the text refer to both the original Latin and the English translation.

9. Germain G. Grisez, *Contraception and the Natural Law* (Milwaukee: Bruce Publishing Co., 1964), pp. 76–106.

10. Dietrich von Hildebrand, *The Encyclical Humanae Vitae: A Sign of Contradiction* (Chicago: Franciscan Herald Press, 1969), pp. 35–49. See also William E. May, *Human Existence, Medicine and Ethics* (Chicago: Franciscan Herald Press, 1977), pp. 67–86.

11. Pope Pius XII, Address to the Italian Catholic Union of Midwives, October 29, 1951, *Acta Apostolicae Sedis* 43 (1951): 835–854; English translation: *The Catholic Mind* 50 (January 1952): 49–64.

12. For this development and for the most comprehensive history of the teaching on contraception see John T. Noonan, Jr., *Contraception: A History of Its Treatment by the Catholic Theologians and Canonists* (Cambridge: Harvard University Press, 1965).

13. Pope Pius XII, Address to the Fourth International Convention of Catholic Physicians, September 29, 1949, *Acta Apostolicae Sedis* 41 (1949): 557–561. For a development of other papal references to artificial insemination and for current theological discussion see John F. Dedek, *Contemporary Medical Ethics* (New York: Sheed and Ward, 1975), pp. 97–101.

14. Rodger Van Allen, "Artificial Insemination (AIH): A Contemporary Re-analysis," *Homiletic and Pastoral Review* 70 (1970): 363–372. Bernard Häring, *Manipulation: Ethical Boundaries of Medical Behavioural and Genetic Manipulation* (London: St. Paul Publications, 1975), pp. 194–195.

15. See, for example, Leandro Rossi, "Diretto e indiretto in teologia morale," *Rivista di Teologia Morale* 3, no. 9 (1971): 37–65; idem, "Il limite del principio del duplice effeto," *Rivista di Teologia Morale* 4, no. 13 (1972): 11–37.

16. Some of these opinions can be found in *Avortement et respect de la vie humaine,* Colloque du Centre Catholique des Médecins Français (Paris: Éditions du Seuil, 1972).

17. For a synthetic approach to human sexuality in the light of contemporary Catholic moral theology see Philip S. Keane, *Sexual Morality: A Catholic Perspective* (New York: Paulist Press, 1977).

18. For an argument in favor of euthanasia in some circumstances see Daniel C. Maguire, *Death by Choice* (Garden City, New York: Doubleday, 1974). For a review of recent literature and a rejection of euthanasia in the light of Catholic teaching see Kevin D. O'Rourke, *Hospital Progress* 57, no. 11 (November 1976): 68–73.

19. See my *New Perspectives in Moral Theology* (Notre Dame, Indiana: University of Notre Dame Press, 1976), pp. 212–276.

20. For a discussion of these theories see Richard A. McCormick, *Ambiguity in Moral Choice* (Milwaukee: Marquette University Press, 1973). McCormick has closely followed these developments in his "Notes on Moral Theology" which appears every year in *Theological Studies*.

21. Anthony Kosnik et al., *Human Sexuality: New Dimensions in American Catholic Thought* (New York: Paulist Press, 1977), pp. 88–98.

22. *Acta Apostolicae Sedis* 68 (1976): 77–96; English translation: *The Catholic Mind* 74 (April 1976): 52–64.

23. Roger Aubert, *Le pontificat de Pie IX,* Histoire de l'église depuis les origines jusqu'à nos jours, XXI (Paris: Bloud & Gay), pp. 254–261.

24. Murray developed the historical aspects of his thesis in a series of articles in *Theological Studies*. On the issue under discussion see especially John Courtney Murray, "Leo XIII: Separation of Church and State," *Theological Studies* 14 (1953): 145–214. For a synthetic presentation of his position see John Courtney Murray, "The Problem of Religious Freedom," *Theological Studies* 25 (1964): 503–575. For a study of Murray's teaching on this point see Faith E. Burgess, *The Relationship between Church and State according to John Courtney Murray, S.J.* (Düsseldorf: Rudolf Stehle, 1971).

25. See, for example, my book *Christian Morality Today* (Notre Dame, Indiana: Fides Publishers, 1966), pp. 47–91.

26. For a brief overview of this period see Shannon, *The Lively Debate*, pp. 32–75.

27. Ibid., pp. 90–94.

28. For a quite complete study of the various reactions to the encyclical see Selling's dissertation, "The Reaction to *Humanae Vitae.*"

29. Karl Rahner, "Zur Enzyklika *Humanae Vitae*," *Stimmen der Zeit* 93, no. 9 (1968): 193–210; English translation: *Theological Investigations XI: Confrontations I* (New York: Seabury Press, 1974), pp. 263–287. For a somewhat similar position see Norbert Rigali, "The Historical Meaning of the *Humanae Vitae* Controversy," *Chicago Studies* 15 (1976): 127–138.

30. This theory was first proposed by Peter Knauer, "La détermination du bien et du mal moral par le principe du double effet," *Nouvelle*

Revue Théologique 87 (1965): 356–376; also idem, "Überlegungen zur moraltheologischen Prinzipienlehre der Enzyklika *Humanae Vitae*," *Theologie und Philosophie* 45 (1970): 60–74.

31. For a similar position see P. J. McGrath, "On Not Reinterpreting *Humanae Vitae*," *Irish Theological Quarterly* 38 (1971): 130–143.

32. Joseph A. Komonchak, "Ordinary Papal Magisterium and Religious Assent," in *Contraception: Authority and Dissent*, ed. Charles E. Curran (New York: Herder and Herder, 1969), pp. 101–126.

33. Daniel C. Maguire, "Morality and Magisterium," *Cross Currents* 18 (1968): 41–65. See Avery Dulles, "The Theologian and the Magisterium," *Proceedings of the Catholic Theological Society of America* 31 (1976): 235–246.

34. Yves M. Congar, "Pour une histoire semantique du terme 'magisterium'," *Revue des sciences philosophiques et théologiques* 60 (1976): 85–98; idem, "Bref historique des formes du 'magistere' et des ses relations avec les docteurs," *Revue des sciences philosophiques et théologiques* 60 (1976): 99–112.

35. Michael D. Place, "The Response Due to Papal Solicitude: A Study of Selected Eighteenth Century Theologians" (S.T.D. dissertation, Catholic University of America, 1978). For an overview of some recent approaches see Richard A. McCormick, "Notes on Moral Theology," *Theological Studies* 38 (1977): 84–114.

36. Curran et al., *Dissent in and for the Church*, pp. 199–200. See Edward F. Sheridan, "Canadian Bishops on Human Life," *America* 119 (October 19, 1968): 349–352.

37. Pope Pius XII, "Address to an International Congress of Anesthesiologists," November 24, 1957, *Acta Apostolicae Sedis* 49 (1957): 1031; English translation: *The Pope Speaks* 4 (1958): 396–397.

38. Edwin F. Healy, *Medical Ethics* (Chicago: Loyola University Press, 1956), pp. 381–383.

39. Michael J. Walsh, "The Holy See's Population Problem," *The Month* 7 (1974): 632–636.

40. John P. Boyle, *The Sterilization Controversy: A New Crisis for the Catholic Hospital* (New York: Paulist Press, 1977).

3: Moral Theology, Psychiatry and Homosexuality

The subject of homosexuality is currently being discussed at great length in both the psychiatric and theological literature. Both psychiatrists and theologians disagree in their evaluation of homosexuality. These sharp discussions within and between these two disciplines raise once again the very significant question of the relationship between psychiatry and theology. The purpose of this chapter is twofold: first, to discuss the relationship between theology and psychiatry; second, to develop an approach to the morality of homosexual relations and homosexual acts. The perspective will be that of Roman Catholic theology but with an appreciation of the ecumenical dimension of contemporary theology.

I. Relationship between Theology and Psychiatry

Moral theology and psychiatry have many similar interests, and as a result potential conflicts can arise rather easily. Both disciplines examine human behavior. Specifically, some very fundamental questions are touched by both—freedom, guilt, interior peace, sexuality. In addition the sacrament of penance in Roman Catholicism celebrates the peace of God through the reconciliation of the sinner with the community and with the risen Lord. What is the relationship between the peace of the sacrament and the peace that comes with the help of psychiatry? The overlappings of the two disciplines are very obvious.

The Relationship in Its Historical Development

The relationship between theology and psychiatry in its historical development generally took the form of Catholicism's reaction to and relationship with the theory of Freud. Generally speaking, the first reaction within Catholicism to Freud was quite negative. Catholicism and Freud seemed diametrically opposed, for Freud was an atheist, a materialist and a determinist. In addition his whole approach seemed to be hedonistic.[1] The antipathy between Catholicism and Freud has often continued on the level of popular understanding.[2]

Catholic scholarship, especially in France in the 1930s, began to take a more positive approach to Freud by sorting out those areas in which the church and theology could learn from Freud from those areas in which Freud could not be accepted. The greatest contribution in the reassessment of Freud can be found in the two-volume work of Roland Dalbiez published in 1936.[3] Subsequently a large number of French Catholic authors entered into dialogue with Freud and tried to bridge the gap between Freud and Catholicism.

In 1949 Madame Maryse Choisy, a French psychiatrist, and Leycester King, S.J., professor of psychology at Oxford, sponsored the first international congress of Catholic psychotherapists and psychologists.[4] Articles and books carrying on the dialogue appeared in French especially in publications such as *Psyche,* founded by Madame Choisy in 1946, as well as in *Études Carmelitaines, Supplément de la vie spirituelle* and *Cahiers Laënnec.*

The fifth annual conference of this Catholic group was held in Rome in 1953. Pope Pius XII received the participants in an audience and addressed them.[5] The spirit of dialogue pervaded much of the papal address. At the end the pope assured his hearers that the church follows their work and practice with warm interest and best wishes. Psychotherapists labor on a terrain which is very difficult, but their activity is capable of producing precious results for medicine, for the knowledge of the soul in general, and for the religious dispositions of human beings and their development.

The Christian psychotherapist must always consider the human person from a fourfold perspective: as a psychic unit and totality which cannot be reduced to one particular dimension; as a structured unit in itself in which there can be no true opposition between the psychological and the metaphysical, or ontological, aspect of human existence; as a social unit which refutes the error by defect which reduces all dynamic tendencies in human beings to unconscious urges and refutes the error by excess which in the name of altruism and going out to others forgets about a proper love of self; as a transcendent unity whose human existence can never forget the relationship to God. Specifically, three topics are considered under this last heading. There is nothing against faith if psychology discovers a religious instinct in human beings. Second, in addition to neurotic or morbid guilt which psychotherapy tries to heal, there is also a true guilt of the sinner before God. Third, the transcendent orientation must always show respect for God and his likeness as reflected especially in moral norms and in human actions. At times the individual will not be formally or subjectively guilty for his actions, but material sin can only be tolerated and never approved by the therapist. Thus, in general, Pope Pius XII accepted the dialogue with psychiatry and psychoanalysis by recognizing that there can and should be a harmonious relationship between psychiatry and Catholicism but pointing out that psychiatry must always respect the total human being and the moral law.[6]

The ensuing dialogue often distinguished various levels in Freud's thought—the philosophical, the psychological and the therapeutic. On the philosophical level Freud was an atheist, materialist and determinist. Accordingly there is a definite and irreconcilable conflict between his philosophy of human nature and Catholic philosophy.[7] However, authors like Albert Plé even played down these differences. Freud was looking only at the premoral, or the subhuman, aspect of the human act. It is true that he scarcely mentions reasonable human acts, but he is a physician of the mentally ill, most of whom are operating on the premoral or subhuman level. At times there are occasional expressions in Freud about freedom, self-control, the higher part of human nature, joy in intellectual work and altruistic love.[8]

On the level of psychology somewhat the same distinctions occur. Freud fails to give importance to the rational aspect of psychology. He overemphasizes the instinctive, the irrational and emotional elements in human nature.[9] Plé again tries to be somewhat more accepting of Freud by showing how his position is compatible with that of Thomas Aquinas; the two can complement one another in the realm of psychology.[10] On the level of therapy many authors recognized that Freudian psychoanalysis has made great contributions to the knowledge of human beings and our unconscious. Psychoanalytic theory is neutral and can be used by believers or nonbelievers. There are some dangers, but through psychoanalysis Freud has provided a valuable means for contributing toward human development, growth and maturity.[11]

This dialogue with and openness to Freud especially on the level of psychoanalysis as therapy also took place in the United States. In 1950 the Guild of Catholic Psychiatrists held their first meeting. Their journal, *The Bulletin of the Guild of Catholic Psychiatrists,* began in 1953. In the first volume the compatability between Freudian therapy and Catholic principles is affirmed.[12] However, it is fair to say that the intellectual level of the discussion in this country never reached the same height as it did in France. The translation of some important, groundbreaking French articles into English was warmly welcomed by Catholic psychiatrists in the United States.[13]

The dialogue with and acceptance of Freudianism as complementary to Roman Catholic philosophy and understanding became accepted into the mainstream of Catholic thought. However, suspicions and tensions continued to exist on all levels of the church, not merely in the widespread popular belief that the church itself was opposed to psychiatry and psychoanalysis.

In 1952 a then minor Vatican official, Msgr. Pericle Felici, wrote in the monthly bulletin for the clergy of Rome that it is difficult to excuse from mortal sin those who adopt the curative method of psychoanalysis and those who voluntarily submit to it. Many observers saw the later papal statement as a correction of the impression given by the above analysis.[14]

Another incident showing tension involved the decision of the Congregation of the Holy Office to put on the index of forbidden books a study written by Marc Oraison. The book *Vie chrétienne et problèmes de la sexualité* was originally a doctoral dissertation written by Oraison, who was a priest, physician and psychoanalyst. Oraison, by the way, continues in his work and has published many subsequent books, including one on homosexuality.[15] In this book under discussion Oraison accepted the Catholic teaching on the grave objective immorality of sexual sins. However, since most human beings are so immature sexually and so dominated by unconscious motives, it is only rare that grave subjective mortal sin exists in sexual matters. The book was condemned on March 18, 1953, but the condemnation was not publicly announced until January 3, 1955. Orasion submitted to and accepted this negative judgment.[16]

On July 15, 1961, the Congregation of the Holy Office issued a *Monitum,* or warning, about psychoanalysis. The *Monitum* mentioned the existence of dangerous opinions about sexual sins and imputability and also indicated that psychoanalytic training is not necessary for all priests. Priests and religious are forbidden to practice psychoanalysis without permission, but this merely represents a restatement of canon law which prohibits to clerics the practice of medicine and surgery. The fourth point in the document ordered that priests and religious of both sexes are not to undergo psychoanalysis unless their ordinary permits it for a grave reason. Although not denying the complementarity of faith and psychiatry, this document in itself and in its general understanding in the popular press gave a more negative impression of this relationship. Many theologians in interpreting the last part of the *Monitum* distinguished between psychology and psychiatry, on the one hand, and psychoanalysis on the other. Psychoanalysis here is to be interpreted in the very narrow and strict sense.[17]

This section has tried to give an overview of the relationship between theology and psychiatry which generally became one of dialogue, complementarity and harmonious working together despite dangers and problems that could easily exist.

What Should the Relationship Be?

After a review of the historical development of the relationship the question arises: What should be the relationship between theology and psychiatry? This query forms part of the larger question of the relationship between theology and the empirical sciences. In general the relationship should recognize an overall harmony and complementarity, but also some tensions and possible dangers.

First, there should exist a general harmony and complementarity between theology and the empirical sciences, including psychology and psychiatry. In this context I am writing in terms of the tradition of Roman Catholic theology, but I propose this position as normative for the entire theological enterprise.

The Roman Catholic faith and theological traditions have insisted on the bold assertion that faith and reason cannot contradict one another. Chapter One has already pointed out that this fundamental premise constitutes the cornerstone of the Catholic theological tradition. Truth is one. Faith and reason can never be opposed.[18] The history of Catholic theology shows the influence of such an approach, but also at times, especially after the Reformation and in the nineteenth century, the practice of Catholic theology did not live up to its theory. In the beginning the early responses to Freud betrayed a mistrust of reason and of science.

However, the Second Vatican Council in the Pastoral Constitution on the Church in the Modern World reaffirmed the best in our tradition when it treated the relationship between faith and science: "If methodological investigation within every branch of learning is carried out in a genuinely scientific manner and in accord with true moral norms, it never truly conflicts with faith" (no. 36).[19]

A second reason for the general complementarity between theology/faith and reason/science is grounded in Catholic theology's acceptance of the goodness of the human.[20] Just as faith and reason are basically harmonious, so too Catholic theology accepted a complementarity between nature, or the human, and supernature, or grace. According to the traditional understanding grace in no way contradicts nature or is opposed to nature, but, rather, grace builds on nature. Catholic theology accepted and made its own the principle that nothing human can be foreign to the Christian. Today there are different ways of expressing the relationship between nature and grace, but the basic affirmation of the goodness of the human remains.

On this basis Catholic moral theology founded its theory of natural law. The epistemological question for Christian theology asks where the Christian finds true ethical wisdom and knowledge. Is it merely in the sacred scriptures, in Jesus Christ, in revelation and in grace? Catholic theology responded that human reason on the basis of human nature can be a source of ethical wisdom and knowledge. How do we know what God wants us to do? What is right and wrong in God's sight? Do we appeal immediately and directly to the will of God? The Catholic tradition has answered the last question in the negative. God's will is revealed mediately in and through the humanity which we have. We are to act in accord with our God-given human nature. We must make every effort to learn the meaning of our humanity, for in this way we come to discover what it is God wants us to do and to be. Again there have rightly been many objections to the traditional concept of natural law in Catholic thought, but the fundamental insight endures. As was pointed out in Chapter One, the Catholic tradition espouses a basic openness to reason and the human and to whatever reason can tell us about the human.

Although there is a complementarity between theology and the sciences in general or psychiatry in particular, there is not a perfect identity. As a result there will always be some tensions and possible conflicts. First, empirical sciences in general, as important and significant as they are, do not consider the totality of the human. There exists the transcendent aspect of the human which in some ways lies beyond the empirical. The scientific is only a part of the human. The human realities of love, hope, joy and searching for truth have a transcendent dimension about them. Likewise, to live the Christian understanding of the paschal mystery with its law of the cross and its belief in life in the midst of death shows the transcendent aspect of human existence.

Aspects of this limitation of the sciences can be seen in some of the recent discussions in modern medicine and genetics. Sometimes there has been a tendency not to accept the limitations of the scientific. Genetics can do great things to better human existence, but the realities of pride, sloth, anger, hatred, acquisitiveness and an unwillingness to share love, life and goods with others cannot find an ultimate remedy in genetics. Human sinfulness still remains a part of our existence, and we know only one Messiah. On the other hand I disagree with those who are unwilling to see the positive contributions that science can and should make. Especially in the area of genetics and modern medicine one often hears the complaint that human beings should not play God. However, through our scientific advances there is no doubt that we have more power now than we have ever had before. There are some circumstances in which we can and should do what might be described by some as playing God. Our decisions about who receives scarce lifesaving technologies will involve the decisive judgment about who lives and who dies.[21] Yes, there is a danger of using the limitations of science to prevent and oppose legitimate growth and progress, while at the same time one can never forget that the heights and the depths of what it means to be human transcend the level of the scientific.

A second source of tension arises from the fact that there are many empirical sciences dealing with the human. Moral theology looks at the human action from the broadest possible perspective and horizon. The empirical sciences have a more particular horizon and perspective. For example, one can consider the human from the aspect of sociology, psychology, pedagogy, biology, and so on. All these are particular aspects of the human. In this finite world in which we live very often nothing is perfect from every single perspective. At the very minimum one must admit that the perspective or horizon of one science is not always identical with the truly human horizon. One illustration of this reality can be found in the discussions common to many sciences about the ethical nature of experimentation. Experimentation is absolutely essential to the growth of science. However, there are moral and human limits to what is acceptable experimentation. Even though some experiments might be helpful and important from the viewpoint of increasing scientific knowledge, there are times when it is necessary in the name of the human to say no to them.

One can never totally identify any one science with the human. In practice, just because something is possible or even good from the perspective of one science, it does not follow that we should always do it. Genetics might in the future find it possible to clone (produce genetic twins) famous and success- ful people. What a boon it would be, according to some geneticists, if the human race had ten thousand Einsteins, ten thousand Martin Luther Kings, or ten thousand Mother Teresas! But there are many other aspects that must be considered. What about the psychological problems created for all these "identical twins"? What about the problem of identity among themselves and with the famous twin they are supposed to imitate? No one science can claim to be identical with the truly human.

Third, problems exist for the moral theologian and ethicist when there is a difference of opinion within a particular science. The moral theologian must be open to the data of all the sciences but cannot be an expert in most of the empirical sciences. The problems become immensely more complex when scientists themselves disagree. Within every science there are often different opinions about theory, methodology and practical conclusions. In economics one can follow Fried- man, Galbraith or Marx. In psychology the differences go all the way from Skinner to Erikson. Experts in the field cannot agree, but ultimately human beings have to make decisions and cannot postpone these until all the evidence is in from the experts. Part of the contemporary crisis of culture comes from the fact that all of us as human beings must make decisions in the midst of great complexity and of some uncertainty about which approach is best. The ethicist or moral theologian who studies the morality of human acts faces this same problem. Thus, there exists a number of tensions between the scientific and the human perspective.

In the specific area of psychiatry there are many illustrations of these tensions. In the 1950s and later an interesting discussion took place in Catholic theology about the relationship between sanctity and psychic health. In its bald terms the question was phrased: Can a neurotic be a saint and vice versa? It was often argued that one could be a neurotic and a saint. Sanctity does not ultimately depend on human psychic structures. Although sanctity can exist in persons with deformed psychic structures, anyone in the Catholic tradition with its acceptance of the goodness of the human and the positive relation between grace and nature must always work for the shining forth of sanctity in whole and healthy psychic structures.[22]

The terms neurotic and immoral do not necessarily mean the same thing or describe the same reality. There are neurotic forms of behavior which are not immoral and vice versa. Lying often occurs under stress situations without any neurosis present. However, this does not mean that lying is not morally wrong. The very fact that neurotic and immoral are not identical points to significant differences between psychiatry and moral theology. Also moral theology recognizes the disagreement existing within psychiatry on many theoretical and practical issues.

II. The Morality of Homosexual Acts

The first part of this chapter has studied the relationship between psychiatry and theology. The second half should logically focus on how moral theology approaches the evaluation of homosexuality and how it employs psychiatric data. First, moral theology must be open to the data and findings of psychology, of psychiatry and of all the sciences about homosexuality. No one should study the morality of homosexuality without such data.

A Christian theologian must consider other sources in addition to the data of the sciences. Christian moral theology first of all gives great significance to the teaching of the scriptures. The exegetical question concerns the proper understanding of what the scriptures themselves mean in their references to homosexuality. Then this scriptural teaching must be applied to the contemporary situation. On both these questions there are divided opinions within the theological enterprise. Moral theology likewise pays special attention to the Christian tradition, but again there exist the questions of knowing exactly what the tradition teaches and of applying this understanding correctly in our contemporary circumstances. The Catholic theologian is also guided by the official teaching of the hierarchical church as was developed at great length in Chapter Two. Human ethical reasoning also furnishes an important aspect of the approach. In general, moral theology tries to develop a coherent theory which gives due weight to all these different factors as it tries to evaluate individual questions.

As we pointed out above, immorality and psychological or psychiatric disorders are not identical. The problem is even more complex because of the lack of agreement within psychiatry on the nature of homosexuality, about which there have been many divergent opinions over the years. Is it a disease? A symptom? A neurosis? A personality disorder? An arrested stage of development? A normal condition? Perhaps the current trends in the literature are best illustrated in recent actions by the American Psychiatric Association. In 1973 the trustees of the American Psychiatric Association by a unanimous vote with some abstentions ruled that homosexuality should no longer be listed as a "mental disorder" in its official nomenclature of mental disorders. A new category called "sexual orientation disturbance" describes those whose sexual orientation is to the same sex and who are bothered by such an orientation or wish to change it. Later a minority of about 40 percent of the members did not support such a change. In addition there is still no agreement on the etiology of homosexuality. Various theories have been proposed about the cause of homosexuality—organic factors including hormonal influences, genetic factors and psychological or environmental conditions.[23]

The above paragraphs describe the way in which moral theology should approach the question of the morality of homosexual actions with special emphasis on the data of psychiatry and its relationship to the theological-ethical analysis. I have already developed at great length my approach to homosexuality.[24] There is no need to repeat that analysis, but in the light of misinterpretations and of the need for greater clarity this section will explain more fully the position already proposed.

In general there are three positions which can be taken with regard to the moral evaluation of homosexual actions. The first, which has been the traditionally accepted teaching in general and is the official teaching of the hierarchical magisterium in Roman Catholicism, affirms that homosexual acts are always wrong. In the Catholic tradition the procreative purpose, the male-female aspect of sexuality and a faculty-act analysis serve as the basis for this moral condemnation of homosexual acts. However, this position can and does admit that, subjectively, homosexual acts may not always be gravely sinful because of diminished imputability on the part of the person.[25]

A second position maintains that homosexual acts are neutral. The morality of the sexual act depends upon the quality of the relationship. The moral determination does not rest on whether the act is heterosexual or homosexual, but rather the quality of the relationship of the persons determines the morality.[26]

A third generic position can most aptly be called a mediating position. There are a number of different ways in which mediating positions can be developed. I proposed a position based on what I call a theory of compromise. Basically, I want to develop a theory which can coherently incorporate two presuppositions which at first sight might seem opposed or contradictory. Obviously my own ethical judgments form the basis for these two different presuppositions that I want to hold together.

First, for an irreversible or constitutional homosexual, homosexual acts in the context of a loving relationship striving for permanency can be and are morally good. There is great debate in the literature about whether a constitutional or irreversible homosexual can truly be changed to heterosexuality. For theoretical as well as practical reasons (time, expense) it seems that the irreversible and constitutional homosexuals cannot and should not be changed. This presupposition accepts the general understanding that the homosexual has no control over one's own sexual orientation. There is no personal fault or guilt whatsoever which brings about the homosexual condition. An individual has the psychic structure of inversion independently of one's own willing and doing. I also maintain that not all homosexuals are called to celibacy or sublimation. Not all homosexual acts of irreversible homosexuals are morally good. There must be the context of a loving relationship striving for permanency. Here, too, one must take account of the fact that social pressures work against a more permanent type of relationship between homosexual partners.

On the other hand, I want to maintain that the ideal meaning of human sexual relationships is in terms of male and female. I interpret the existing data from the scripture, the historical tradition and contemporary insight in this manner. Since heterosexual relationships are the ideal, all should strive in this direction, for there is a normative aspect involved here. My theoretical position has two very significant practical corollaries. In terms of education I do not think that youngsters on the onset of puberty should be taught that sexuality is neutral. One is not morally free to make a choice for one or the other. However, even at this stage it should be judiciously pointed out that for the irreversible homosexual homosexual acts in the context of a loving permanent relationship are not morally wrong. A second practical corollary of the ideal of heterosexuality insists that for the struggling adolescent who may go through periods of sexual development the goal should be toward heterosexuality.

Many mediating positions have basically the same general presuppositions as I have outlined above. Such mediating positions are open to rebuttal from both sides. Two recent Catholic studies on homosexuality have challenged my position. John Harvey, arguing for the traditional position, disagrees and insists that homosexuals, like all others who are not married, are called to avoid sexual indulgence.[27] John McNeill adopts a modified version of the second position (quality of the relationship is determinative provided the person is an invert) and disagrees with me for holding that heterosexual relations remain the ideal.[28] Since I have previously defended my presuppositions, it is not necessary to do so again.

With these presuppositions I have tried to develop a theory which coherently explains this reality. Working in the Roman Catholic theological, ethical tradition, I was trying to find in that tradition the resources from which I could construct a coherent explanation incorporating the two general positions outlined above.

In the past the Catholic moral tradition in general and its position on homosexuality in particular did not go far enough in my perspective. One solution is to invoke the distinction between objectively wrong but not always subjectively sinful approach and recognize that this lack of subjective guilt tends to be the rule in the case of the invert. A somewhat similar theory involves the justification of homosexual acts as the lesser of two evils.

From my perspective these approaches still look upon the act as being objectively evil. My position, as previously enunciated, clearly stated that, objectively, homosexual acts for the irreversible homosexual in the context of a loving union tending to permanency are objectively good; but at the same time the ideal and normative human meaning of sexuality are in terms of male and female.

Both Harvey and McNeill have misunderstood my position.

Harvey maintains that according to Curran one must freely sin, and this is a contradiction in terms.[29] At the very least this is an interpretation which I did not hold and, in my judgment, one which in no way follows from my position. McNeill ends his first long discussion of my theory with the conclusion that according to Curran homosexuals must do everything in their power to correct their condition, or at least abstain from an active expression of it — and consequently bring any homosexual love relationship to an end.[30] My conclusion was that for the invert (to use the word which McNeill rightly uses) who is an irreversible homosexual homosexual acts within the context of a loving relationship can be and are objectively, morally good. I spoke about reluctantly accepting such a reality to emphasize that while morally good, these actions still were less than the ideal.

To justify the objective goodness of homosexual acts in such cases it is necessary to appeal to something other than subjective realities. The Catholic ethical tradition has characteristically insisted on an ontological, or metaphysical, basis for morality. *Agere sequitur esse* — morality follows from our being. We should act in accord with who and what we are. In this case the invert has a different psychic structure and a different sexual humanity; consequently the invert's action can and should correspond to this different being. Homosexual acts are grounded in the homosexual psychic structure of the invert.

From my presuppositions it is also necessary to find a way to maintain that heterosexual acts are the ideal, for human sexuality is to be understood in terms of a male-female relationship. How can something be objectively good for some people and yet not the ideal and also objectively wrong for others. How can this type of apparent ethical relativity be justified?

Theological Basis of Compromise

My theory develops and applies in a new way an approach which has existed in the Catholic tradition and was recently emphasized again by Josef Fuchs.[31] The Fathers of the Church with an insistence on the history of salvation distinguished in practice a twofold natural law. There were differences between human beings in the state of paradise before the fall and human beings existing after the fall or sin. In this concept primary natural law corresponds to the state of human existence before the fall, whereas secondary natural law corresponds to the state of human existence after the fall. There is a relativity about natural law, for the material demands of natural law differ in the various situations in the history of salvation. Secondary natural law comes about because of the transforming significance of the invasion of sin into human history.

The distinction between primary and secondary natural law must be seen in the light of another distinction between absolute and relative natural law. Absolute natural law is based on the ontological, abstract human nature viewed in itself. As such this human nature has never existed. Abstract human nature is always incarnated in a different time of the history of salvation. This absolute natural law based on human nature, absolutely considered, is existentially open to different determinations depending on the different contexts of the history of salvation. In the order before the fall these concrete situations are different from those after the fall. Here, then, is the basis for the distinction between the primary and secondary natural law, both of which are aspects of relative natural law. In all these different situations in the history of salvation the absolute natural law is applied. Notice that the absolute natural law is not modified or truly changed in the different historical situations. The formal demands of the absolute natural law remain the same, but they are abstractions which are then applied differently in different situations. The principles of the absolute natural law do not formally change in the changing situations of salvation history; they are changed materially in accord with the accidental changes in the different situations of salvation history.

Examples of secondary, relative natural law abound. Human society, family, marriage, and the state all belong to the absolute natural law. They are part of human existence as such. However, there are certain characteristics of these realities which exist only in the history of salvation after sin. The state in the present condition involves coercion, but this does not belong to the absolute natural law, for sin makes it necessary. Killing in self-defense, just war, capital punishment, revolution and the toleration of evil in society are all examples of relative natural law recognizing the presence of sin. Specific institutions such as slavery and private property are thus called into existence because of the situation of sin in the world. Before the fall there would have been no place for slavery or for private property. The historical situation after the fall brought about certain applications of the absolute natural law in the light of the presence of sin in the world. Fuchs reminded Catholic theology about this approach in its own tradition.

In my judgment Catholic moral thought in the manuals of theology as well as in the changing theology of the 1960s ultimately did not give enough importance to the reality and the effects of sin. Too often in the past the Catholic notion of natural law tended to see only the natural and metaphysical aspects and forgot about the realities brought about by the continuing presence of sin. The failure to give enough importance to the reality of sin became even more pronounced in the 1960s when an attempt was rightly made to overcome the dichotomy between nature and supernature. Undoubtedly there existed in Roman Catholic thought too great a dichotomy between the gospel and our daily life, between the kingdom of God and the world in which we live. However, in trying to overcome this dichotomy perhaps the pendulum swung so far that we forgot our finitude, our sinfulness and the fact that the fullness of the eschaton is in the future. The temptation existed to see everything as grace and gospel. I insisted on the need to recognize the continuing presence of sin, for ultimately the Christian is called to struggle against the power of sin, although I did not want to exaggerate its influence. I developed a stance or perspective for moral theology which calls for moral theology to view all reality in the light of the fivefold Christian mysteries of creation, sin, incarnation, redemption and resurrection destiny. Failure to give due importance to any one of these aspects results in an imbalance in one's theological stance or perspective.[32]

My insistence on the presence of sin referred not only to what has traditionally been called original sin but also to the continuing presence of sin in the world. Sin becomes incarnate in the various structures of human existence. The sin of the world which has been developed by some contemporary theologians must clearly be distinguished from personal sin and guilt.[33]

One must never forget there is a twofold aspect about the sin of the world. On the one hand, the Christian is called to struggle against sin. The whole of the Christian message calls for the Christian in union with Jesus to strive through the power of love to overcome sin. The call to conversion reminds the individual of the need continually to change one's heart as well as struggle to change the conditions of the world in which we live. It seems at times that the theory of the fathers of the church failed to recognize this aspect of sin. They too readily justified and accepted the reality of slavery as being brought about by the evil of sin and did not struggle enough to do away with such an institution. On the other hand, one must admit that in our imperfect world, in which the fullness of grace is not yet here, there will always remain some aspects of the sin of the world in our life. This is the truth that was recognized in the early centuries of the church.

Sin can become incarnate in the social and political structures of human existence. I want to extend this outlook to recognize that the sin of the world can also affect some individuals without affecting others. The psychic structure of the irreversible invert constitutes such a manifestation of sin in the world. This theory is compatible with all the different approaches to the etiology of homosexuality. If homosexuality is caused by poor psychological and environmental relationships, it is even easier to see in the psychic makeup of the irreversible homosexual the effects of sin in the world. Since it is irreversible, it cannot and should not be changed. The individual person bears no personal moral guilt for this condition. Just as private property is morally justified as a result of sin in the world, so in the same way do I justify homosexual acts for the irreversible homosexual in the context of a loving relationship striving for permanency. At the same time this is not the ideal, and those who are not irreversible homosexuals have a moral obligation to strive for a loving heterosexual union.

Probably I should have developed at somewhat greater length the strictly ethical aspects of this theory. It is obvious that the presence of sin in the world cannot justify every single action. It has been pointed out above that the fathers of the church too readily and too easily justified the institution of slavery rather than struggling to abolish such a form of oppression. On the level of ethical theory it is necessary for one to consider all the values involved and on the basis of proportionate reason to decide whether or not something is objectively good. In the light of my understanding of the different moral values involved and of the meaning of sexuality, homosexual acts could then be justified in the context of a loving, permanent relationship.

Since I have first proposed my position, some other Catholic moral theologians have applied the theory of proportionate reason justifying premoral or ontic evil to the case of the irreversible homosexual. There are cases in which the ontic evil of homosexual acts does not become an objective moral evil because in the circumstances of a stable relationship there is a proportionate reason for a true homosexual who is not called to celibacy to have homosexual relations with one's partner.[34]

In the preceding chapter I have expressed some reservations about the theory of premoral or ontic evil as still giving too much importance to the physical and failing to recognize that because of finitude nothing will be perfect from every single perspective. Noncontraceptive marital intercourse is not a moral ideal as such.

From a theological perspective it is helpful to distinguish various types of conflict situations. Objective conflict situations can arise primarily from finitude, from the presence of the sin of the world and from eschatological tension. In the question of homosexuality I see the conflict situation arising primarily from sin in the world and not from finitude. In this view heterosexual relations remain a true ideal, but for the irreversible homosexual, actions in the context of a relationship striving for permanency are objectively good. Their moral goodness is grounded in the psychic makeup of the individual.

In practice I arrive at much the same conclusion as the theory of premoral or ontic evil, but I want to emphasize the diverse ultimate groundings of conflict situations and the differences that follow from a conflict based on finitude and one based on the presence of the sin of the world.

In this second half of the chapter I have tried to explain at some length the theological and ethical rationale behind the theory of compromise which I have employed to explain coherently that homosexual acts for the irreversible homosexual in the context of a loving union striving for permanency are objectively good. Yet the ideal, normative meaning of human sexuality is in terms of heterosexual relationships. In pastoral practice this calls for a new and different approach.

NOTES

1. As an example of such an approach see Rudolf Allers, *The Successful Error* (New York: Sheed and Ward, 1940).

2. John J. Hayes, "Chaplain's Letter," *Bulletin of the Guild of Catholic Psychiatrists* 3, no. 2 (December 1955): 2.

3. Roland Dalbiez, *La méthode psychoanalytique et la doctrine de Freud* (Paris: Desclée de Brouwer, 1936).

4. Louis Beirnaert, "L'attitude chrétienne en psychothérapie," in *Expérience chrétienne et psychologie* (Paris: Editions de L'Épi, 1964), p. 249. This volume is a collection of Beirnaert's previously published articles.

5. *Acta Apostolicae Sedis* 45 (1953): 278–283. For an English translation see *The Catholic Mind* 51 (1953): 428–435.

6. For a favorable commentary on this address see Beirnaert, pp. 247–259.

7. John C. Ford and Gerald Kelly, *Contemporary Moral Theology I: Questions in Fundamental Moral Theology* (Westminster, Md.: Newman Press, 1958), pp. 320–321.

8. Albert Plé, "Moral Acts and the Pseudo-Morality of the Unconscious," in *Cross Currents of Psychiatry and Catholic Morality,* ed. William

Birmingham and Joseph E. Cunneen (New York: Pantheon Books, 1964), pp. 178–187. Plé, like Beirnaert, has been a strong defender of Freud in Catholic circles. See the influential article on Freud which he wrote for the International Theological Commission, Albert Plé, "L'apport du Freudisme à la morale chrétienne," *Studia Moralia* 12 (1974): 135–155.

9. Ford and Kelly, *Contemporary Moral Theology I*, p. 324.

10. Albert Plé, "St. Thomas and the Psychology of Freud," in *Cross Currents of Psychiatry and Catholic Morality*, pp. 84–109.

11. See, for example, Joseph Nuttin, *Psychoanalysis and Personality: A Dynamic Theory of Normal Personality* (New York: Sheed and Ward, 1953). It is interesting to note the similarities in the Catholic reaction to Freud with the reaction to Marx and the willingness as time went on to distinguish the various levels in the thought of these two significant authors.

12. James E. Hayden, "The Perspective of a Catholic Psychiatrist," *Bulletin of the Guild of Catholic Psychiatrists* 1, no. 3 (April 1953): 25–39.

13. Francis J. Braceland, "Preface," in *Cross Currents of Psychiatry and Catholic Morality*, pp. v–x. This volume brought together articles translated from the French which had appeared in the journal *Cross Currents*. This journal since its inception in 1950 has made great contributions to American Catholic intellectual life, especially during the time before the Second Vatican Council when its articles made American Catholics aware of some of contemporary European theology.

14. Paul Vanbergen, "L'église et la psychoanalyse," *La Revue Nouvelle* 48 (1968): 102–107.

15. Marc Oraison, *The Homosexual Question* (New York: Harper and Row, 1977).

16. Ford and Kelly, *Contemporary Moral Theology I*, pp. 175–180.

17. John J. Lynch, "Notes on Moral Theology," *Theological Studies* 23 (1962): 233–239; René Carpentier, *Nouvelle Revue Théologique* 83 (1961): 856–861.

18. This position was strongly affirmed at the Fifth Lateran Council (1513) and the First Vatican Council (1870). See *Enchiridion symbolorum definitionum et declarationum de rebus fidei et morum*, ed. H. Denzinger, A. Schönmetzer, 32nd ed. (Barcelona: Herder, 1963), n. 1441, 3017.

19. After this paragraph in the text of the document there is an official footnote to a recent work on Galileo. In the context of earlier conciliar discussions it seems that the document here intends to warn against another Galileo case. For this interpretation see unofficial footnote 99 in *The Documents of Vatican II*, ed. Walter M. Abbott (New York: Guild Press, 1966), p. 234.

20. For a fuller development of this understanding and its ramifications in moral theology see Josef Fuchs, *Natural Law: A Theological Investigation* (New York: Sheed and Ward, 1965).

21. For a discussion of genetics including many different approaches see *The New Genetics and the Future of Man,* ed. Michael P. Hamilton (Grand Rapids, Michigan: William B. Eerdmans Publishing Co., 1972).

22. Louis Beirnaert, "La sanctification dépendelle du psychisme?" in *Experience chrétienne et psychologie*, pp. 133–142; also Augustine P. Hennessy, "Maturity and Spirituality," *Proceedings of the Catholic Theological Society of America* 17 (1962): 181–194.

23. For a summary of the psychological, psychiatric and sociological positions proposed about homosexuality see Herant A. Katchadourian and Donald T. Lunde, *Fundamentals of Human Sexuality,* 2nd ed. (New York: Holt, Rinehart and Winston, 1975), pp. 332–339. For a summary of the relevant empirical data in the context of moral theological evaluations see John R. Cavanagh with John F. Harvey, *Counseling the Homosexual* (Huntington, Indiana: Our Sunday Visitor Press, 1977), pp. 30–90; André Guindon, *The Sexual Language: An Essay in Moral Theology* (Ottawa: University of Ottawa Press, 1976), pp. 299–377; Philip S. Keane, *Sexual Morality: A Catholic Perspective* (New York: Paulist Press, 1977), pp. 71–91; Anthony Kosnik et al., *Human Sexuality: New Dimensions in American Catholic Thought* (New York: Paulist Press, 1977), pp. 57–60, 186–218.

24. "Homosexuality and Moral Theology: Methodological and Substantive Considerations," *The Thomist* 35 (1971): 447–481. The same study is reprinted in my book *Catholic Moral Theology in Dialogue* (Notre Dame, Indiana: University of Notre Dame Press, 1976), pp. 184–219.

25. Sacred Congregation for the Doctrine of the Faith," "Declaration on Sexual Ethics," par. 8. The official text is found in *Acta Apostolicae Sedis* 68 (1967): 77–96. An English translation in pamphlet form is available from the Publications Office, United States Catholic Conference, 1312 Massachusetts Ave., N.W., Washington, D.C. 20005.

26. E.g., Gregory Baum, "Catholic Homosexuals," *The Commonweal* 99 (February 15, 1974): 479–482.

27. John F. Harvey, "Contemporary Theological Views," in Cavanagh, *Counseling the Homosexual,* pp. 235–237.

28. John J. McNeill, *The Church and the Homosexual* (Kansas City: Sheed, Andrews and McMeel, Inc., 1976).

29. Harvey, "Contemporary Theological Views," p. 236.

30. McNeill, *The Church and the Homosexual,* p. 35.

31. Fuchs, *Natural Law,* pp. 85–122.

32. Charles E. Curran, *New Perspectives in Moral Theology* (Notre Dame, Indiana: University of Notre Dame Press, 1976), pp. 47–86.

33. Piet Schoonenberg, *Man and Sin: A Theological View* (Notre Dame, Indiana: University of Notre Dame Press, 1965), pp. 98–123.

34. Philip S. Keane, *Sexual Morality: A Catholic Perspective* (New York: Paulist Press, 1977), pp. 84–90; also John F. Dedek, *Contemporary Medical Ethics* (New York: Sheed and Ward, 1975), pp. 80–86.

PART TWO

Social Ethics

4: American Catholic Social Ethics, 1880–1965

Catholic ethics in the United States has seldom reflected on its own historical development. Nevertheless, a Catholic social ethics did develop in this country and played a very significant role in the life of the church. Church historians have devoted time and energy to studying this movement, but unfortunately Catholic ethicists have not reflected on it. This chapter will not reduplicate the historical work that has already been done; nor will it consist primarily in explaining the substantive positions of different authors. Rather, the scope of this study is to analyze American Catholic social ethics from the perspective of the relationship between "American" and "Catholic" with special emphasis on the theological and ethical methodologies employed.

I. Historical Background

After 1880 there emerged what Aaron Abell, the foremost historian of American Catholic social thought, has described as Catholic social liberalism, which was to become the mainstream of Catholic social thought in the United States down to contemporary times. According to Abell three factors characterize Catholic social liberalism: a crusade for social justice, cooperation with non-Catholics and the rapid Americanization of the immigrants.[1]

In the nineteenth century the primary problem facing the

Catholic Church in the United States was its relationship to the American ethos. Could one be both Catholic and American at one and the same time?[2] This question has remained central down to the present day. Native and Protestant Americans tended to be suspicious of Roman Catholics who, as mostly an immigrant people, spoke often in a foreign language, constituted a distinct minority and owed allegiance to a foreign ruler. Prejudice, bias and even violence against these immigrants often existed in all parts of the United States. But there was another side to the dilemma. Rome tended to be suspicious of American Catholics. America was the land of freedom, but in the nineteenth century Roman Catholicism strongly attacked the concept of freedom that was then present in Europe. The problem of freedom, seen especially in terms of religious freedom, was to remain a source of tension until the 1960s.

In the earlier part of the nineteenth century the practical aspect of this question centered on the Americanization of the Catholic immigrants. Is the American ethos compatible with the Catholic faith? One side argued that the immigrant Catholics should maintain their language, their culture and their differences from other Americans. Any loss of distinctiveness would result in a loss of faith. Such a position was frequently taken by German-American Catholics.[3] The other side saw no incompatibility between the Catholic faith and the American ethos. In fact, Orestes Brownson and Isaac Hecker, the founder of the Paulists, saw American people in their environment and mentality as ripe for Catholic teaching and conversion provided only the teaching was properly understood and that some of the authoritarian rigidities that had arisen in reaction to the Protestant reform were rightly discarded. The hierarchical leadership of the American Catholic Church generally solved the problem in favor of the Americanization of the immigrants.[4]

In the last two decades of the nineteenth century the position asserting no basic incompatibility between American and Catholic was solidified and applied to questions of social ethics under the leadership of Bishops Ireland, Spalding, Keane and especially Cardinal Gibbons, the head of the

American hierarchy.[5] Four historical events of that period deserve mention here in this context. Most significant was the support given by Cardinal Gibbons and the American Catholic Church to the Knights of Labor. In July 1886 Rome reaffirmed its earlier condemnation of the Knights of Labor in the province of Quebec, Canada. Despite opposition from two of the eleven American archbishops, Gibbons, with prodding and support from Ireland and Keane, strongly defended the Knights of Labor in a memorandum submitted to the Congregation for the Propagation of the Faith, which in 1888 decreed that the Knights of Labor could be permitted and tolerated.[6]

Gibbons in his brief to the congregation responded to the charges of indifferentism and of dangers to the faith because the Knights of Labor were a nondenominational organization and Catholics would be mixed with Protestants, secularists and even atheists. Gibbons saw no ultimate harm coming from this, and he pointed out that only through organized effort could labor obtain justice. A condemnation of the Knights of Labor by the church would make the church appear to be against the poor and the worker, and also the church would be out of tune with the political powers in this country. The accusation of being un-American—that is to say, alien to our national spirit—is the most powerful weapon which the enemies of the church can employ against her. Supporting progressive reform and labor was both the American and the Catholic thing to do. Separate Catholic labor unions would be neither appropriate nor effective in this country.[7]

A second significant event concerned Fr. Edward McGlynn, a New York priest who was excommunicated by Archbishop Corrigan of New York for his support of Henry George. George, running for the office of mayor of New York in 1886, advocated a single tax theory according to which all the increased value of land should be taxed. Since increased land value was not attributed to the owner, it should be given back to the people in the form of taxes. Corrigan also attempted to place George's book *Progress and Poverty* on the index. The more liberal bishops were upset with the excommunication of McGlynn because it played into the hands of those who would condemn the church as being against the poor and as not allowing freedom of political thought within the church. Here again the liberals ultimately won. The McGlynn case was reopened in 1892, and he was ultimately reconciled with the church. The Holy Office decreed that Henry George's doctrines were deserving of condemnation but refrained from promulgating and officially making public the decree.[8]

Circumstances surrounding two national, lay Catholic congresses in Baltimore in 1889 and in Chicago in 1893 showed the same approach. The speakers, especially in the Chicago congress, definitely favored social reform, opposed the abuses of excessive wealth and defended the rights of the worker. The bishops took care to make sure that the congresses adopted a more liberal, reform-minded tone and avoided controversial issues such as the temporal power of the papacy. In his address to the 1893 Columbian Catholic Congress in Chicago, Archbishop Satolli, the papal delegate to the United States, urged the delegates to go forward with one hand bearing the book of Christian truth and the other the Constitution of the United States.[9]

In the last decade of the nineteenth century American Catholic liberals (to use the term of Professor Robert Cross) had to yield some ground, especially in terms of Roman approval. There were different causes: exaggerations and misunderstandings of what liberals such as Ireland, Keane and Hecker stood for; hyperbolic and flamboyant statements by American liberals; political pressure from conservatives in Europe and in the United States. In 1899 Pope Leo XIII sent a letter to Archbishop Gibbons (*Testem benevolentiae*) condemning ideas associated with Americanism—the need to modify doctrines in accord with the times in order to attract converts; a deemphasizing of external guidance, of the supernatural, of passive virtues and of religious vows; discussions with heretics.[10]

The liberals responded that these positions were not really held in the United States but were misunderstandings based on defective translations of Hecker's writings. Conservatives replied that the letter was badly needed to correct abuses in

America. At the very minimum the condemnation showed how American Catholics continually had to struggle to overcome the suspicions of Americanism on the part of Roman authorities and European Catholics.[11] Undoubtedly Leo's letter had an effect in dampening the cause of the American liberals, especially in the area of doctrine, but it does not seem to have seriously affected the more practical question of social ethics and the working with non-Catholics on common societal concerns. Thus history shows the problematic that faced the American Catholic Church in general and social ethics in particular—the compatibility or incompatibility between Catholic and American.

II. Catholic Ethical Methodology

Catholic theology itself provided an impetus to the approach which saw basic compatibility between the American ethos and environment and the Catholic understanding. Especially from the time of Leo XIII Catholic social ethics had been developed methodologically in terms of natural law theory. In theological ethics the first methodological question concerns the source of ethical wisdom and knowledge for the Christian. Catholic theology has traditionally accepted that ethics is based on faith and reason, on revelation and on natural law; but the primary, and at times almost the sole, emphasis has been on natural law.[12] Chapter One showed that the acceptance of reason, the human, and natural law in the Catholic tradition is grounded in the importance of mediation.

Perhaps the best example of the Catholic approach is seen in the introduction of Pope John XXIII's encyclical *Pacem in terris* issued in 1963. The laws governing human existence are to be found in the nature of man where the father of all things wrote them. The creator has imprinted in man's heart an order which conscience reveals to him and enjoins him to obey. By these innate laws human beings are taught how to live in peace and harmony with other human beings in human society. Such an approach is not based on scripture, revelation and redemption but primarily on reason, nature and creation. If anything, nature and supernature are clearly separate and almost dichotomized, so that the social life of the Christian is seen almost exclusively in terms of nature.[13]

Such an approach stresses what the Catholic or Christian shares with all others — human nature and human reason. The distinctively Christian aspect of the supernatural, grace and redemption does not enter decisively into the picture. Consequently such a methodology opens the door to recognize that in theory one shares much ethical wisdom and knowledge with all human beings and in practice Catholics could collaborate and cooperate with all people of goodwill to work for justice and peace. Pope Leo XIII in his famous encyclical *Rerum novarum* of 1891 on the condition of the workers appeals to this "common opinion of mankind . . . found in the careful study of nature and in the laws of nature."[14] The natural law thus provides a bridge by which American Catholics can find agreement in theory and collaboration in practice with other Americans in working for the betterment of society.

Rerum novarum also provided the basic substantive positions for much of what characterized the mainstream of American Catholic social ethics in the twentieth century. Such an ethic proposes a middle course between the evils of laissez faire capitalism, which so exalts the freedom of individuals that it forgets about justice and obligations to others, and the opposite evil of socialism, which so stresses the collective that the rights of the individual are trampled on. The pope supported nonrevolutionary labor unionism as a means for obtaining justice for the worker. The state has a positive role to intervene and make sure that justice is protected through social legislation, although the state cannot take over functions belonging to others. Thus both the unique situation of the Catholic Church in the United States and the theological methodology employed in Catholic social ethics set the stage for the mainstream approach of American Catholic social ethics which can properly be described as reformist and gradualist. Yes, there were some problems and difficulties in the American economic and political system, but the American system was not radically out of tune with Catholic ethics. Catholics collaborating with others in society could bring about the necessary reforms of the existing structures.

III. John A. Ryan

The best illustration of the mainstream of reforming or liberal Catholic social thought can be found in the Bishops' Program of Social Reconstruction issued by the Administrative Committee of the National Catholic War Council on February 11, 1919. This forward-looking document was very much in tune with the progressive reforming element in American society in the first two decades of the twentieth century.

Rather than proposing a comprehensive scheme of reconstruction, the bishops focused on those reforms that seemed desirable and obtainable within a reasonable period of time. The short-term aspects of the program called for: continuation of the United States Employment Service to deal with unemployment after the war; continuation 'of the National War Labor Board with its emphasis on a living wage and labor's right to organize; sustaining the present wage scales; housing for the working class; reduction of the cost of living with government checks on monopolies and perhaps even government competition for monopolies; an enactment of a legal minimum wage; provision by the state for insurance against illness, unemployment, old age and other disabilities; labor participation in industrial management; vocational training; state laws against child labor. In the light of the defects of the present system fundamental and long-term reforms were mentioned—cooperation, copartnership and the call for the majority of workers to become owners, at least in part, of the instruments of production. However, the primary emphasis was on the gradualist approach. Some even condemned the approach as being socialistic, but this is not an accurate description of what is primarily a progressive and reform-minded document. Notice, too, how its appeal based on reason alone was to all people and contained little that was distinctively Christian except for a closing paragraph calling for a reform in spirit and a return to Christian life and Christian institutions.[15]

The author of the document was John A. Ryan, who for almost half a century was a leader and symbol of liberal, reforming social Catholicism. As author of important theoretical works such as *A Living Wage* (1906) and *Distributive Justice* (1916) and as a professor at The Catholic University of America, he was a leader in Catholic social theory.[16] As director of the Social Action Department of the National Catholic Welfare Conference from 1920 until his death in 1945, he educated Catholics, directed programs and actively collaborated with many people on a practical level in pursuing his goals of social reform. There were occasional problems with some more conservative members of the American hierarchy, but Ryan remained a firm spokesperson in the cause of social reform and justice—one whose views were appreciated by Catholics and non-Catholics alike.[17]

A more detailed evaluation of Ryan's ethical methodology will show how such an approach was appropriate for the substantive ethics of a reformer or liberal who accepted the fundamental goodness of the American system, pointed out deficiencies and believed that people of goodwill could work together to bring about the required changes toward a greater social justice.[18]

First, Ryan employed a natural law theory which from the theological perspective meant an emphasis on human nature and human reason. At best one finds in *A Living Wage,* Ryan's doctoral thesis first published in 1906, a very occasional reference to or citation from scripture, but there is no sustained development of a biblical theology. Such a methodological approach is completely different from that of his contemporary, the Protestant social gospel theoretist Walter Rauschenbusch, whose first significant work on social ethics, *Christianizing the Social Order,* was published by Macmillan, Ryan's publisher, in 1907.[19] Rauschenbusch based his ethics primarily on the concept of the kingdom of God and making that kingdom present in this world, and he moved from the biblical teaching to moral conclusions. A little later Ryan wrote that he disagreed with the Protestant approach which too often identified religion with humanitarianism. The kingdom of God is in heaven, and the church is primarily interested in the salvation of souls in comparison with which temporal goods are utterly insignificant. The church must teach us how we are to live in this present world, and this explains the social mission of the church and its function in teaching social ethics.[20] Ryan's own works were generally well received and well reviewed in the secular press, especially by progressives who agreed wholeheartedly with his reforming proposals and the reasons on which they were based.[21]

Second, Catholic natural law theory emphasizes order and harmony. The divine plan, or law, is itself an ordering. The vision shaped by natural law theory does not see relationships in terms of hostility, opposition and conflict but rather understands that all are called to work together harmoniously for the common good, which then redounds to the good of the individual. In Catholic natural law theory there is no opposition between the common good and one's individual good. Ryan's major work on *Distributive Justice*, first published in 1916, follows this basic approach by considering the proper distribution of the products of industry among the four classes that contribute to these products—landowners, capitalists, businessmen and laborers.[22]

Ryan added his own distinctive developments to the basic natural law emphasis on harmony and balance—the principle of expediency. The ultimate test of the morality of any social system is its bearing on human welfare. In the matter of social institutions moral values and genuine expediency are in the long run identical.[23] Ryan the economist and Ryan the ethicist collaborated to work out this theory of harmony and expediency. Influenced by John A. Hobson, an economist from The Johns Hopkins University, and others, Ryan proposed an economic theory of underconsumption according to which prosperity exists in our society only if the wage earners have the money to buy goods.[24] The payment of a living wage is a moral obligation based on the rights of the individual laborer to the goods of creation, but industry by paying such a living wage to all its workers will thereby secure its own continued prosperity. Good morality and good economics are in harmony. Ryan in 1932 declared it a fundamental task for Catholic Action "to bring about the identification of morality and expediency in our industrial system, by persuading all classes that prosperity cannot be maintained unless the receivers of wages and salaries obtain a considerable increase in purchasing power."[25]

Third, Catholic natural law theory sees the state as a natural society based on the social nature of human beings who are called to band together with others to accomplish what as individuals they cannot do. Again there is a basic harmony between the individual and the state, not an opposition as if the state had the primarily negative function of preventing sinful human beings from harming one another. Ryan maintains that the end of the state is to promote the welfare of its citizens, as a whole, as members of families and as members of social classes. Thus Ryan readily calls upon the state to bring about a greater justice in industrial relations by legislating a minimum wage, prohibiting child labor, and providing for insurance against unemployment and disabilities. This dependence and reliance on the state as the primary factor in social reform is characteristic of Ryan's thought, especially before 1931.

Fourth, Ryan insisted on distributive justice as the primary category, not commutative justice, which views the problem too narrowly in terms of the rights of one individual vis-à-vis another. In accord with this position Ryan maintained that the primary ethical consideration rests on the fact that the goods of creation exist for all human beings. This primary consideration governs everything else. As a result Ryan stressed more the limits of private property than did the early papal encyclicals. The natural right of ownership is always qualified by the higher common right of use which is based on the universal destiny of the goods of creation for all human beings. In Ryan's understanding of property the emphasis is on the human person's needs as the primary title to property.[26]

Private ownership (he considered private ownership

primarily in terms of land ownership) is a natural right, but of the third kind or class. Private ownership is not an intrinsic good (a right of the first class such as life); nor is it directly necessary for any individual (like marriage as a natural right of the second class). Private land ownership is necessary as a social institution providing for the general welfare and hence is indirectly necessary for the welfare of the individual. This is what Ryan meant by calling it a natural right of the third class. The utlimate justification for private property in Ryan's thought lay in its ability to obtain the end, or objective, of property better than any other system.[27] Some have disagreed and pointed out that Ryan should have based his argument for private property more on metaphysical considerations and the inherent rights of the human person.[28]

Fifth, John Ryan's natural law methodology was much more inductive and empirical than the natural law of the manuals of Catholic theology—a fact that was heavily influenced by his teachers Thomas Bouquillon in moral theology and William Kerby in sociology.[29] Some of the features already alluded to fit in with a more inductive methodology. Ryan was an economist and acknowledged the limits of dealing with ethical problems merely in the light of philosophy and theology. The acceptance of the public welfare as the determining criterion, the principle of expediency, and the use of economics to determine what was expedient in practice all characterized his more inductive understanding of natural law. A more inductive methodology will always be more in tune with the existing situation even though reforms are called for.

On the basis of his ethical methodology one can see how Ryan was a liberal, a reformer and the leading figure in American Catholic social liberalism in the first half of the twentieth century. There is no doubt that Ryan and his followers were far out in front of the majority of Catholics, and often their thoughts were not translated into either teaching or action at the grass-roots level. At the same time Ryan was frequently under attack from conservative groups and individuals both inside and outside the church.

Ryan was not a radical but a reformer who tried to change

and modify the system with the help of much broad-based support. Unlike many reformers, however, he was apparently never satisfied with the changes and reforms that were made. In my judgment his methodology kept him always open to demanding new and further reforms. Although his basic theory did not change much after his more theoretical writings in the first two decades of the twentieth century, there was a development in his understanding of the reforms necessary in keeping with what was required by the public welfare. Patrick Gearty points up four different phases in the development of Ryan's thought on the economic order. The first stage extending to 1913 emphasized legislative reform to combat social problems. Beginning with his debate with the socialist Hillquit, Ryan advocated a more widespread ownership of property so that workers would become part owners of the tools they used. After World War I he developed a third stage called industrial democracy and advocated labor's sharing in management, profits and ownership. The fourth phase after Pope Pius XI's encyclical *Quadragesimo anno* of 1931 advocated the occupational group system.[30]

However, many of the criticisms and defects of a reforming position and of natural law theory apply to Ryan's theory. From the theological perspective he obviously did not integrate the supernatural and the natural orders as well as subsequent theology is trying to do. Likewise, Ryan's theory tends to forget the reality of sin and its many ramifications in human lives and relationships. His emphasis on social and institutional reform seems to imply that there is no great need for change on the part of individuals. Personalists contend that the primary center for change is the heart of the individual person and that it is not enough just to talk about changing the structures of society. In addition, his perspective did not allow him to see the deeper incompatibilities that might be existing between the American economic system and the gospel message, or in his case the natural law. The other approaches to be explained later involve further criticisms of Ryan's approach.

One final point of historical importance deserves mention in this context. The election of 1928 with the defeat of Al Smith brought out many anti-Catholic prejudices and saddened Ryan immensely because he thought these attacks against Catholics were totally unfair and uncalled for.[31] Ryan himself became a part of the controversy as opponents of Smith cited Ryan's book on *The State and the Church,* which upheld in theory the obligation of the state to support the one, true church, although it pointed out that in practice this had application only to the completely Catholic state. Ryan himself doubted that such a state still existed in the world, and certainly not in the United States today. Most probably such an obligation would never apply in the American future, but one cannot yield on principles of unchanging and eternal truth. Logically it could happen even in the United States that non-Catholic sects may so dissolve to such a point that the political proscription of these may become feasible and expedient.[32] Ryan who had done so much to advance the cause of Roman Catholicism in the eyes of many non-Catholics in the United States because of his efforts at reform of the social economic order was not able to bridge this gap between Catholicism and Americanism with regard to the political order and the question of religious liberty. Religious liberty would still remain a problem for Roman Catholics in the United States for a few more years.

IV. German-American Catholics

In addition to the mainstream approach exemplified by the reformist and gradualist approach of Ryan there were two other significant approaches in the first half of the twentieth century that deserve mention—the German-American Catholics and the Catholic Worker Movement. German-American Catholics formed a Central Verein in 1855 as a national federation of all the German Catholic benevolent societies existing throughout the country especially on the parish level. The group took an interest in social reform in the light of the injustices of the industrial order and established the Central Bureau in 1909 to carry out this work. A journal *Central-Blatt and Social Justice* was started to publish articles in both German and English to educate the members about social justice. The leading individual in the movement was Frederick P. Kenkel, who was the key figure in the formation of the Central Bureau and remained its active director until his death in 1952 at the age of 88. Kenkel and the Central Bureau have been described as conservative reformers—but their general conservativism in all matters made them much more discontent with the existing industrial society in the United States and therefore more radical in their reform proposals than the liberal or meliorist reformers in the mainstream.[33]

In opposition to both capitalism and socialism they advocated a fundamental reorganization of society based on a corporate, or organic, society which called for a hierarchical ordering of all elements in society in which the state respected the lesser social groupings and did not usurp their functions. The economic order was to be run by vocational groups in which labor and capital were not opposed to one another as in the more liberal approach but in which labor, capital and management working together in a particular industry were united in running that industry for the common good of all.[34]

Again, both their understanding of the relationship between Catholicism and the American ethos and their theological methodology influenced the conclusions to which they came. In the basic question of the relationship between Catholic and American the German-American Catholics stressed much more the differences and incompatibilities. They had generally opposed the rapid Americanization of the immigrants, and they held onto their language, customs, social groupings and their faith. In fact the Central Verein as an organization fostered this German consciousness. They were not readily disposed to accept Americanization, and their journal often pointed out the problems with the idea of freedom behind the political and economic orders in American society. German-American Catholics feared liberalizing Catholics went too far in their acceptance of things American. They also brought with them from Germany their traditional suspicions of and even hostility toward Protestantism, so that they were not willing to work together with Protestant groups, even with German Protestant groups.

From their German origins many learned opposition to the entire nineteenth-century liberalism and its ramifications in political, social and economic life. In reacting against the nineteenth-century political, social and economic development, German-American Catholics often embraced a romanticism which glorified the Middle Ages and the past. There was a heavy emphasis on agrarianism and the evils of the city and the industrial world.[35] Kenkel himself has been described as a romantic and utopian who gradually became even more alienated from American culture and industrial society. Kenkel was heavily influenced by some German-Catholic thinkers, especially by Karl von Vogelsang, a romantic visionary who proposed an extreme corporatism in Germany in the nineteenth century.[36] Von Vogelsang's solidaristic opinions in Germany in the nineteenth century differed from the more realistic and reforming approach of Hitz and of the later von Kettler.[37]

Although *Central-Blatt and Social Justice* was not a theological journal as such, theological methodology definitely influenced the position of the Central Verein. They too employed the natural law method which appealed to reason and human nature and not to the supernatural and revelation. However, their approach to natural law was more deductive and abstract in comparison with Ryan's more inductive and concrete methodology. Beginning with the concept of human nature, the human person and society, the solidarists deduced the way in which such a society should be structured. The traditional emphasis of Catholic theology on hierarchical ordering and harmony in this theory resulted in the call for an organic society in which all the parts work together for the good of the whole.[38]

Ever fearful of socialism, they insisted on what was later called the principle of subsidiarity, which limited intervention by the state and left many things in the hands of intermediate bodies. Kenkel, for example, opposed Ryan's call for a constitutional amendment to prevent child labor because he saw it as undue exercise of the power of the federal government in a matter that should be handled on the local level, even though he himself was opposed to child labor.[39]

Such a deductive, abstract approach also influenced their stance concerning how change is to be brought about. The ideal proposed is quite critical of the existing structures, but little or nothing is said about how to effectuate their program in practice. Kenkel and the Central Verein were opposed to the gradualist approach of the mainstream liberals as exemplified in the latter's calling upon the state to legislate reform and in their strong backing for labor unions. Not only were these reforms not radical enough for Kenkel but they actually hindered the ultimate achievement of the corporate society. Unfortunately, the Verein never did address the question of how this ultimate reform was to be brought about.

Another weakness of such a method concerns its abstract, universalist and ahistorical approach. No one can ever approach reality from such an impartial and universal perspective. We are all the creatures of our own historical and cultural times and places, so that we should never be deceived into thinking that ours is a perfectly neutral, universal and abstract perspective. In fact, it seems the romantic vision of the medieval world actually influenced and colored the method and conclusions of the Verein. The idea of society which they deduced from their understanding of the nature of the human person and of human society was that medieval ordering to which they were so attracted.

The approach and the conclusions of Kenkel and the Central Bureau stand in contrast and even in opposition to the mainstream liberal approach. Their influence unfortunately was limited to the German community, and in the last few years the *Social Justice Review* (this new name was given in 1940) seems to have lost its social vision and concentrated on decrying the abuses of the contemporary church and world.

V. The Catholic Worker

A second significant position differing from the mainstream liberal reformers is associated with the Catholic Worker Movement, which is truly a movement inspired by Peter

Maurin and Dorothy Day and not an organization. This movement, which began in 1933, is often characterized as radical because of its opposition to the existing social and economic order. In place of the structures of the contemporary industrial society they proposed to establish farming communes which would put into practice the axiom from each according to abilities and to each according to need and also to found houses of hospitality in which committed Catholics, voluntarily sharing the lot of the poor, offer food and shelter to the victims of industrial society. They propagated their ideas through discussions and through their paper *The Catholic Worker* started by Dorothy Day in 1933 and still published by her today.[40]

In terms of cultural influences there were not the dramatic and well-defined characteristics which colored the approach of Kenkel and the Central Verein. Perhaps the most significant factor that influenced the movement and others similar to it was the depression. The depression beginning in 1929 showed up the inequities of the economic system and the need for change. To Dorothy Day and her followers problems caused by the depression merely highlighted the radical incompatibility between the gospel and the existing industrial order.[41]

Dorothy Day and Peter Maurin were convinced of the need continually to clarify their ideas and communicate them with others, but neither of them pretended to be a theologian or an ethician. Perhaps the most systematic statement of their approach is found in the writings of Paul Hanly Furfey, a sociologist from The Catholic University of America who wrote a number of books explaining the approach of Catholic personalism or radicalism from the 1930s to the present.[42] Although Dorothy Day and Peter Maurin never developed their approach in any systematic or theological way, the general outlines of their understanding are quite clear.

The Catholic radicals did not employ a natural law approach but instead adopted a method based entirely on the scriptures and the supernatural. Furfey himself called for a supernatural sociology and a pistic society emphasizing the unique importance of grace, redemption and the supernatural.[43] Their approach was distinctively Christian and Catholic, highlighting the differences with all other approaches and eschewing cooperation with others that would merely result in watering down the gospel message. Not reform but radical change was necessary because the existing social and economic orders were basically incompatible with the gospel message.

The inequities of the system stand out starkly in the light of the eschatological ethics based on the gospel teaching of Jesus. *The Catholic Worker* constantly stresses the horrible condition of the poor and the unequal distribution of wealth in our society. From the very beginning they pointed out the horrendous injustices based on racism in American culture. They were strong pacifists and even lost leadership and followers because of Dorothy Day's continued support of pacifism during World War II.[44]

Christian personalism characterized the Catholic Worker approach. First, the heart of the individual had to be changed. The basic problems were much deeper than mere structural reform, for all first had to be willing to accept the gospel and practice a harsh and dreadful love. By voluntary poverty one shows one's love and solidarity with the poor. In accord with personalism one must respect the freedom of others, for too often the objective world impinges itself on the individual and turns the individual into an object. They were very much opposed to structure in any form even in their own movement, since they looked upon structure as a source of objectivization and the denial of the personal. For this reason they, unlike the liberals, were very much opposed to state intervention and even gloried at times in the name of anarchist. A true communitarism could be built only on a true personalism.

The approach of the Catholic Worker stressed the notion of gospel witness and was based on a deontological understanding that the Christian must bear witness to the gospel no matter what happens. As a result, they were not primarily interested in the effectiveness of the approach which they adopted. Some Christian radicals in the contemporary environment have tended to stress more the gospel as an effective means of social change. The Catholic Workers did not deny the effectiveness of the gospel, but they saw their role primarily as one of bearing witness to the gospel and letting God bring about whatever God would want in his own good time. As an effective means of social change to be embraced by many, it seems that the Catholic Worker Movement will never receive high grades. However, as a witness to a belief which involves a strong, personal commitment, the Catholic Worker Movement evokes the admiration of most people.

Their insistence on a social ethic based on eschatology and on the scriptures tends to result in fundamentalistic and overly simplistic solutions. They make no effort at any kind of reform of the people who come to them because they think this would be against their tenets of personalism. For fear of coercing and taking away the freedom of the individual does the Catholic Worker Movement really fail to engage the person in the depths of one's own being? Christian love seems much more complex than the Catholic Worker recognizes. Also one can question if such an eschatological ethic really appreciates the imperfections and the conflicts which will continue to exist in the present world in which we live. To her credit Dorothy Day herself acknowledges inconsistencies in her own approach because it is ultimately impossible to live out the full eschatological gospel message at all times. However, there are other Christians who wonder if one does not have to take a more realistic approach to the world in which we live.

VI. The Mainstream after World War II

In the first half of the twentieth century John A. Ryan symbolized and led the mainstream position of American Catholic social liberalism with its willingness to accept a compatibility between the American system and Catholic ethics, although it constantly called for continuing reform in the economic area in order to improve the system. After Ryan's death and after World War II this approach continued but seems to have lost some of its reforming zeal and to have accepted even more the basic compatibility between being

American and being Catholic. Historical circumstances again influenced this changing emphasis.

The economic inequalities and inadequacies which the depression pointed up were never structurally solved. Increased productivity and consumption connected with World War II brought a new and greater prosperity to Americans in general, so that the problem of structural change did not seem acute. The general prosperity affected Roman Catholics, who after the war truly moved into the middle class of American society with many able to buy a house in the suburbs, to own a car perhaps for the first time, and to send their children to college. The American dream was apparently becoming true for many Catholics who were no longer on the bottom of the economic and social ladder in this country.

After the war American and Catholic interests merged even more in the common fight against communism. Catholics had long before pointed out the danger of communism and were accused by many in the 1930s of siding with fascist and totalitarian regimes because of their fear of the communist menace. In the late 1940s and 1950s the United States and the Roman Catholic Church were identified as the two bastions of the free world standing up to the communist menace. All these factors influenced the approach of Catholic social ethics at this time.

John F. Cronin, a Sulpician priest with a doctorate in economics, continued the Ryan tradition as the best-known American Catholic author dealing with problems of economic and social justice. Cronin was also assistant director of the Social Action Department of the National Catholic Welfare Conference. He wrote textbooks on economic problems and books on Catholic social principles and Catholic social action. His best known work which was often used as a textbook in Catholic colleges and seminaries in his *Social Principles and Economic Life* published in 1959, after having been published in a slightly different form in 1950, and later revised in 1964 to include the social thought of Pope John XXIII as expressed in his two encyclicals *Mater et magistra* and *Pacem in terris*.

Cronin continued the methodology and approach of John

A. Ryan, but there were significant differences in part attributable to the changing circumstances mentioned above. Cronin placed much greater weight on authoritative church teaching than did Ryan—although this significant methodological development of giving more importance to authoritative church teaching had gradually been developed over the years in Roman Catholic social thought, including Ryan's. Cronin began each chapter with excerpts of authoritative papal and episcopal statements on the particular topic, and after having set out this teaching, he then followed with his own development of the issues. Looking back at Ryan, it is amazing how few references he has in his major theoretical writings to the papal documents, and how they in no way occupy the central place in the development of his thought. One can understand how even Ryan as the years went on appealed more and more to papal teaching to give his own thought more of an authoritative weight and acceptance in the Catholic Church.

Although continuing to call for reform, Cronin is also more apologetic and defensive about the American system than Ryan was. In speaking about social problems today, Cronin pointed out that the competitive individualism of the postmedieval period is no longer the dominant form in our society and that great changes have occurred in our economic structure. However, three points have become particularly clear in the mid-1960s—the persistence of poverty in certain areas, the increasing challenge of automation and the stubborn fact of unemployment. These points should not belittle the achievements of the American economic system, but they indicate that social reform is an ongoing challenge. Our living standards are unquestionably high. The problem of income distribution has been greatly improved, and more Americans have moved into the middle class. But we cannot be complacent because material prosperity can never be the ultimate goal of society. The objectives of Pope Pius XI still remain true—the need for an organized effort to serve the common good and greater cooperation in economic life.[45]

Cronin's methodological approach is less dynamic and more

static than Ryan's, so that the reforms he indicates are not as great. In the 1950 version of his work Cronin strongly defends Pope Pius XI's program of the organic or corporate society as the ideal type to be brought about in practice here in the United States.[46] But by 1964 Cronin changed views and agreed with Pope John XXIII's giving in his encyclicals only a passing mention to Pope Pius XI's program for organized economic life. According to Cronin Pope John's approach is more practical, pastoral and evolutionary.[47] However, both Pope John and Cronin are much more optimistic about the entire economic structure and order than was Pius XI. In contrast to Ryan, Cronin in his day is very suspicious of the dangers of overcentralized power in the state and often warns against giving too much of a role to the state, even though Pope John called for more state intervention than had his predecessors.[48]

Cronin was still a reformer in the order of social justice, but he was less a reformer than John A. Ryan. The practical involvements of the two individuals well illustrate this point. John Ryan was labeled by some as a socialist. He anticipated the reforms of the New Deal and later cooperated with many of the New Deal programs. His biographer used as the title of the life of Ryan an accurate and, in this author's view, obviously laudatory description of Ryan—the Right Reverend New Dealer—first used in derision by Father Charles Coughlin. On the other hand, John Cronin was acknowledged as their expert on communism by the American Catholic bishops, with whom he worked to fight communism. He became friendly with Congressman Richard Nixon in his crusade against communism and helped him in the Hiss case. Cronin later became the primary speech writer for Nixon when he was vice-president, although this working relationship did not continue after 1960.[49]

It should also be pointed out that the changing times should also have brought a greater awareness of changing issues and problems. The central problem was no longer the plight of the worker. On the national scene there was the growing recognition of the tremendous problem of racism and the continuing poverty of many people in the midst of the American plenty.

Cronin to his credit recognized these problems but really did not emphasize them, and they received a comparatively cursory treatment from him. In addition, as was becoming clear in some of the papal statements at the time, it was now necessary to consider problems in a worldwide perspective and not just on the basis of a local or national outlook. What effect does the American economic system have on the rest of the world? These problems were certainly present in the 1950s and early 1960s and were being raised by some people, but again one must recognize that they only became conscious problems to many in the subsequent years.

VII. John Courtney Murray

The theologian who contributed the most to solving the problematic of the compatibility of Catholic and American was the Jesuit John Courtney Murray. Murray was more of a systematic and academic theologian than any of the others considered so far. He concentrated more on the political aspect of the question than on the economic aspect. In his own mind Murray proved there was a total compatibility between being American and being Catholic. To the Roman ecclesiastics he showed that religious liberty as practiced in the United States is compatible with Catholic thought. To non-Catholic Americans he argued that Catholics have no difficulty accepting the American political system because it is based on natural law.

Murray's work in religious liberty was preceded by an interesting debate between himself and Paul Hanly Furfey on the question of intercredal cooperation. Murray understood intercredal cooperation, as he was discussing it in the early 1940s, as the working together of people of different creeds in the interest of social justice and reconstruction. It is precisely the natural law which Catholics hold in common with all others which is the basis of a cooperation animated by the common religious tenets and beliefs that are held. Mixed or intercredal cooperation is based, not on the supernatural, divine unity of the hierarchical church, but rather on the natural, spiritual unity of the human race which recognizes belief in God as the fundamental principle of the social order and upholds obedience to that moral order. To be effective such work needs to be organized, and the organization itself can be interconfessional without any danger of indifferentism or of *communicatio in sacris*.[50]

As it might be expected, Furfey held the opposite position. We have been ineffective in changing society precisely because we have been too uncritically cooperative with others. In being overanxious to cooperate with liberals and others we have kept our distinctively Catholic social doctrine in the background. We need to become more aggressively Catholic, not less.[51] Note how the different methodological approaches have influenced the substantive question.

The Murray-Furfey debate actually centered quite heavily on the interpretation of papal documents, especially *Singulari quadam* of Pope Pius X issued in 1912 in response to a question in Germany of whether Catholics could participate in non-Catholic (mixed or neutral) trade unions.[52] Murray interprets the document's conclusion that such participation can be tolerated and permitted as acknowledging the legitimacy of such organized interconfessional activity. Furfey interprets the document not as acceptance and encouragement of such organized cooperation but as a reluctant toleration much like the toleration of mixed marriages. Murray brings to his interpretation of the document an historical, critical hermeneutic—the need to sort out the doctrinal principles from the contingent historical aspects of the question. The pope according to Murray balances off the two poles of the unity of the church and of a concern for the common good to accept ultimately a social peace (not a unity of faith) based on a practical agreement on fundamental religious and ethical principles.

In addition to illustrating how different methodologies approach the practical ramifications of the question of being Catholic and American, this controversy has an importance beyond itself because it indicates the methodological approach which Murray himself would ultimately develop in dealing with the question of religious liberty. The four important elements present in this debate which were further developed by Murray are: natural law, an historical understanding of natural law, recognition that a social peace in the political order does not imply a unity of faith but can coexist with different faiths, and an historical, critical hermeneutic as applied to authoritative papal statements.

According to Murray the church-state and religious liberty questions must be seen in the light of the Catholic tradition which asserts both the distinction between the church and state and the harmony (*concordia*) between the two. The concept of natural law with its recognition of the distinction between the order of grace and the order of nature strongly calls for a distinction between the secular order and the sacred order. One can and should distinguish between the two societies—the church and the state.[53] But what about the harmony between them? In 1945 Murray approached the problem of religious liberty under its ethical aspect and saw the following as important factors in the solution of the problem: God, the moral law, human conscience, and the state (civil authority and its function of effectively directing citizens to the common good of the organized community).[54] However, in his consideration of the state Murray accepts the fact that the state as such has an obligation toward God—to acknowledge God as its author, to worship Him as He wills to be worshipped and to subject its official life and action to His law. The state has the obligation directly to promote public religion and morality as central elements of the common good. From such a perspective Murray could only affirm the basic outline of the older Catholic approach to religious liberty.[55]

As he himself mentions later, his final position rests on acknowledging the distinction between society and the state. The state plays only a limited role within society, for it is only one order within society—the order of public law and public administration. There follows from this the important distinction between the common good which is the care of society as a whole and the more limited concept of public order whose care devolves on the state and which consists in an order of justice, an order of public peace and an order of public morality. Murray is here describing the limited constitutional state.[56]

Natural law theory without further modification was not enough to prove religious liberty, especially if one wants to acknowledge that the state as such has obligations toward God. What was needed was a more historically conscious understanding of natural law. A more historically conscious methodology begins not with an abstract notion of the state from which it deduces certain obligations but with the existing concrete reality, in this case the limited constitutional state. Here was the key methodological and substantative point in solving the problem of religious liberty.[57] The function of the state is limited and does not extend into areas beyond its competency, which is the peace of the earthly city. Yes, there is a harmony between the two societies (the church and the state), and the state does have the obligation of the care of religion; but this is fulfilled when the order of constitutional law recognizes, guarantees and protects the freedom of the church.[58]

Religious freedom understood in this perspective differs completely from the religious freedom often proposed in Europe by Continental liberalism and condemned by the popes. The first amendment of the American constitution with its nonestablishment clause is neither an article of faith nor of theology but rather an article of peace. The first amendment thus corresponds to the need for the public peace and consequently is good law based on the limited function of constitutional government. Continental liberalism upheld the juridical omnipotence and omnicompetence of the state and left no room at all for the church and the order of the sacred. The Continental theory of the omnicompetent state derived from a philosophy that extolled the autonomy of reason and had no room for religion or the church. In the American system of a limited constitutional government the separation of church and state was based on articles of peace and not on faith in the autonomy of reason.[59]

A large portion of Murray's writings on church and state

concentrated on interpreting through an historical, critical method the authoritative teaching of the church especially as it was expressed in the encyclicals and documents of Pope Leo XIII. According to Murray one must recognize the historical-polemical aspect of Leo's writing based on his attack on Continental liberalism with its omnicompetent state. The doctrinal aspect in Leo's writings includes the concept of the two societies, the freedom of the church, the state as based on human nature, the need for harmony between the two societies and the orderly cooperation between the two societies.[60]

Murray contends that Leo's defense of the confessional state belongs to the polemical-historical aspect rather than the doctrinal aspect of his teaching and that Leo XIII himself recognized this fact.[61] The condemnation of the separation of church and state likewise belongs to the polemical-historical part of his writings, since it is based on the particular realities of Continental liberalism.[62] Murray's historical, critical approach and his acceptance of the development of doctrine definitely paved the way for the fathers of Vatican II, who ultimately were able to adopt a new approach to religious liberty.[63] Chapter Two has indicated some shortcomings in Murray's theory of development in the teaching of the hierarchical magisterium on church and state. There exists more discontinuity than Murray is willing to admit.

In theory, John Courtney Murray was able to remove one of the most significant obstacles in the way of reconciling the Catholic understanding and the American political order and ethos. John Ryan had been unable to do this, but Murray by employing a more historically conscious natural law approach (Ryan had worked in the economic area with a more inductive and historically minded approach) was able to solve the dilemma and recognize that religious freedom could be totally reconciled with the Catholic self-understanding.

But the final victory was not yet achieved merely on the basis of Murray's writings. In the middle 1950s Murray was forbidden by Roman authorities to write any more on this particular topic. It was only after many struggles at the Second Vatican

Council that the church officially accepted the teaching on religious liberty, even though the drafts originally proposed to the council went against such a teaching. Religious liberty was *the* American issue at the council both in terms of the American public and press and the concern of the American bishops. Murray himself had no part in the preconciliar debates, nor was he invited to the first session of the council. However, Cardinal Spellman invited him to the second session, and Murray through his own speeches and those he wrote for many American bishops and especially through his active work on the drafts had a great influence on the final document.[64]

Murray in his writings also solved the other half of the American and Catholic compatibility question—the suspicion on the part of Americans that Catholics did not really accept the American political system and ethos. In 1960 Murray published a collection of his essays under the title *We Hold These Truths: Catholic Reflections on the American Proposition*. Murray's basic thesis was simple and audacious. Not only is there no incompatibility between the American proposition and the Catholic understanding, but it is precisely the natural law, which has been accepted and preserved in the Catholic Church, which is the basis for the American proposition. The public philosophy of America is based on the proposition of the Declaration of Independence that we hold these truths to be self-evident that all men are created equal and have certain inalienable rights. "The point here is that Catholic participation in the American consensus has been full and free, unreserved and unembarrassed, because the contents of this consensus—the ethical and political principles drawn from the tradition of natural law—approve themselves to the Catholic intelligence and conscience."[65]

What is the meaning of the natural law on which the American proposition and consensus are based? Murray affirms that there are four metaphysical premises of natural law: 1) a realistic epistemology that asserts the real to be the measure of knowledge; 2) a metaphysic of nature with nature as a teleological concept, so that the form of a thing is its final cause; 3) a natural theology; 4) a morality based on the order of nature which is not an order of necessity but rather an order of reason and therefore of freedom.[66]

Murray pushes the point even further. He recognized that the American university with its acceptance of pragmatism has long since rejected the whole notion of the American consensus about the truths we hold in common and the natural law basis upon which they rest. It is paradoxical that a nation which had thought of its own genius in Protestant terms actually owes its origins and its continued stability to the natural law tradition accepted by Roman Catholicism. If we are to continue as a nation, we must renew the tradition which is no longer accepted by the university in general or by contemporary Protestant thought.[67]

Our proponent of compatibility between American and Catholic was not an uncritical observer of the American political scene, as is exemplified in his criticism of pragmatism and the lack of rational analysis in some Protestant thought. Contemporary American thought is troubled by a vacuum of any overall political moral doctrine with regard to war and the use of force.[68] In general there is a moral vacuum because the doctrine of natural law is dead. But in his last chapter Murray proposes that the doctrine still lives and the resources in the natural law tradition could make it the dynamic of a new age of order and of rational progress.[69]

Murray thus makes a bold case for the proposition that Catholics not only can accept the American proposition, but the proposition itself is based on Catholic natural law theory. Personally I do not think he has proved his point. At best there is a common ground morality behind the consensus proposition, but there is not and need not be agreement on ultimate metaphysical and philosophical premises. Murray's thought, however, represents the culmination of that long struggle to prove that Catholicism, an immigrant and minority religion, is at home in the American ethos.

No sooner had Murray achieved this final goal of proving the compatibility between American and Catholic when the synthesis was strongly questioned. Dissatisfaction with the problems of the poor, of race and of an unpopular war in

Southeast Asia all occasioned the phenomenon of dissent within the American culture in general and especially within American Catholic culture. Likewise, from the methodological viewpoint the theories proposed at the Second Vatican Council presupposed a methodology no longer based solely or primarily on the natural law. The council documents recognized the need to overcome the dichotomy between the supernatural and the natural, to place scriptures at the heart of all theology, and to make belief in the kingdom of God more relevant to daily life. But to develop this any further would go beyond the scope of this present chapter which intends to cover only the period up to 1965. The purpose here has been to analyze the story of American Catholic social ethics in terms of its most central problematic—the relationship between Catholic and American and the underlying theological methodologies with which this problem was approached. Other American Catholics, such as Charles Coughlin and Joseph McCarthy, undoubtedly exercised great influence in American political life, but this chapter has been primarily interested in social ethical methodology and the various theories developed in American Catholicism.

NOTES

1. Aaron I. Abell, ed., *American Catholic Thought on Social Questions* (Indianapolis and New York: Bobbs-Merrill Co., 1968), pp. xxiii–xxvi; 141–262.

2. For an historical study of the question especially in the later part of the nineteenth century see Robert D. Cross, *The Emergence of Liberal Catholicism in America* (Cambridge: Harvard University Press, 1958). The relationship between Catholicism and Americanism obviously has frequently been discussed. For an overview showing many facets of the relationship see Thomas T. McAvoy, ed., *Roman Catholicism and the American Way of Life* (Notre Dame, Indiana: University of Notre Dame Press, 1960).

3. Emmet H. Rothan, *The German Catholic Immigrant in the United States (1830–1860)* (Washington, D.C.: Catholic University of America Press, 1946).

4. Abell, *American Catholic Thought,* pp. 3–51. In this particular book Abell includes selections from significant authors and documents and supplies his own introductions and commentaries. For his own historical study see Aaron I. Abell, *American Catholicism and Social Action: A Search for Social Justice 1865–1950* (Notre Dame, Indiana: University of Notre Dame Press, 1963). The first chapter treats the development of the Catholic minority.

5. Cross (p. vii) describes the tendency to promote a friendly interaction between Catholicism and American life as Catholic liberalism.

6. Henry J. Browne, *The Catholic Church and the Knights of Labor* (Washington, D.C.: Catholic University of America Press, 1949).

7. The text of Gibbons' brief, including differences between the French and the English versions of it, can be found in Browne, *The Catholic Church,* appendix III, pp. 365–378.

8. For a favorable account of McGlynn's life and thought see Stephen Bell, *Rebel, Priest and Prophet: A Biography of Dr. Edward McGlynn* (New York: Devin-Adair Co., 1937).

9. Abell, *American Catholicism and Social Action,* pp. 100–122. The Satolli speech is cited on p. 112.

10. Thomas T. McAvoy, *The Great Crisis in American Catholic History, 1895–1900* (Chicago: Henry Regnery Co., 1957).

11. McAvoy; summarized in Cross, *The Emergence of Liberal Catholicism,* pp. 199–203.

12. Jean-Yves Calvez and Jacques Perrin, *The Church and Social Justice* (Chicago: Henry Regnery Co., 1961), pp. 36–53.

13. Pope John XXIII, *Pacem in Terris,* ed. William J. Gibbons (New York: Paulist Press, 1963), n. 1–7; the original text is found in *Acta Apostolicae Sedis* 55 (1963): 258–259.

14. Pope Leo XIII, *Rerum Novarum* in *The Church Speaks to the Modern World: The Social Teaching of Leo XIII,* ed. Etienne Gilson (Garden City, New York: Doubleday Image Books, 1954), p. 200. no. 11; original text: *Acta Sanctae Sedis* 23 (1890–91): 645.

15. "The Bishops' Program of Social Reconstruction," in Abell, *American Catholic Thought,* pp. 325–348.

16. John A. Ryan, *A Living Wage* (New York: Macmillan, 1906); idem, *Distributive Justice* (New York: Macmillan, 1916).

17. For biographical information see Ryan's autobiography, John A. Ryan, *Social Doctrine in Action: A Personal History* (New York: Harper and Brothers, 1941), and especially Francis L. Broderick, *Right Reverend New Dealer John A. Ryan* (New York: Macmillan, 1963).

18. For a detailed description of Ryan as a liberal and reformer as contrasted with radicals and conservatives see David J. O'Brien, *American Catholics and Social Reform* (New York: Oxford University Press, 1968), pp. 120–149. O'Brien's valuable study contains a very informative short section on how the papal encyclicals were suscepti-

ble to different interpretations (pp. 22–28) as well as a concluding chapter on "Catholicism and Americanism" (pp. 212–227).

19. Ryan had sent the manuscript to Richard T. Ely, an economist and Protestant proponent of the Social Gospel, who talked Macmillan into publishing the book if Ryan would pay for the printing plates. Ryan, *Social Doctrine in Action,* pp. 80–81.

20. John A. Ryan, "The Church and the Working Man," *Catholic World* 89 (1908–09): 776–778.

21. Broderick, *Right Reverend New Dealer,* pp. 46–47.

22. Ryan, *Distributive Justice,* p. xiii.

23. Morris Hillquit and John A. Ryan, *Socialism: Promise or Menace?* (New York: Macmillan, 1914), p. 58.

24. George C. Higgins, "The Underconsumption Theory in the Writings of Monsignor John A. Ryan" (M.A. dissertation, Catholic University of America, 1942).

25. John A. Ryan, *Seven Troubled Years* (Ann Arbor, Michigan: Edwards Brothers, Inc., 1937), p. 59.

26. Ryan, *Distributive Justice,* pp. 356ff.

27. Ibid., pp. 56–60.

28. Patrick W. Gearty, *The Economic Thought of Monsignor John A. Ryan* (Washington, D.C.: Catholic University of America Press, 1953), pp. 130ff.; Reginald G. Bender, "The Doctrine of Private Property in the Writings of Monsignor John A. Ryan" (S.T.D. dissertation, Catholic University of America, 1973), pp. 114ff.

29. Broderick, *Right Reverend New Dealer,* pp. 31–33.

30. Gearty, *Economic Thought,* pp. 254–297. For a description of Ryan as a continuing reformer see Neil Betten, "John Ryan and the Social Action Department," *Thought* 46 (1971): 227–246.

31. Broderick, *Right Reverend New Dealer,* pp. 170–185.

32. John A. Ryan and Moorhouse F. X. Millar, *The State and the Church* (New York: Macmillan, 1922), pp. 38–39.

33. The best source for the history and description of this movement is Philip Gleason, *The Conservative Reformers: German-American Catholics and the Social Order* (Notre Dame, Indiana: University of Notre Dame Press, 1968). For a study of German-American Catholics in the later part of the nineteenth century see Colman J. Barry, *The Catholic Church and German Americans* (Milwaukee: Bruce Publishing Co., 1953). On the particular subject under discussion, but of much less value than Gleason, see Sister Mary Elizabeth Dye, *By Their Fruits: A Social Biography of Frederick Kenkel, Catholic Social Pioneer* (New York: Greenwich Book Publishers, 1960) and Mary Liguori Brophy, *The Social Thought of the German Roman Catholic Central Verein* (Washington, D.C.: Catholic University of America Press, 1941).

34. The social thought of the Central Verein was often expounded in long articles which appeared in installments in *Central-Blatt and Social Justice.* In addition to Kenkel the most authoritative spokesper-

son was William J. Engelen, S.J., a college professor. See, for example, Engelen, "Social Reflections," *Central-Blatt and Social Justice* 12 (1919–20): 203–205, continuing in twenty installments ending in 14 (1921–22): 178–180; also Engelen, "Social Observations," *Central-Blatt and Social Justice* 14 (1921–22): 219–221, continuing in five installments ending in 14 (1921–22): 357–359.

35. E.g., W. J. Engelen, "Social Reconstruction (VII)," *Central-Blatt and Social Justice* 18 (1925–26): 147–148.

36. Gleason, *Conservative Reformers,* pp. 140–143, 200–203.

37. For an analysis of the German situation see Edgar Alexander, "Social and Political Movements and Ideas in German and Austrian Catholicism (1789–1950)," in *Church and Society,* ed. Joseph N. Moody (New York: Arts Inc., 1953). pp. 325–583.

38. A concise summary of this approach as found in the writings of the German Jesuit Henry Pesch is given in W. J. Engelen, "Social Reconstruction XIII: Rev. Henry Pesch, S.J.," *Central-Blatt and Social Justice* 19 (1926–27): 77–79, 111–112, 147–148, 183–184, 219–220.

39. Frederick P. Kenkel, "Some Arguments against the Proposed Child Labor Amendment," *Central-Blatt and Social Justice* 18 (1925–26): 114–116, 150–152.

40. The best book on the movement in general is William D. Miller, *A Harsh and Dreadful Love: Dorothy Day and the Catholic Worker Movement* (Garden City, New York: Doubleday Image Books, 1974). Additional bibliography may be found there, especially references to books written by Dorothy Day including her autobiographical works and collections of her articles from *The Catholic Worker.* On the particular question of social ethics see O'Brien, pp. 182–211. I am also grateful for help from the research being done at Catholic University by Stuart Sandberg.

41. Neil Betten, "Social Catholicism and the Rise of Catholic Radicalism in America," *Journal of Human Relations* 18 (1970): 710–727; O'Brien, *American Catholics,* p. 211.

42. For my detailed analysis and critique of Furfey's thought see Charles E. Curran, "The Radical Catholic Social Ethics of Paul Hanly Furfey," in *New Perspectives in Moral Theology* (Notre Dame, Indiana: University of Notre Dame Press, 1976), pp. 87–121.

43. Paul Hanly Furfey, *Fire on the Earth* (New York: Macmillan, 1936), pp. 1–21; idem, *Three Theories of Society* (New York: Macmillan, 1937).

44. A sampling of articles from *The Catholic Worker* can be found in *A Penny A Copy: Readings from the Catholic Worker,* ed. Thomas C. Cornell and James H. Forest (New York: Macmillan, 1968).

45. John F. Cronin, *Social Principles and Economic Life,* rev. ed. (Milwaukee: Bruce Publishing Co., 1964), pp. 17–25.

46. John F. Cronin, *Catholic Social Principles* (Milwaukee: Bruce Publishing Co., 1950), pp. 213–253.

47. Cronin, *Social Principles and Economic Life*, pp. 130–140.

48. Ibid., pp. 90ff., 140ff.

49. Gary Wills, *Nixon Agonistes* (New York: Signet Books, 1971), pp. 34–39.

50. John Courtney Murray, "Intercredal Cooperation: Its Theory and Its Organization," *Theological Studies* 4 (1943): 257–286.

51. Paul Hanly Furfey, "Intercredal Cooperation: Its Limitations," *American Ecclesiastical Review* 111 (1944): 161–175.

52. In addition to the articles mentioned in the preceding notes and some other interventions of less importance the debate continued: John Courtney Murray, "On the Problem of Cooperation: Some Clarifications," *American Ecclesiastical Review* 112 (1945): 194–214; Paul Hanly Furfey, "Why Does Rome Discourage Socio-Religious Intercredalism?" *American Ecclesiastical Review* 112 (1945): 365–374.

53. John Courtney Murray, "Leo XIII: Separation of Church and State," *Theological Studies* 14 (1953): 200–201.

54. John Courtney Murray, "Freedom of Religion I: The Ethical Problem," *Theological Studies* 6 (1945): 235.

55. Ibid., pp. 266ff.

56. John Courtney Murray, *The Problem of Religious Freedom* (Westminster, Md.: Newman Press, 1965), pp. 28–30.

57. John Courtney Murray, "The Declaration on Religious Freedom," *Concilium* 15 (May 1966): 11–16.

58. Murray, *Problem of Religious Freedom*, p. 32.

59. John Courtney Murray, "Civil Unity and Religious Integrity: The Articles of Peace," in *We Hold These Truths* (New York: Sheed and Ward, 1960), pp. 59–60.

60. Faith E. Burgess, *The Relationship between Church and State according to John Courtney Murray, S.J.* (Düsseldorf: Rudolf Stehle, 1971), pp. 116–120.

61. John Courtney Murray, "Leo XIII: Two Concepts of Government II: Government and the Order of Culture," *Theological Studies* 15 (1954): 16–21.

62. Burgess, *Relationship between Church and State*, pp. 114–115.

63. Raymond Owen McEvoy, "John Courtney Murray's Thought on Religious Liberty in Its Final Phase," *Studia Moralia* 11 (1973): 240–260.

64. For developments in the conciliar period itself see Richard Regan, *Conflict and Consensus: Religious Freedom and the Second Vatican Council* (New York: Macmillan, 1967).

65. Murray, *We Hold These Truths*, p. 47.

66. Ibid., pp. 327–328.

67. Ibid., pp. 40–41.

68. Ibid., p. 273.

69. Ibid., pp. 334–336.

5: Social Ethics: Future Agenda for Theology and the Church

This chapter will discuss the future agenda for the church in the area of social ethics and the relationship of church and society. The perspective will be that of Catholic social ethics with a realization that a truly Catholic social ethics is ecumenical both in terms of its relation to other Christian thought and action and in relation to all people of good will. We will consider the question against a broad general background but give special importance to the perspective of Catholic social ethics in the United States.

A first consideration logically should focus on the issues involved. What are the particular problems and questions facing the world and the church in the area of social ethics?

One point is certain. There will be no lack of issues. The future agenda can and must learn from what Christians and others have been doing in the past as well as from a true discernment of the problems of the present and the future. The Second Vatican Council grouped the issues of church and society under five headings — marriage and the family, culture, socioeconomic life, life of the political community, and the fostering of peace.[1] The World Conference on Church and Society sponsored by the World Council of Churches in Geneva in 1966 divided its material into four sections — economic development, nature and function of the state, structure of international cooperation, and man and community in changing societies.[2] Recently the "The Call to Action" Conference under the auspices of the American bishops treated the following areas: church, ethnicity and race, family, humankind, nationhood, neighborhood, personhood, work.[3]

Theology as such has no exclusive insight into discerning the social problems facing the world and the church today. Theologians, like all other individuals and groups within society and the church, must try to learn from all possible sources what are the primary issues facing the world and society today. Any true discernment process, recognizing the importance given to participation by Pope Paul VI in *Octogesima adveniens,*[4] must call for the cooperation of all in discerning these problems—especially minorities and those who are oppressed and suffering. Newer problems have emerged in the last few years, but questions concerning peace, the poor and discrimination because of race or sex will continue to be very significant questions.

From the theological perspective the more significant questions concern method—how theology should approach such social questions and how the church should carry out its social mission. These are the two main tasks to be pursued in this study. However, these more methodological questions might best be raised in the context of a particular substantive issue. Social economic issues will be chosen to focus the methodological questions.

In the midst of the myriad social issues facing society, it is difficult to select one issue as primary, but the social economic issue would have to be considered very important, if not primary. The papal encyclicals starting with Leo XIII concentrated on social economic issues; in the United States there was a strong emphasis on social justice in the writings of Catholics. Social economic justice in the encyclicals and in the American Catholic literature centered on the economic questions of safeguarding the rights of workers—a living wage, right to join unions, provision against illness and sudden catastrophe, right to own property.

The changed economic circumstances in the United States obviously influenced a decreased interest in social economic questions in the past few decades. The war economy of World War II artificially solved the problems of the depression.

Catholics who used to be the poor of the land moved into the middle class after that war. The new poor (especially the blacks) were not Roman Catholic, and it was somewhat easy for the church to forget about them. Even the Spanish speaking who are Roman Catholic were easily overlooked. American Catholics struggling to prove they could be loyal Americans tended not to be critical of America the land of opportunity. The post-World War II struggle in which Roman Catholicism and the United States were the two bulwarks of the free world against the Communist menace only served to heighten the identification of American and Catholic and made Catholics less critical of their own society, as was explained in the last chapter.[5]

However, the social economic problem still remains. In the United States such questions as tax reform and welfare reform, although they are not radical questions, show the importance of the socioeconomic sphere. Even more fundamental are the problems of poverty still existing in the United States. The most significant development highlights the worldwide nature of the question.[6] The developing nations of the world feel the inequities of the present economic order. Liberation theology coming from the South American experience calls for a radical change in the economic structures of society. North Americans must look beyond their narrow boundaries to see the problems in their global scale. Issues such as peace, human rights, and sexual equality are always important questions, but the proper distribution of the goods of creation remains very significant. John Coleman Bennett has recently called attention to the importance of economic ethics.[7] Thus social economic questions can well serve as illustrations of how both theology and the church should approach social ethics and social action.

I. Theological Approaches

Various questions of theological methodology and approaches will be raised, but initially some assumptions coming from recent developments in social ethics will be mentioned. First, Catholic social ethics can no longer work out of the model of the nature-supernature, kingdom-world dichotomy which too often characterized Roman Catholic thought in the past. The gospel and the kingdom must be positively related to the world and the social problems facing human existence. The second assumption concerns the need for an historically conscious approach which will be much more inductive.

Both these assumptions are comparatively recent in Catholic social ethics. The Pastoral Constitution on the Church in the Modern World is the first document of the hierarchical magisterium to incorporate such approaches. Note the emphasis on overcoming the dichotomy between faith and the world, the gospel and our daily life, and also observe the methodology which begins the discussion of particular social questions by an inductive reading of the signs of the times. These two approaches are even more evident in the Medellín Documents issued by the South American Bishops in 1968. Although these characteristics did not appear in official Catholic Church documents before 1963, now they can correctly be assumed as necessary aspects of any Christian social ethics.

A third assumption recognizes the need for critical reason and an emphasis on praxis. Moral theology in general and social ethics in particular obviously are more disposed to accept such an emphasis. Again there will be differences in the amount of emphasis given to critical reason and praxis, but still one must underscore the importance of such aspects in social ethics today.

Mediation

Chapter One has emphasized that Roman Catholic theology has traditionally been characterized by an acceptance of mediation. Catholic theologies of the church and of natural law illustrate this fact. God and God's presence to us is mediated in and through the church. God's plan for human action is primarily known, not directly and immediately from God, but rather in and through our understanding of the human. The divine plan in no way short-circuits the human reasoning process, but precisely in and through human reason reflecting on our existence we arrive at what God wants us to do.

Contemporary emphasis on the gospel and on the kingdom calls for some kind of mediation. The hermeneutic problem in understanding the scriptures recognizes the need for a mediating principle going from the gospel to contemporary existence. How does one go from the gospel or the concept of the kingdom to the particulars of the social, economic and political world in which we live?

Contemporary liberation theologians such as Gutierrez also recognize the need for a mediating principle. Gutierrez acknowledges three distinct levels of liberation which affect each other but are not the same—political liberation, the liberation of man through history and liberation from sin.[8] Gutierrez calls for a mediation through utopias and eschews a politico-religious messianism which does not sufficiently respect the autonomy of the political arena. Faith and political action will not enter into a correct and fruitful relationship except through utopia. Utopia is characterized by three elements—its relationship to historical reality, its verification in praxis and its rational nature.[9] Hugo Assmann calls for a mediation through a sociological analysis based on Marxism[10] and thus seems to argue for a very specific mediation.

Perhaps the American scene can offer another mediating principle—distributive justice. The previous chapter has indicated that the Catholic tradition in the United States has emphasized distributive justice as seen in the significant book of that title by John A. Ryan. Ryan used distributive justice as the canon for the proper distribution of the products of industry among their producers.[11] In contemporary philosophical writing much more importance has been paid lately to questions of justice and distributive justice.[12] The concept of distributive justice thus enables Catholic ethics to enter into dialogue with many other philosophers and people of good will.

The particular social questions that are being raised in the

American context today emphasize problems that readily fit under the category of distributive justice—making medical care available for all, which will be considered at length in the next chapter, income maintenance programs guaranteeing a minimum income for all; an equitable tax system doing away with regressive taxes such as sales taxes or the existing social security tax.[13] The rubric of distributive justice addresses the very significant question of the proper distribution of the goods of this world. Questions of the international economic order can readily be approached in and through this understanding.

Distributive justice as a mediating concept properly emphasizes the biblical concept that the goods of creation exist for all human beings.[14] Too often, especially in the United States, a rugged individualism and a poor concept of freedom have characterized the understanding of the ownership of goods. Distributive justice avoids the pitfalls of a narrowly individualistic concept of justice and rightly emphasizes the Christian belief that God destined the goods of creation for all human beings.[15] The concept of distributive justice remains quite generic, and there can be and will be disagreements about particular ramifications and societal structures. However, it seems to me that distributive justice serves quite well as a mediating concept between the gospel demands and the realities of the present situation.

Mediation and Specificity

The acceptance of mediation recognizes the relative autonomy of the human, human reason and scientific data and their interpretation. Political, social and economic data and their interpretation must be respected by theological ethics in coming to its conclusions. Theological ethics can and should offer guidance for our choices in these societal matters, but such choices are heavily dependent on scientific data and their interpretation, which cannot be short-circuited by theological and ethical judgments. As was pointed out in Chapter Three theology cannot say which psychological theory or which sociological interpretation is more adequate for interpreting the reality in question.

Some so stress the autonomy of the human, human reason and human sciences that they contend that theological ethics is imcompetent to draw any such specific conclusions about what should be done in practice.[16] I deny this assertion. Human judgments are not merely economic, social or political judgments. They are truly human and moral judgments, even though they involve a great deal of complex scientific data and interpretation. It is precisely because of being mediated through the specifics of human sciences that particular human, moral and Christian judgments cannot claim to be the only possible Christian interpretation. Sometimes it is rather easy to identify the concrete solution with the Christian approach as in the condemnation of torture or the blatant violation of human rights. But in many cases the Christian solution cannot be so readily identified with any one approach primarily because of the fact that the final judgment relies quite heavily on scientific data and their interpretation. In practice it will often be impossible to claim that there is only one possible Christian solution and no other. This position has been generally accepted in Catholic thought as was mentioned in Chapter Two. Take, for example, proposals made for nuclear disarmament or different ways of providing basic medical care for all.

Eschatology

Eschatological considerations have exerted a strong influence on contemporary theology. In the light of eschatology and of the fullness of the kingdom the present social, political and economic conditions are shown to be imperfect and in need of change. The status quo can never be totally accepted by one who has an eschatological vision. The call to improve the structures of our world must always beckon the Christian.

At the very minimum an eschatological vision provides a negative critique of existing structures. However, ultimately such a critique should also call for a positive response which works to bring about change. The eschatological vision and the understanding of the kingdom can furnish positive aspects in terms of the values, goals, ideals and attitudes that must be present in all Christian approaches. These positive aspects alone do not arrive at concrete solutions. As mentioned above, such values must be mediated through the scientific data and their interpretation in coming to grips with concrete problems.

An eschatological vision calls for a continual effort to change the social, political and economic structures in which we live. However, the fullness of the eschatological vision will never be totally achieved. The Christian recognizes the power of sin in the world and the need to struggle continually against the forces of sin. The kingdom will never be perfectly present in this world; its fullness lies beyond our grasp. Imperfection and lack of completeness will characterize our structures. Likewise, one must reject the naive optimism of Protestant liberalism which identified any change as necessarily good.

Too often in the immediate past some people readily accepted the need for social action and social change, but they quickly became disillusioned when such change did not occur. If the experience of the last decade teaches us anything, it is the need for a long-term commitment to bring about the kinds of social changes which are necessary. Romantic visionaries might be willing to give a bit of their time or a certain amount of effort in trying to bring about change, but they too readily become discouraged in the light of the long-haul situation. Consequently, the virtue of hope strengthens the individual to continue commitment to the struggle even when success seems all too absent. Relatively oppressive and unjust structures will not be changed readily or quickly.

Since the fullness of the eschaton serves as a negative critique on all existing structures, the Christian recognizes that the kingdom cannot totally be identified with any one specific approach. The Christian must always be willing to criticize all things—including one's own vision and tactics in the light of the eschaton. Too often Christians have too readily identified the gospel or the kingdom with their own cause, country or philosophy. American Protestants of earlier generations too readily identified the kingdom of God with the United States.[17] Chapter Four showed that immigrant Catholics at times strained too mightly to prove there was no incompatibility between being American and Catholic.[18]

Such a critical eschatological perspective calls for continual vigilance and self-criticism. The danger, however, always remains that people will use this as an excuse to do nothing and thus accept the status quo. The eschatological vision should never be employed as an excuse for noninvolvement. Christian theology must be willing to criticize all ideologies and their approaches, but there are still some approaches which are more adequate than others and must be adopted in practice. The Christian and eschatological vision must be willing to become incarnate in concrete historical, cultural and political circumstances even though one recognizes the risks involved. In this context I prefer to use the term strategies to refer to the particular approaches that Christians can use in changing social structures. These strategies can and should be very specific, but they can never be absolutized and removed from critical reflection. In this way one avoids the dogmatization of many forms of ideological theories.

An eschatological understanding together with a recognition of mediation also tends to argue against the acceptance of any overly simplistic solutions to social problems. My own innate theological "prejudice" also argues for such complexity. It is too simplistic to reduce all ethical problems to any one type of opposition. Social problems cannot simplistically be reduced to just any one factor be it that of class, sex, race or country. However, it can be that one of these aspects is more significant in a particular situation and thus furnishes the strategy that must be employed in that situation in order to overcome the oppression and injustice.

Although eschatological considerations are most important, I do not think eschatology alone (especially apocalyptic eschatology) can serve as an adequate basis for the development of moral theology or social ethics. I have proposed that the stance or logically first step in moral theology embraces the fivefold Christian mysteries of creation, sin, incarnation, redemption and resurrection destiny. The failure to incorporate all of these aspects stands as a negative critique of such past approaches as Catholic natural law, Lutheran two-realm theory, liberal Protestantism and Neo-Orthodoxy. More positively, such a stance provides the basic horizon or perspective within which moral theology and Christian social ethics should be developed.

Personal and/or Structural Change

Catholic social thought in general and especially since the nineteenth century has emphasized the need and importance of structural change. It is not enough merely to call for personal change and a change of heart. Catholic ethics has traditionally recognized structures and institutions as necessary aspects of human existence, even to call them natural organizations in the sense that human beings are social by nature and thus called to form groups, institutions and structures to creatively accomplish what human beings alone are incapable of doing. Liberal Catholic social thought in the United States has often been associated with the call to reform the social, political and economic structures of society.[19] At times some elements of radical Catholic social reform have so stressed the personal element they have not given enough importance to the need for a change of structures.[20]

From my perspective both changes of heart and changes of structure are necessary in social ethics. Unfortunately these two aspects too often are separated, and the need for both is not stressed. The "Call to Action" Conference sponsored by the American bishops in Detroit in the fall of 1976 rightfully called for structural changes but said little or nothing about the need for change of heart and all the educational and motivational aspects that can help bring about such a change.

The present nature of the economic change required in the world is of such a nature that it cannot be accomplished without a somewhat radical change of attitude on the part of individual persons and especially individual persons existing within the more wealthy nations of the world. When change itself is not too radical, then there is no need for great personal change of heart and attitudes. This has been the assumption and the premise of liberal social reformers in the United States. The myth of ever-greater growth insisted that change means that more people share more equitably in the ever-growing progress—especially material progress. Progress implied more for everyone with no need for anyone to give up what one already enjoys.[21]

Already there are signs even in the United States that such an approach cannot deal with the extent of the problems that are being faced today. The energy crisis might call for a great change in life-styles and attitudes of many Americans. Ecological problems have made us very suspect of the older notion of progress and of the promise that the future will be bigger and better than the present or the past. Especially in the context of the international economic order the rich nations of the world are called to a more radical type of change which cannot be accomplished without a change of heart of individuals and all that is entailed with such a change. Americans must be willing to give up some of their high material standard of living in order that other people on the earth might have an equitable share of the goods of creation. Recent proposals to the effect that small is beautiful remind us of the profound kinds of changes that are necessary. Thus, good theological ethical theory combined with the understanding of the magnitude of the problems that we are facing especially in the areas of socioeconomic ethics reminds us of the need for both personal change of heart and structural change. Any theological ethics which fails to recognize both will tend to be inadequate.

Harmony and Conflict

Catholic social thought, with its traditional emphasis on the natural law as an ordering of reason, has tended to see the world and society in general in terms of order and harmony rather than in terms of conflict and opposition. Catholic theory has seen no true opposition but rather concord between law and freedom. Good law does not restrict our freedom but rather tells human beings to do that which by nature they are called to do. Hierarchical ordering dominated our understanding of human nature as well as our understanding of human society and of the church, with the lower aspects serving the higher. All the individual parts work together in proper coordination and subordination for the good of the whole. When applied to the economic order, this outlook called for the cooperation of all the individual elements and units in the economic order—capital, labor and management—working together for the common good. The corporate society proposed by many Catholic theorists and espoused by Pope Pius XI in *Quadragesimo anno* inculcates such an emphasis on hierarchical ordering and working together for the common good.[22] At times in practice there was an innate realism which recognized the existence of problems and the need for some conflict in such questions as war, strikes and disagreements; but the heavy emphasis in Catholic theory was on order and harmony.

The harmony-conflict question surfaces above all in views of society and the relationship among the classes existing in society. In the economic order Marxism talks about a class struggle between the poor and the rich. How should Catholic ethics look at such conflictual understandings of human existence? In general, Catholic social thought in my judgment must give more importance to conflict with a somewhat decreased emphasis on order and harmony. A recognition of the presence of sin as well as a more historically conscious methodology will put less influence on order and harmony than in the pre-Vatican II Catholic approach. There is also a need to develop a theology of power. However, a greater recognition of the role of conflict does not mean that all social relationships should be seen in terms of conflict or that conflict is the ultimate and most fundamental way of viewing the human scene.

Christianity ultimately calls for love and reconciliation. Love of enemies has been a hallmark of Christian teaching and preaching—if not, unfortunately, of Christian action. Christian social ethics can never forget the appeal to the human person as person to change one's own heart and to work for a change of social structure. Conflict for the Christian cannot be the ultimate nor can it be accepted for its own sake. However, on this side of the fullness of the eschaton, conflict at times can and will be an acceptable strategy in Christian social ethics. As a strategy, it can never become an ideology or an ultimate explanation of reality. However, there will be more conflictual situations than Catholic social ethics was willing to admit in the past. Thus, for example, conflict among classes might be a necessary strategy in bringing about social change, but conflict can never be the first or the ultimate or the most important reality.

Somewhat connected with conflict is the question of violence which must be faced in our contemporary world. Here the Catholic tradition in its just war tradition worked out an understanding that accepted violence in a just cause but at the same time insisted on limiting the violence. There are some today who call for a total pacifism, but I cannot accept such an absolute approach.

Detached and Participant Perspectives

What is the better perspective for arriving at good ethical judgments—that of a participant or that of a detached observer? Emphasis on critical reason and praxis shows the importance of active participation in the ongoing work itself. However, the need for critical reflection on praxis also calls for some type of self-criticism and detachment.

In my judgment there are advantages and disadvantages to both perspectives. History shows that the detached observer does not realize the extent of the problems faced by certain people or societies. White, middle-class, male theologians and ethicists have not been as aware of the injustices existing for other races, the poor and women as they should have been. If one is not involved in the oppression and injustice, there is a tendency not to realize its existence.

On the other hand, the participant can be so involved in a particular struggle that one fails to see other important aspects. I, for example, can never reduce social conflict totally to a struggle of the poor against the rich. I believe that this at times can be very true, but I also believe that there are other social problems such as the evils of sexism and racism. Those who in the past fought the cold war against communism failed to recognize the divergent aspects among different communist countries and also were unwilling to criticize the free world. Advocates of feminine rights correctly recognize the wrongs done to women in society, but at times some tend to overlook the rights of the fetus. The ultimate advantages and disadvantages of both models call for the need for both perspectives in any theological or ethical enterprise.

Social Ethics As a Reflexive, Systematic Discipline

Theological social ethics by its very nature constitutes a reflexive, systematic discipline. Its discourse can be described as second-order discourse as distinguished from first-order discourse (e.g., preaching). Any second-order discourse will not have as immediate an effect upon action and change as first-order discourse. I affirm that social ethics should have some effect on social change, but I recognize there are other realities that have an even greater effect on social change. Chapter One developed at greater length this understanding of the role of moral theology.

II. Role of the Church

Having treated some questions of theological methodology in the area of social ethics especially in the light of economic questions, this chapter will now consider some ecclesial aspects centering on the social mission of the church. Again, the focus is on the Roman Catholic Church, but what is said applies to all Christian churches. In addition to what is developed in this section there is a great need for ecumenical witness and action in the social mission of the Christian churches.

Importance of the Social Mission of the Church

One cannot stress enough the importance of the social mission of the church. *Justice in the World,* the document released by the Synod of Bishops in 1971, strongly states: "Action on behalf of justice and participation in the transformation of the world fully appear to us as a constitutive dimension of the preaching of the Gospel, or, in other words, of the church's mission for the redemption of the human race and its liberation from every oppressive situation."[23]

The social mission of the church has thus been recognized as a constitutive dimension of the church. The challenge remains to make this a living reality on the pastoral level in the life of the church. Pastoral creativity and imagination must put flesh and blood on the bare bones of this statement. The force of the statement should not be lost—without a social mission the church is not truly church, for it is missing a constitutive aspect. This is true of the church on all levels of its existence but especially on the level of the local church. The parish community must be not only a worshiping community but also a serving community. How to bring this about in practice is perhaps the primary pastoral problem facing the church at the present time.

Peculiar circumstances on the American Catholic scene make this pastoral ministry more difficult but even more imperative. The mainstream of American Catholicism tried to prove there was no basic incompatibility between being American and being Catholic. The older distinction between natural and supernatural was used to point out the different spheres. The great contribution of the American church at the Second Vatican Council was in the advocacy of religious freedom and the separation of church and state. The subtle danger was to separate American and Catholic on the one hand and state and church on the other into two separate spheres. In such a way there was no incompatibility between them, but also the church or the gospel readily lost any influence on the state or the secular. Catholics had a different faith from other Americans, but this did not affect their participation in the national life and questions facing society. There was a fear of admitting anything distinctively Christian or Catholic that one could bring to bear on the social and political orders. The Catholic ethos in the United States tended to eliminate faith, the gospel and the supernatural from political, social and economic theory and life. There is all the more need in the United States for a creative pastoral ministry making the social mission of the church a constitutive part of the church.

There have been some creative developments in the last few years in social ministry. The church and groups in the church can act as catalysts for various forms of community organizations. These community organizations can then work effectively for social change. Here the role of the church is neither patronizing nor paternalistic but rather enabling. Also, church groups can and should act as advocates for the poor and disadvantaged.[24]

Limits on the Social Mission of the Church

The proper understanding of the social mission of the church, as well as the call for creative ministerial intiatives to make the social mission of the church a constitutive part of the church, calls for a recognition of the limitations involved in both comprehending and structuring the social mission of the church. First, the social mission is only a part of the total mission of the church. There are many other aspects of the mission of the church, involving especially the preaching of the gospel and the liturgical celebration of the presence of the risen Lord in our midst with the concomitant hope that he will come again. The social mission should not be seen as opposed to these other aspects, for these other aspects by their very nature call for a social mission dimension. But the church cannot be reduced only to the social mission.

Second, there are many individuals and groups apart from the church who are working for the betterment of society. Catholics and other Christians must avoid the narrow triumphalism of claiming to be the only ones working for social justice and struggling against the forces of oppression. Such a proposed understanding is unfair to all the other individuals and groups who have dedicated themselves to working against injustice.

Third, individual Roman Catholics are not only members of the church community but they belong to many other groups, communities and societies which are also working for the betterment of society. One cannot and should not go back to a Catholic ghetto concept according to which the Catholic does not become involved in ecumenical, secular and other groups working for social change. Any structuring of the social mission of the church must recognize that the social mission of individual Catholics must not be totally or perhaps even primarily in terms of Christian groups or organizations as such. Fourth, there has been much discussion in moral theology in the last decade about the existence of a specifically Christian ethic. My contention is that from the viewpoint of specific ethical content as well as that of proximate goals, attitudes and dispositions such as self-sacrificing love, care for the poor and struggling against oppression there is no distinctively Christian social ethical content. Obviously this is a disputed point, but at the very minimum one must be willing to recognize that Christians have no monopoly on social ethical wisdom or insight.

Pluralism

Different aspects of pluralism have been mentioned already in the discussion of theological methodology. First, there can be a legitimate pluralism on the level of theological methodology itself. Many would not agree with the methodology I proposed. Some, for example, would call for a more radical approach that would advocate a Christian witness to peace and voluntary poverty.

Second, there will be a pluralism because of the different possible scientific theories and interpretations of the data involved in complex social ethical questions. Third, on these specific issues the very complexity of the issues argues against the possibility of claiming with absolute certitude that there is only one possible Christian approach or solution.

The history of American Catholic social ethics as developed in the last chapter reminds us of the pluralism of approaches that existed even among those who did not accept the status quo. John A. Ryan put heavy emphasis on the role of the state to bring about reform. German-American Catholics distrusted the state and called for a very thoroughgoing reform on the model of the corporate society. The Catholic Worker Movement espoused a radical personalism that distrusted all organization and even gloried in the name of anarchism. History thus indicates the pluralism which has existed in social ethics.[25]

It is interesting that Catholic social theory has traditionally recognized a legitimate diversity or pluralism on concrete questions facing society.[26] Chapter Two has proposed that dissent, or more positively pluralism, will be increasingly present on some questions of more personal and individual ethics such as contraception, sterilization, divorce and even abortion and euthanasia. The basic reasons stem from the distance of such questions from the core of faith and from the complexity of these specific questions because of which one cannot claim that a particular solution is so certain that it excludes the possibility of error. One cannot speak about *the* Christian solution to specific concrete problems as if there were no other possible Christian alternative. In an era where pluralism is being recognized even in the area of personal morality, one cannot logically deny its existence in social ethics. In both areas theology must continue to discuss the important question of the limits of pluralism.

Ecclesiological Consequences

My understanding of mediation, eschatology and pluralism concluded that often Christians and the church can agree in pointing out what are the problems and difficulties existing in society (a negative critique). In season and out of season the whole church should preach and respond to the basic gospel message of conversion which calls for Christians to struggle against the presence of sin not only in our hearts but also in the social structures of society. On the level of the general there should be more agreement among Christians and within the churches on the values, goals and ideals to be present in society, but as one descends to particular plans and strategies, the very complexity of these issues will often mean that it is increasingly difficult to speak about *the* Christian solution.

In this area above all one sees the importance and need for smaller groups within the church. Groups of Christians can and should join together to work for a common purpose and employ a common strategy. In many ways the liberation theology of South America has grown up in the context of such small groups of committed Christians banded together to work for overcoming oppression. In the United States the Catholic Worker movement and other such apostolates illustrate the same basic reality. The peace movement in the United States in a more informal way sponsored the existence of such groups.

Although there have been some such groups present in the United States in the past, it seems that they were not as numerous as in other countries. Perhaps this is because a Catholic Action approach with an emphasis on cell units was not as common in this country as elsewhere. However, I believe it is very important and essential for the good of the church to have a variety of small groups existing within the church.

In the last few years in the United States a number of smaller groups working for social justice and change have come into being. Think, for example, of the Justice and Peace organizations which have sprung up in dioceses and in religious communities. Network, a group of women religious lobbying for social change, has attracted attention and support. There are many different types of groups which can and should exist. At times one might find various church groups on different sides of the same issue as has happened on the Equal Rights Amendment. At times even the bishops can function as such a group within the church.

In this view one sees the church, whether on a local, national or international level, as a larger community in which serious dialogue takes place about what the gospel calls us to do in terms of changing societies. Individuals and smaller groups within the church would be able to do what larger groups and the entire church itself might not be able to do. I would hope that in this way many individual Christians would feel a vocation to join such particular groups in their witness to poverty, peace, social justice, and other vital issues.

There is still at times a role for the total church and its leadership, whether on a local, national or international level, both in terms of teaching and of acting on specific social problems. A whole church body either on a parochial or national or even worldwide basis can and should at times address specific moral questions. However, in so doing there are some cautions that must be taken into account. First of all, since such questions involve technical data and expertise, those who are addressing such problems must make sure that they have competently mastered all the details which are involved. Second, it will be impossible to speak out or act on all the issues facing society because of a lack of expertise, but the more significant questions can and should be chosen. Third, they should recognize that other Christians might disagree with the particular position that is being taken. In this way the position is proposed in the name of the church but with the recognition that even individual members of the church might disagree with a particular aspect of it. Here the moral credibility of the teaching is most significant.

In looking to the question of the future agenda of the church in the area of social ethics this chapter has purposely avoided a substantive consideration of the various issues. Instead, an attempt has been made to consider the theological methodology that should be involved in such discussions and also the ecclesiological implications of the social mission of the church.

NOTES

1. Pastoral Constitution on the Church in the Modern World, nos. 46–93. For a reliable English translation see *The Documents of Vatican II,* ed. Walter M. Abbott (New York: Guild Press, 1966).

2. *World Conference on Church and Society: Official Report* (Geneva: World Council of Churches, 1967).

3. The final recommendations of this conference were printed in *Origins: N.C. Documentary Service* 6, no. 20 (November 4, 1976) and no. 21 (November 11, 1976): 309–340.

4. Pope Paul VI, *Octogesima adveniens,* no. 22. This and other important documents on social justice can be found in *The Gospel of Peace and Justice: Catholic Social Teaching since Pope John,* ed. Joseph Germillion (Maryknoll, New York: Orbis Books, 1976).

5. David J. O'Brien, *The Renewal of American Catholicism* (New York: Oxford University Press, 1972), pp. 138–162.

6. Pope Paul VI, *Populorum progressio,* no. 3, in Gremillion, *The Gospel of Peace and Justice,* p. 388.

7. John C. Bennett, *The Radical Imperative* (Philadelphia: Westminster Press, 1975), pp. 142–164.

8. Gustavo Gutierrez, *A Theology of Liberation* (Maryknoll, New York: Orbis, 1973), pp. 36–37; 176.

9. Ibid., pp. 232–239.

10. Hugo Assmann, *Theology for a Nomad Church* (Maryknoll, New York: Orbis, 1976), pp. 116, 138ff.

11. John A. Ryan, *Distributive Justice* (New York: Macmillan, 1916). See also John A. Coleman, "Vision and Praxis in American Theology," *Theological Studies* 37 (1976): 3–40.

12. John Rawls, *A Theory of Justice* (Cambridge, Mass.: Belknap Press of Harvard University, 1971); Robert A. Nozick, *Anarchy, State and Utopia* (New York: Basic Books, 1974).

13. Bennett, *The Radical Imperative,* pp. 152–154.

14. E.g., Ryan, *Distributive Justice,* p. 358.

15. Recent documents of the hierarchical magisterium have stressed this universal destiny of the goods of creation. See Pastoral Constitution on the Church in the Modern World, no. 69, in Gremillion, *The Gospel of Peace and Justice,* pp. 305–306; *Populorum progressio,* nos. 22–24, in Gremillion, *The Gospel of Peace and Justice,* pp. 393–394.

16. Such an understanding is proposed by Paul Ramsey in his critique of the World Conference on Church and Society held in Geneva in 1967. See Paul Ramsey, *Who Speaks for the Church?* (Nashville: Abingdon, 1967), p. 53.

17. Martin E. Marty, *Righteous Empire: The Protestant Experience in America* (New York: The Dial Press, 1970).

18. O'Brien, *The Renewal of American Catholicism.*

19. Aaron I. Abell, *American Catholicism and Social Action: A Search for Social Justice* (Notre Dame, Indiana: University of Notre Dame Press, 1963).

20. E.g., Paul Hanly Furfey, *Fire on the Earth* (New York: Macmillan, 1936); see also William D. Miller, *A Harsh and Dreadful Love: Dorothy Day and the Catholic Worker Movement* (Garden City, New York: Doubleday Image Books, 1974).

21. Such an assumption in my judgment lies behind many aspects of the social reform ideas of John A. Ryan, especially his theory of underconsumption. See George C. Higgins, "The Underconsumption Theory in the Writings of Monsignor John A. Ryan" (M.A. dissertation, Catholic University of America, 1942).

22. Harold F. Trehey, *Foundations of a Modern Guild System* (Washington, D.C.: Catholic University of America Press, 1940).

23. Justice in the World, no. 6, in Gremillion, *The Gospel of Peace and Justice*, p. 154.

24. For the importance of church organizations as advocates for the poor see *Towards a Renewed Catholic Charities Movement* (Washington, D.C.: National Conference of Catholic Charities, 1971).

25. David J. O'Brien, *American Catholics and Social Reform* (New York: Oxford University Press, 1968).

26. Frans H. Mueller, "The Church and the Social Question," in *The Challenge of Mater et Magistra*, ed. Joseph N. Moody and Justus George Lawler (New York: Herder and Herder, 1963), pp. 13–33. For confirmation of this in recent documents of the hierarchical magisterium see *Octogesima adveniens*, nos. 59–61, in Gremillion, *The Gospel of Peace and Justice*, pp. 510–511; Justice in the World, no. 37, in Gremillion, *The Gospel of Peace and Justice*, p. 521.

6: The Right to Health Care and Distributive Justice

Developments in biomedical research and technology have brought to the fore many new problems. Lately attention has begun to focus on the social aspects of these questions, especially a just distribution. The just distribution of health and medical care has its roots in the problem of dividing up a finite amount of resources.

There are many different aspects of the basic problem of distribution. One aspect concerns the relationship of medical resources to other needed resources—education, food, clothing, defense, transportation, environment. How much should be invested in these different needs? What are the priorities among these different needs?

Even if these priorities were solved, there remains the still-difficult question of a just distribution within health care and medical care themselves. It is impossible to do everything. What should have priority? Should we spend more for exotic lifesaving devices such as artificial hearts or for a better delivery of maternal and prenatal health care? How does one deal with the priorities existing within medicine and health care? A third aspect of distribution concerns the allocation of scarce medical resources. Who shall receive the necessary life-giving resources when only a limited number are available and those who do not receive the resources will probably die?

There is a fourth aspect of distribution which refers to the recipient of medical or health care. On what basis is health care to be obtained by the individual person in our society? There is much discussion in contemporary American society about this aspect of distribution. The problem obviously begins with the fact of the poor distribution of health care in our society; some people even talk about a crisis in the delivery of health care.[1]

Recent developments such as Medicare and Medicaid have tried to insure more just and adequate access to medical care for the aged and the poor, but these programs still fall short of these goals.[2] Other problems of unjust distribution arise from the number and distribution of personnel and facilities in different geographic sections of the country and in urban or rural settings.[3] Existing private insurance programs do not cover all the citizens of our country. Perhaps 20 percent of the population under sixty-five have no private hospital insurance, but this includes a disproportionate number of the working poor, of blacks and of people living in the south. Over a million Americans are uninsurable according to present plans. Many people who are self-employed or who are employed in small firms must pay very large premiums for even limited coverage. Only half the population has any major medical coverage. There are often limits on the amounts to be paid in many insurance policies. Today the middle class is very aware of the financial hardship which can be brought about by prolonged or catastrophic illness in the family.[4]

In addition to these apparent injustices and inadequacies of the present system, one must also mention the problem of the escalating cost of health care in our society. Health care expenses have risen at the rate of about 12 percent per year during the decade of 1966–1975. At the current time 8.3 percent of the gross national product is being spent for health care.[5] A higher percentage of the gross national product in the United States is spent on health care than in most countries which have a system of socialized medicine such as Great Britain or Sweden.[6] Public policy planners are very aware of the need to contain costs.

This chapter will discuss justice and the distribution of health care to individuals in the society, although it is evident that the presence and influence of the other questions of distribution cannot be totally neglected. Legislators have been proposing various bills to deal with the problem. The ethical question underlying the discussion is often phrased in terms of the right to health, the right to medical care or the right to health care. These phrases have become slogans in our contemporary society. The primary focus of our study is the existence of such a right and its grounding. For the moment the precise object of the right will be bracketed, but reference will be made to the right to health care. Is there such a right and what is its basis?

Ethical considerations about the proper distribution of goods in society have also recently been discussed not only in the context of health care but in the broader context of ethical theory and of the proper distribution of all goods in society. Until a few years ago the predominant ethical perspective both in theory and in practice in the distribution of health care in the United States seems to have been a form of utilitarianism. Utilitarianism strives to bring about the greatest good of the greatest number.[7]

In ethical theory in the last few decades there has been strong criticism of the utilitarian approach. Distribution involves not only the total amount of the goods but also the important question of how goods are distributed. The total amount distributed is not the only question. Other considerations most often in terms of justice and rights must enter into the question of proper distribution. The rights of individuals might be violated even though the total amount of goods produced is greater. The greatest good of the greatest number can readily give too little importance to the rights of the individual. The utilitarian canon of distribution seems to neglect the important question of the fairness or justice of the distribution by concentrating only on the total amount produced.[8] Utilitarian theorists are aware of these charges often made against the system and have tried to respond to them.[9]

There is a similarity here with another problem of distribution—the allocation of scarce medical resources when there are not enough to go around. Some advocate a theory based on the contribution to society (especially future contributions).[10] However, others insist on the equal dignity of all human beings and do not want to maintain that some lives are of more value, dignity or importance than others. To protect the equal dignity of all lives, this position proposes a random selection procedure (first come, first served; or lottery).[11]

In more recent ethical writings great emphasis has been given to the language of rights and justice in order to protect the individual (especially the poor) in the distribution of goods within society. Rights' language had been used previously in ethical theory in a very individualistic way (e.g., Thomas Hobbes). In fact, such an individualistic understanding of rights strongly argues against any right to health care. In this conception a right defines a freedom of action. The basic right of the individual is the right to life. To sustain life one produces economic values in the form of goods and services that one should be free to exchange with others. Goods and services are thus owned in order to sustain life by one's own physical and mental effort. Just as the customer has no right to the baker's bread, so the customer has no right to the doctor's services. Medical care is neither a right nor a privilege; it is a service. The concept of medical care as the patient's right is immoral because it denies the most fundamental of all rights—that of the doctor to sell one's own services as the means of supporting her/his life.[12]

Behind such a theory lies a very individualistic concept of society. Robert Sade, whose denial of a right to health care was summarized in the preceding paragraph, logically maintains that the only proper function of government is to provide for the defense of individuals against those who would take their lives or property by force. The state is thus seen as coercive and its function is minimal—to prevent physical harm to individuals. The state should not further impede the liberty of individuals. Sade remarks that it is frequently overlooked that behind every law is a policeman's gun or a soldier's bayonet.[13]

I. Equalitarian Justice

Proponents of a right to health care do not accept such a view of rights. Their primary purpose of establishing a right to health care is to insure the rights of all, especially the poor, to be provided with health care. However, supporters of theories of justice in health care do not all agree on the ultimate meaning of justice and its ramifications. It is impossible to review here all the different theories of justice and their applications to health care. Justice as equality, one of the most significant contemporary theories, will be considered at length and critiqued. Then a different theory of distributive justice, which has been overlooked in the contemporary discussions, will be proposed as theoretically and practically more adequate.

The most simple way of stating the thesis of justice as equality is that similar cases should be treated similarly. Such an approach has many benefits. It has a very sympathetic ring in the popular mind. It is also in keeping with many developments and currents in contemporary ethical theory. Such a theory is formal. The problems connected with the question of what is the proper amount of treatment or of medical care are avoided by merely asserting that equal treatment should be given to all. Such an approach is built upon the fundamental ethical principle of universalizability: No arbitrary exception should ever be made. Whatever is done in this particular situation for this particular sick person should be done in all similar situations. The formal character of such an approach avoids any arguments concerning principles and intuitions. Finally, such a theory is most compatible with the goal of equal access to health care for all. If this is the goal, there is no better way to justify it than by a principle of justice understood in terms of equality. Now two different authors who have developed the concept of justice as equality will be considered.

Gene Outka has made an intriguing argument for what he admits is only a prima facie case that every person in the resident population should have equal access to health care delivery.[14] Outka develops an argument which recognizes that justice as equality (not his words) is a necessary but not sufficient approach. Since the statement of equality is purely formal, it could justify no treatment for all just as much as some treatment.

In any division of distribution within society one must

discuss the various canons or titles of distribution—merit, desert, social contribution, need. Meritarian concerns, for example, are present in the justice governing the teacher assigning grades to a student. The grade should correspond to the quality of the work done by the student. Awards granted within a society are justly distributed primarily by taking account of the contributions made to society. In the area of health care Outka rejects distribution based on merit or on social contribution. The reason for medical care is ill health. An irrational state of affairs is held to obtain if those whose , needs are the same are treated unequally when the need (illness) is the ground of treatment.

Outka must prove that the right to health care rests on need and the other canons of distribution such as desert, merit or social contributions do not enter into the picture. To do so Outka emphasizes the distinctive character of health crises. Health crises seem nonmeritarian because they are beyond our control and responsibility. We are equal in being randomly susceptible to disease, for there is little or nothing we can do about these crises. Medical treatment thus differs from other basic needs such as food and shelter, for these latter two factors are at least predictable. One can hold that responsibility increases with the power to predict, but we are not responsible for cancer or the health crises that befall us. Medical need is a classical case of uncertainty.

Outka thereby makes the case for equal access to health care on the fact that need is the governing criterion and that similar cases must be treated similarly. However, he admits this is only a prima facie case. Collisions between equal access and efficiency or insatiable needs do exist, so at times the distribution of medical care in less than optimal situations will not be based solely on the goal of equal access. If all our money were spent on the most ill people in society, there would be nothing to spend for others. In conflict cases actual solutions should be those most compatible with the goal of equal access; for example, random selection when there are not enough resources to go around.

Outka perceptively recognizes the complexity of the problem and the fact that justice as equal access cannot always be obtained. Outka also realizes that meritarian concerns might have some effect on health, but the application of such a recognition is very limited in practice. The author understands that he has made the best case possible for his position by speaking of need in terms of health crises. He purposely excludes speaking about prevention. However, his position is somewhat vulnerable as a result.

By insisting on the crisis aspect of medical care Outka can more readily prove the thesis that need is the only canon of distribution because personal responsibility does not enter in. However, it seems that he actually proves a narrower theory—equal access to medical care in crisis situations. Health care and medical crises are not exactly the same thing. Outka seems to move too readily and too quickly from crisis to care. In addition to the logical difference between crisis and care, many contemporary authors are showing how important personal responsibility is with regard to health care. (This matter will be discussed later at greater length.)

Outka insists on the distinctiveness of health care and both distinguishes and even separates health care from other basic human needs such as food and shelter. He realizes that he is limiting the question and considering the distribution of health care in an isolated context, but justifies considering only one aspect of a complicated question at a time. However, does this not indicate the somewhat formal and too abstract nature of his theory? In reality one cannot abstract from the question of the distribution of all the goods within society. There are significant theoretical and practical benefits in a more unified theory which can be applied to other important goods as well.

The somewhat formal and abstract nature of his approach is also evident in recognizing that some collisions will exist in practice, so that some modifications in the theory of justice as equality are necessary. There is great wisdom in such flexibility, but perhaps it indicates that these other considerations should have been discussed earlier in constructing the theory.

Robert Veatch has also proposed an equalitarian theory of just health care delivery.[15] Veatch does not spend as much effort on justifying the choice of equalitarian justice as does Outka, but he shows how this approach should be modified and applied in practice. Accepting a basic equal claim of all as far as health care goes, Veatch enunciates the principle that justice requires that everyone has a claim to the amount of health care needed to provide an opportunity for a level of health equal, as far as possible, to the health of other persons. Such a formulation avoids the problem that a group of the medically sick who are the most ill could end up with all our health care resources. The neediest have a just claim only when something fruitful can be done. With the recognition that health care does not necessarily produce health, the duty of society is to provide an opportunity of equal health care. Both merit and compensatory justice have been proposed as modifiers of the equalitarian theory, but in general in the area of health Veatch wants to keep these considerations to a minimum.

In the light of the complexity of the problem Veatch recognizes that justice cannot be the only criterion for allocating health care. Often the medically least well-off prefer inequality in order to promote their own medical welfare. Claims of justice may be overturned (although this should be minimized as much as possible) by efficiency, aggregate utility, cost factors and other right-making characteristics.[16] Veatch thus admits that other ethical claims, especially that of efficiency, can modify the claims of justice.

As such the concept of justice as equality is a formal concept which says little or nothing about the real problem of distribution and of priorities within society. Both in theory and in political practice it is not helpful to talk about rights to certain things without seeing the problem in the context of the total question of distribution.[17] Such an approach also ignores the very difficult problem of determining the priorities within health care and medicine. The federal dollar today is paying for much health education, research and service, but the urgent question remains about what should be our priorities. Often the question is addressed today in terms of preventive medicine versus crisis medicine. Veatch explicitly recognizes that something might be unjust but nevertheless right because of other right-making considerations such as efficiency. Such a distinction seems to stem from the failure to integrate the whole question of distribution into justice. Justice is one thing and distribution is another.

In my judgment these problems point to a more serious and underlying defect in the notion of justice as equality—a view of society which is too individualistic and does not give enough importance to the social reality as such. The concept of society presupposed in the justice as equality theory is still too individualistic rather than distributive. If the problem is one of just distribution of goods within society, then it should be impossible to see a contradiction between justice and right distribution. Justice as equality despite its attempts to overcome the charge of individualism and protect the rights of poor individuals in society still suffers from an individualistic concept of justice and of society. To speak about the rights of individuals apart from the question of distribution seems to understand society as the means for individuals to achieve their own good. There is present the notion that society exists only to insure the good of individuals, but this destroys any understanding of society as more than an aggregate of individuals cooperating only to achieve their own good.

The remainder of this chapter, in keeping with the suggestion made in the previous chapter, will explicate a theory of distributive justice which has been developed within the natural law tradition. In the recent discussions of the right to health care this theory has generally not been represented.[18] However, such a theory seems to overcome some of the problems already mentioned and offers a theoretical framework for grounding, analyzing and applying in practice the right to health care. The theory as proposed here does not accept all the metaphysical presuppositions and historical conditionings surrounding the natural law tradition.

II. The Understanding of Society

A correct understanding of the right to health care and the distribution of resources must rest on a proper understanding of society. The perennial problem in such considerations is to avoid the Scylla of individualism and the Charybdis of collectivism. Society is more than just an aggregate of individuals, and yet society is not merely a collectivity in which the individual is lost or submerged for the good of society or of others. Although its proponents might not advert to it, an equalitarian theory of justice implies too individualistic a view of society. There is an ethical tradition which wants to give more importance and meaning to society and the community without at the same time subordinating the individual to the community. This tradition insists on the common good, not just the private good of individuals, as the purpose of society.

Society and the state as a part of society are not voluntary associations which individuals decide to join merely for their own purposes. Human reality calls us to live in society because human beings must exist in social and political relationships. The state is a natural society based on the social realities of human beings, not something which exists only at the whim and voluntary choice of individuals or something that exists solely or primarily because of the need of individuals to protect themselves and their rights against one another and other outside forces. The human being has a social dimension to one's existence as is illustrated in the many relationships necessary for human living. Both the quest for perfection and weaknesses of the human person call upon the person to live in society, including the political society of the state. The goal of human perfection calls for relationships in reciprocity with others. Human needs and deficiencies require us to work together with others to achieve and accomplish what cannot be accomplished by individuals alone.

The end or purpose of human society is the common good. The common good of human society differentiates the human society from other groupings. In an animal society there is a public good but no common good because there are no persons. Here the animal is merely a part of the whole, and the good of the whole can claim the sacrifice of the individual. However, the good of human society is not merely the individual good or the total aggregate of the individual goods of the persons who constitute the society. In such a conception there is really no society and no truly social fabric.

The distinctive character of human society is the fact that it is a whole containing other wholes. The end of society is the common good, but a common good of human *persons* who are not merely parts of a whole. The common good is common both to the whole and to the persons who comprise it. The common good avoids the extreme of collectivism, because it demands that the good be distributed to the persons who make up society. The common good of a human society ceases to be that when it denies the personhood of its members. The common good not only refers to the various spiritual and material goods existing within society but above all involves the ordered relationships existing in society.

There is a reciprocal and even somewhat paradoxical relationship between the individual and society. In one sense the individual is a part of and subordinated to the community. In another sense the person is transcendent and can never be subordinated to the community. The relationship between individual and community is one of reciprocity; however, precedence is due to the person insofar as all social questions arise and must be resolved in relation to the person.[19] According to Johannes Messner it is wrong to ascribe primary being to society and only secondary being to the individual, but it is equally wrong to ascribe primary being solely to the individual and only secondary being to society.[20] Jacques Maritain recognizes the same tension. On the one hand the person as person, or totality, requires that the common good of the temporal society flow back upon it and even transcends the social whole. On the other hand the person as individual, or part, remains inferior and subordinated to the whole and must serve the common work.[21]

Society thus has a meaning, a significance and a reality which is more than the mere aggregate of individuals. Likewise, the common good of society has a meaning, a significance and a reality which is more than and different from the aggregate of the individual goods. In keeping with this understanding of society and of the common good one can consider the question of rights and justice.

The language of rights is the language of claims—not merely of desires and hopes. In general a right can be described as that which is due someone as one's own. The objective right, or the material, is that which is owed, which might be a thing (money) or an action or even an omission. From the subjective viewpoint a right is the inviolable moral power of an individual to do, to have or to demand something for one's own good. The essential elements of a right are four: the subject of the right, or the person; the object, or the matter, of the right; the title, that is, the fact by reason of which one claims the right; and the term, or the person or persons who are affected by the right and have the corresponding duty.[22]

There are various titles which ground one's rights. Obvious examples include a contract or a law. In addition to the rights which come from legal enactments or from a voluntary contract, there exist fundamental human rights which belong to all persons. The metaphysical grounding of such rights is disputed, but I would see the basis of them in the dignity of the human person, coming ultimately from the fact of creation by a gracious God. These basic human rights are enunciated in political documents such as the Bill of Rights of the Constitution of the United States and the Declaration on Human Rights of the United Nations. The basic principle is that the individual person has a right to life and to those things which are necessary for living a decent human life. Lists of such rights often include the right to life, the inviolability of the person, freedom of conscience, of religion, of speech, of association, the right to marry, the right to earn a livelihood and similar ones.[23] One must note the different objects of rights. The right demands sometimes that others do not interfere or at other times that others positively do something. Within society there are not only rights of individuals vis-à-vis one another but there are also rights and correlative duties of individuals vis-à-vis society.

III. Distributive Justice

How is justice then to be understood? Justice generally deals with giving what is due. Within society there are three basic relationships which must be considered—the relationship of individuals to one another, the relationship of the social whole to individuals and the relationship of individuals to the social whole. These three relationships correspond to the three basic forms of justice. Commutative justice orders the relationship of one individual to another individual. Distributive justice orders the relationship of the community as such to its members; legal justice orders the relationship of the individuals to the social whole.[24]

It is important to notice the differences between commutative justice (one to one) and distributive justice (the society to the individual). Distributive justice has to do with the distribution of the common goods or benefits and burdens of the society equally among the members. Commutative justice can determine quite precisely what is due. Justice and equality in commutative justice consist in an equality of one thing to another; for example, on the basis of the contract it is quite clear what is owed. Distributive justice does not arrive at such preciseness. In distributive justice the ordering of justice is whatever corresponds to a proportional equality of the thing to the person. Distributive justice must consider the subject and not just the thing itself as well as the goods or burdens existing within society. In a true sense there is a subjective aspect involved in distributive justice which is not present in commutative justice. For example, the indemnities given for war damages do not depend only on the damage which was done to the property but must also take into account such factors as whether the person was impoverished by the damage or whether the individual had already suffered from other harm such as physical injury from the war. There exists a different kind of equality in the two cases. Commutative justice involves a quantitative or arithmetical equality based on the one thing's relation to another thing, whereas distributive justice rests on a proportional equality which includes a relationship to the person. Not all, for example, should pay equal amounts of taxes.[25]

There are different kinds of goods to be distributed among the members of society. The distribution will depend to some extent on the type of goods to be distributed. There are basic political rights which must be equal for all because of the equal human dignity of all concerned. Here one thinks of such political rights as freedom of conscience, freedom of religion and the other basic freedoms of the person. Health care belongs to what are often called external goods as differentiated from internal goods such as freedom. There are many types of external goods to be distributed within society, including food, clothing, shelter, education, culture, health. In distributing the common goods of society the community must respect the fundamental human rights of all. The common good can never be in opposition to the fundamental rights of the individual person. The discussion of distributive justice will focus primarily on these external goods in general and then make more specific the right to health care.

As it has already been indicated, there is a lack of precision and exactness in distributive justice as compared with commutative justice. Above all there is the very difficult problem of deciding how distribution should take place. What are the titles, or canons, that should be the basis for the distribution of health care and other goods within society? Some have argued that problems of priorities and distribution are so complex that they are almost, if not altogether, incorrigible to rational determination.[26] However, since the distribution of goods within society is a question of such fundamental importance for human existence, we must make some attempts to come to a rational and just theory of distribution. John A. Ryan in his book on distributive justice mentions five canons for a just distribution of the products of industry—equality, need, efforts, productivity, scarcity. He ultimately chooses a sixth— human welfare, which includes all the others, but with a strong emphasis on needs as determining a decent minimum necessary for human life.[27] Toniolo proposes as a norm for distribution the fact that burdens should be distributed according to capacities and goods or advantages distributed according to needs or necessities.[28] Perhaps such an approach is too simple, but at the very least needs furnish a very significant aspect for the division of goods in society.

The most basic right of the individual in society is the right to life. All individual rights are based on the dignity of human life, which also is a necessary presupposition for all other rights. Society exists to assist the individual to achieve true fulfillment. Although health care is not the most fundamental need of the human person, it is of great significance. Health is necessary for the proper and full functioning of the life of the person. The right to health obviously means that the individual has the right not to have one's health unjustly attacked by others. In addition there exist within society goods and services of health care, and society is thus faced with the distribution of health care. The right of the individual in distributive justice cannot be considered apart from society and all its goods and members. There are many needs that individuals have—housing, education, health, food, culture, clothing. The basic formulation is simple: a person has the right to that minimum which is necessary for living a decent human life. Society has an obligation to provide that which is necessary for a decent human life. Obviously there are many relativities that enter into consideration. Much will depend on the goods which are available at the present time in a given society. We must limit our consideration to the society in which we live, although we cannot forget our obligation to other societies. The human person thus has a right to that basic level of health care which is necessary for decent human living.

The ultimate basis for this right is the dignity of the human person and the fundamental need of the human person. Such a right constitutes a true claim that is obligatory for society to honor. There could be different ways in which society provides for this right, but it is truly a claim and not just a wish or a desire. The right to that level of health care which is appropriate for decent human living is based on the concept of the person and of society which has already been described.

However, there are other factors, especially from a viewpoint of religious ethics, which can bolster the existing right to that level of material goods, including health care, which is necessary for decent human living.

The goods of creation exist primarily to serve the needs of all. In the course of time religious thinkers have unfortunately often forgotten the ramifications of this basic teaching found in the Judaeo-Christian tradition. The acceptance of creation reminds us that we are not the ultimate source of the goods we have, but rather we are stewards of what has been given to all of us by a gracious God. The Judaeo-Christian tradition has recognized this throughout its history in various ways such as the jubilee year, the year of forgiveness, and more recently by recognizing the possibility of expropriating large land holdings for the ultimate benefit of the poor.[29]

One example of the failure to recognize the communal destiny of the goods of creation can be found in concepts of private property. There exists no necessary incompatibility between the common destiny of the goods of creation to serve the needs of all and the acceptance of the right to private property, but at the very least the latter right must always be modified by and subordinated to the common destiny of the goods of creation. Too often the right to private property has been seen as an absolute in itself with no limitations. Perhaps in terms of the language that has already been used, private property and the whole question of property have too often been seen in terms of commutative justice and not in terms of an overarching understanding of distributive justice.[30]

Thomas Aquinas justifies the right to own private property as one's own, but he bases his reason not primarily on the dignity and need of the human person as such but rather on the problems and difficulties that would arise in society if people did not own things as their own. In other words, in a more theological language, the existence of private property is justified by the presence of sin in the world. Aquinas accepted the understanding of some of the fathers of the church that without sin there would have been no need for private property. After justifying the right to own private property,

Aquinas quickly adds that the use of private property is not absolute but is governed by the communal destination of the goods of creation to serve the needs of all creatures. One has the right to keep what is necessary for one's sustenance, but there is an obligation to give superfluous goods to the poor.[31]

In the United States Catholic tradition John A. Ryan proposed a very nuanced theory of the right to private property. As we mentioned in Chapter Four, Ryan carefully distinguishes three kinds of natural rights. First, the object of the right is an end in itself, such as the right to life. Rights of the second category have as their object not ends but rather means which are directly and per se necessary for the majority of individuals to achieve their human end, such as the right to marry. Private property belongs to the third class of rights — those which are only indirectly necessary for the individual because they are necessary for human welfare as a social institution. In a very inductive and a posteriori way Ryan justifies the institution of private property as being the best institution at the present time for social or human welfare in general. His reasoning is pragmatic and practical — private ownership works better for society than any other system. However, if socialism would better serve human welfare, then socialism should be adopted.[32]

The communal destiny of the goods of creation and the stewardship role of human beings remind us that an individual cannot arrogate to oneself the goods of creation at the expense of the truly human needs of the neighbor. The God of creation intends creation to serve the basic needs of all. Another religious support for the fact that the individual person has a claim and right to that basic level of external goods which is necessary for decent human living comes from the Christian concept of love, especially love for those in need. There is a difference between love and justice, but one cannot forget the basic thrust of the Judaeo-Christian message on love for those in need.[33]

The argument thus far has seen health care related to other goods (especially what might be called external or material goods) and argues that every human being has a right to that basic level of goods which is necessary for decent human living. There are many such goods—as health, education, food, shelter, culture. How does health care relate to all these others? What is the level necessary for decent human living? What is the relationship between that level of health care and equal access to health care for all?

This question cannot be considered apart from the broader question of the distribution of goods within a given society. Obviously within a socialistic system it is evident that there should be equal access to health care. In this light one could argue for a complete change in the American system of distribution. From the practical viewpoint of change here and now one must work within the context of a nonsocialist policy of distribution. We accept the existence of such a system and argue within it, although we also recognize that the case could be made for a socialist system.

Even within the present American political and economic system the principle that all have a right to that level of material goods necessary for decent human living must be accepted and put into practice. This principle calls for many changes in our present system as illustrated in the question of welfare reform. Health care differs from many of these other goods (as shelter, food, education, culture) so that there cannot be as great a disparity among people in available health care as there might be in other areas. The basic level of health care, in other words, should be quite high because of some special characteristics of health care itself. There are a number of reasons supporting the case for a comparatively high level of health care available for all. However, all considerations must recognize the finite and limited resources existing within society.

First, the reason for health care is found in ill health or the prevention of ill health. There is the same basic need among all. The provision of health care rests only on this need; other goods such as education or culture require a certain level of ability or of interest among the recipients. Health care is more similar to something like protection or security, a need which is basically the same for all people.

Second, a significant aspect of health care involves prevention of ill health and protection of all people living in society. This protection of all through environmental or public health factors such as inoculations must provide basically the same care for all.

Third, even though it might not be the only or the total aspect, ill health is something that often happens to people. The crisis aspect of ill health, its random character and the fact that for some aspects of ill health there is little or nothing one can do to avoid it argue in favor of a more equalitarian division.

Fourth, since many of the advances in knowledge and technology come through governmentally funded research, then the advantages of this research should be made available to all.

Fifth, whenever it is a question of lifesaving devices, then the basic equal dignity of all human beings should be protected. When those who receive the lifesaving devices will live and those who do not receive them will die, justice demands a random selection process. The availability of lifesaving devices should ordinarily not be based on the ability to pay or on contributions to society.

Sixth, to be truly effective and just the program must embrace at least the vast majority of the citizens. The danger lurks that such a system of health care will be inferior. The participation of most of the citizens in the same program helps to ensure that it does not become a second-class system.

All of these reasons point to the conclusion that the basic level of health care necessary for decent human living must involve a sufficiently high level of quality health care.

IV. Advantages and Disadvantages

There are a number of advantages in an ethical formulation of a right to that level of health care which is necessary for decent human living based on the understanding of society and individual rights proposed above. The canon of distributive justice allows one to consider the more fundamental question of the distribution of all goods within society. Both in theory and in practice health care should not be considered alone as something totally unique.

A theory of distributive justice is not only more wholistic but also more realistic insofar as it considers the question of health care in the light of all the other goods of society and the needs of the individuals. One cannot talk about distribution within society without considering both the existing resources or goods to be distributed and the different needs that must be met.

In distributive justice there is a proportional equality and not a purely numerical or quantitative equality. The need to consider the proportional equality between the individual and the common good as well as the other demands upon the common good should at least in principle help focus public debate on matters of justice and rights. Rights language is one of the strongest possible ethical claims. It is no wonder that political and public rhetoric will often use rights language rather than the language of needs or desires or what is fitting. However, as so often happens, one can merely proclaim certain rights without at the same time considering the basic problem of distribution. The abstract claiming of rights and counterrights tends to produce more heat than light unless one is willing to tackle the whole problem of distribution.

Distributive justice by its very nature raises the question of priorities within society itself. On the basis of what has been said thus far, a minimal criterion of distribution is the satisfaction of basic human needs which are necessary for the decent human livelihood of all citizens. The concept of distributive justice also sheds some light on the difficult problems of priorities within medicine and health care itself. The fundamental concern is to provide the health care necessary for decent human living. Today there is much discussion about the priority between preventive and crisis medicine. Our priorities at the present time are heavily in favor of crisis medicine at least in terms of the money appropriated to the two. However, there is no doubt that preventive medicine (vaccines, changes in environment, better personal health habits) has done in the past and does more today to insure more healthy living than crisis medicine. A theory of distributive justice will insist on the need to give more importance to preventive medicine than we do at present. One word of caution should be addressed to supporters of preventive medicine. We are probably not going to come close to the startling progress made in the last century in terms of life expectancy. The grave, more physical causes of shorter life span have already been thwarted. Now we are dealing with more difficult problems, so that one should never expect to have for the future the same type of progress from preventive medicine that existed in the last century.

Unfortunately, the lure of exotic lifesaving devices often attracts us at the expense of other more basic and more simple forms of preventive medicine. In 1972, for example, Congress made funds available for almost everyone who needed kidney dialysis or kidney transplants. This program by the early 1980s may cost more than one billion dollars each year. Is this such an important priority in medical care? Are there not other aspects which are less sensational but ultimately more significant in contributing to health care?[34] The same problem arises in research in medicine, genetics, biology and their respective technologies. Government funding must recognize the basic priority of fundamental human needs rather than exotic and very costly procedures.

Perhaps the question of priorities is nowhere more evident than in the training of doctors. Doctors are most often taught by researchers who rightly are attempting to expand the boundaries of medical science. However, most patients require only ordinary medical care and attention. Are we training doctors for the real work that needs to be done? This perspective raises the whole question about the need of other health professionals dealing with more ordinary problems of patients. Here, too, distributive justice and the need to satisfy basic human needs should call for a great change in the health care delivery system.

In addition, a theory of distributive justice gives more importance to the societal aspect of human existence and avoids the individualism which seems to be latent in the concept of equalitarian justice. In theory and in practice it is necessary to remember that society is not constituted merely for an individual to achieve self-fulfillment. A theory of distributive justice could never admit that an individual's right could be in conflict with the requirements of proper distribution. Justice does include proportional as well as arithmetical equality. The practical ramifications of the need for society to distribute goods in accord with the basic needs of all its members helps to overcome such an individualism.

Briefly consider two cases in which the social aspect of distributive justice argues against a narrow individualism. The obligation of society to provide basic health care to all its people means that health facilities and personnel have to be distributed in such a way as to make this possible. The individual health care person is not totally free to practice wherever and however one wants to. Services and personnel must be provided for all.

Another significant difference based on proportional equality as distinguished from arithmetical equality is illustrated in the Bakke case. Places in medical school were reserved for sixteen minority students, even though the scores they had on academic tests were less than those obtained by white applicants for the same medical school. Justice as equality often tends to see this type of problem merely in terms of arithmetical or quantitative equality. The white person is being discriminated against because of one's skin. Distributive justice is more open to recognize the need for such approaches because proportional equality takes cognizance of differences in the person and differences in the relationship existing between the society and its different members.[35] Distributive justice as a theory can handle much better what is often called compensatory justice than can a theory of justice as equality.

There are some weaknesses and disadvantages in the theory of distributive justice as outlined. First, proportional equality tends to be a vague measure. Not all can agree on what the proportionality should entail. In this brief treatment no attempt was made to outline a whole theory of distribution and all the canons that should govern a just distribution. However, as a minimum, distributive justice recognizes the right of human beings to that level of health care which is necessary for decent human living. Such a criterion is somewhat vague, but by definition there must be relativity in proportional equality. Additional reasons indicated the need for a comparatively high level of health care as that which is necessary for all.

According to some the proposal of a right to health care necessary for a decent human livelihood does not go far enough even if it does include a comparatively high level of care. It is true that the proposal for equal access to health care is by definition more equalitarian and at the same time more radical (although I think it often rests on a presupposition tinged with individualism, at least as proposed under the rubric of justice as equality). If our society were only to accept the concept of distributive justice as outlined here, significant changes would be required. Our welfare program at the present time falls far below this standard, since many people live well below the official poverty level. Medicare and Medicaid have accepted in some respects the principle enunciated here, but in reality, especially in Medicaid because of the differences from state to state, the basic health-care right is not met. The principle of distributive justice proposed here stands as a critique of our existing system.

In a different society one could more easily argue for equal access for all in one unitary health-care system. I do not want to deny that a case might be made for equal access on the basis of distributive justice, but it would be much more difficult to make the case in theory and especially in practice in the light of American political principles at the present time. I am now arguing for a more reforming approach and not a radically new system. The contemporary American society will not accept a single, publicly financed health-care delivery system for all. Even England and the Scandinavian countries do not have such a system.

From another perspective one could argue that the proposal of distributive justice does not take account of the darker side of human existence—what religious ethicists would call the sinful nature of human beings. However, in practice some of our social programs have already to some degree incorporated the idea of what is due to the individual because of the dignity of the person. In theory what is proposed is not a utopia but something more realistic — what is necessary for a basic level of decent human existence.

One final disadvantage, or negative critique, of the theory of distributive justice goes to the foundation of the theory itself. The natural law basis of such a theory has many shortcomings and is generally not accepted in contemporary discussions. The total metaphysical grounding and the teleological basis of traditional natural law, common good and distributive justice theories do not have to be accepted in order to employ the theory proposed here. There is no doubt that an older natural law theory gave too much importance to organic harmony (e.g., the corporate society) and did not give sufficient attention to historicity, change, diversity and pluralism. The theory of common good and of distributive justice outlined here can stand without some of the philosophical presuppositions and historical limitations of the traditional natural law theory. One important aspect of the traditional natural law theory of the state which should not be forgotten in carrying out the distribution of health care is the principle of subsidiarity, which attempts to avoid overcentralization and the dangers of bureaucracy.

V. Ramifications

Finally some ramifications of distributive justice as applied to health care will be considered. First, our treatment has constantly referred to the right as the right to that level of health care which is required for living a decent human life. Notice the object of the right is health care — not health or medical care. Some have proposed the right to health. The preamble to the Constitution of the World Health Organization states that the enjoyment of the highest attainable standards of health is one of the fundamental rights of every human being. Health is defined as a state of complete physical, mental and social well-being and not merely the absence of disease or of infirmity.[36]

It would be difficult to find a broader understanding either of the right or of the definition of health. No one has a right to a state of complete physical, mental and social well-being. This definition proposes a new messianic kingdom produced by human beings through biomedical science and technology. The empiricist and the metaphysician, the atheist and the believer, all can agree that sooner or later we will all die. No one has a right to such well-being as described here. Unfortunately such excesses indicate a messianic view of medicine which is capable of bringing about such a salvific state. Many have reacted today against such an exaggerated view of human powers as specified in the matter of providing health. A firm antidote to such an exaggerated position can be found in Stanley Hauerwas' insistence on medicine as a tragic profession.[37]

Note too the object of the right is not medical care but health care. We recognize today that there are many factors more important than medical care which influence health care — food, environment, shelter, education, personal habits. Recent studies indicate that following some basic rules about sleep, exercise, diet, and curtailment of smoking and drinking has a very significant effect on health care.[38] Rich Carlson ranks the variables affecting health in the following descending order of importance — environment, life-style, society, genetics and finally medical care, which is said to contribute approximately 6 percent of the total health care.[39] One does not have to be a therapeutic nihilist[40] to recognize that health care and medical care are not the same thing. Our society must give more importance and higher priority to the preventive aspects of health care and to the nonmedical factors influencing health. This priority should also be applied in the area of health research.

Distributive justice recognizes that distribution must consider both what is to be distributed and the cost of distribution, which includes the paying for services. The one question cannot be considered apart from the other in reality, although conceptually it is necessary to consider them separately.

In any finite reality there are limits on the amount of medical care that can be distributed. What are the possible limits and how would a system of distributive justice work out such distribution? Veatch proposes three possible limits on the health care distributed—limits based on the amount paid, limits based on the number of dollars or days of hospital care provided and limits based on excluding certain forms of health care.[41] The question of limits recognizes the problem of the rising cost of health care in our society.

A theory of distributive justice which is based on the need and dignity of the individual person cannot base the level of medical care provided on the amount of money paid. These rights cannot depend on how much one pays. The limit in this theory must come from what medical services and care are included, since the theory talks about a level of medical care which is necessary for decent human livelihood. The criterion is somewhat vague, but certain forms of medical care can readily be seen as outside the range—cosmetic surgery, in vitro fertilization, the provision of exotic lifesaving techniques for *all,* much psychiatric care. Hospital care should not ordinarily involve a private room and other types of extra nursing care beyond the basic level.

Other limits have been suggested in terms of number of dollars spent or days of care provided. If a person is in need of basic medical care and is deprived of it merely because one is suffering from a prolonged illness, an injustice is done. Proponents of such limitations are obviously trying to contain costs. Nevertheless, all people in justice should be protected against the financial difficulties coming from catastrophic illness.

An acceptance of the ethical ramifications of a right to a basic level of health care for all would entail some type of national health insurance. In the last few years many different legislative proposals have been offered as to how this program should be financed.[42] How should such a program be paid for? Distributive justice calls for burdens to be distributed on the basis of capabilities.

The vast majority of the cost must come from some form of taxes, but here distributive justice insists on a progressive tax.

Taxes as burdens should be distributed according to ability to pay.[43] A just tax must be one which progressively requires more of those who have a greater income and cannot merely involve the same dollar amount from all or the same percentage (e.g., 3 percent of total income). In the United States a progressive income tax generally exists, although one must recognize the many loopholes involved. Unfortunately, other taxes are quite regressive. The sales tax requires that rich and poor pay the same; the present social security tax is also regressive. Recently proposed tax changes mean that more of our tax dollars are based on regressive taxation such as social security payments. The taxes for health care must rest on a more progressive taxation. Many health-insurance proposals today do not include this provision since often they are based on a tax somewhat similar to social security payments.

However, in the light of the need to contain costs, to prevent unnecessary use and to help with funding (and thereby provide a higher level of care) some cost sharing by individuals would be appropriate. Two important considerations or conditions should be noted. First, the cost sharing should not be made a burden for the poor. Second, the cost sharing should also be related to income—a certain percentage of one's income. Here again proportionate and not arithmetical equality is required. This cost sharing could take the form of either deductibles or of copayments.

A question arises about increased payments based on meritarian concerns. In general should people who expose themselves to health risks have to pay extra or more than those who do not? Thus far our discussion has excluded meritarian concerns in our theory of distribution. As mentioned earlier, there is wide recognition today of the fact that personal responsibility plays an important role in health care. As a result some have proposed that those who risk health by smoking or excessive drinking, for example, should pay more than those who do not.[44] In general, a total theory of distribution must give consideration to meritarian concerns, but meritarian concerns should be minimal in discussing that level of health care which is necessary for all.

In addition, in the area of health care it is practically impossible to make a case for meritarian concerns in terms of increased costs for some. Why? First of all, the way in which many factors enter into health care is not all that certain. We cannot say, for example, just how much effect proper exercise has on health. Second, there are many factors that are important—exercise, sleep, diet. It is impossible to determine exactly how much each part contributes; consequently it is impossible to work out an equitable system. One might say that smokers should pay more than nonsmokers. But what about those who sleep less than seven hours a day? What about those who do not exercise? And then there is the problem of diet. In practice it would be impossible to monitor all these different aspects and to work out a fair system.

The one possible exception to the exclusion of meritarian concerns might be for those whose job or hobby exposes them to more health risks. Especially if there is significantly higher pay connected with the job because of risk, then some type of greater payment might be equitable. One could also argue that hobbies which involve great risk such as skydiving are generally the preserve of the wealthy who can afford to pay more. However, one could also argue that jobs such as coal mining are very dangerous. It seems somewhat difficult to come up with an equitable plan so that it might be better to do away with all meritarian concerns.

One final aspect stems from the fact that health care and services are goods which must be distributed among the members of society. There are many structural problems in our present health-care delivery system which must be corrected. The problems of cost and of maldistribution are compounded by the existing systems of distribution. The need for more preventive medicine has been pointed out. There is no doubt that more personnel are needed and should be employed. However, the health-care personnel needed above all include health-care professionals and paramedical personnel to provide care and services for which a doctor is not necessary. Hospital care should not be required for those who do not need it. The geographical area in which doctors practice cannot be determined only by the marketplace. Also the fee-for-service approach cannot continue as the only or the primary model of health care delivery. Efforts must be encouraged by society to provide different models. One cannot expect radical change overnight in these areas, but it is necessary to move in the directions indicated.

This chapter has endeavored to provide an ethical perspective on the question of the right to health care. The purpose has been primarily to determine what is this right, what is its grounding and what are its practical ramifications. Ethics and the ethician are not able to supply answers for all the concrete problems facing our society. Questions such as medical care ultimately must be decided by prudential choices in the political realm. However, the principles of distributive justice can well serve as the basis for making political decisions about the provision of health care which are both just and feasible.

NOTES

1. Good summaries of the present discussions can be found in special issues of two significant journals: *Current History* 72, no. 427 (May/June 1977) and 73, no. 428 (July/August 1977) and *Daedalus* 106 (Winter 1977), which has also been published in book form.

2. See, for example, *Medicaid Lessons for National Health Insurance,* ed. Allen D. Spiegel and Simon Podair (Rockville, Maryland: Aspen Systems Corporation, 1975).

3. Christine E. Bishop, "Health Employment and the Nation's Health," *Current History* 72, no. 427 (May/June 1977): 207–210.

4. Karen Davis, *National Health Insurance: Benefits, Costs and Consequences* (Washington, D.C.: The Brookings Institution, 1975), pp. 3–4, 34–41.

5. Herbert E. Klarman, "The Financing of Health Care," *Daedalus* 106 (Winter 1977): 215–234.

6. John H. Knowles, "The Responsibility of the Individual," *Daedalus* 106 (Winter 1977): 75; Joseph G. Simanis, "The British National Health Service in International Perspective," *Current History* 72, no. 428 (July/August 1977): 28.

7. For a contemporary utilitarian theory see Joseph Fletcher, "Ethics and Health Care: Computers and Distributive Justice," in

Ethics and Health Policy, ed. Robert M. Veatch and Roy Branson (Cambridge, Mass.: Ballinger Publishing Co., 1976), pp. 99–109.

8. The most significant recent book espousing a theory of justice in opposition to a utilitarian calculus is John Rawls, *A Theory of Justice* (Cambridge, Mass.: Harvard University Press, 1971). Rawls' work has evoked much comment and discussion. See, for example, *Reading Rawls: Critical Studies on Rawls' A Theory of Justice,* ed. Norman Daniels (New York: Basic Books, 1974). Rawls does not discuss health care distribution in this book, but his theory has been applied to health care distribution by Ronald M. Green, "Health Care and Justice in Contract Theory Perspective," in Veatch and Branson, *Ethics and Health Policy,* pp. 111–126.

9. J.J.C. Smart and Bernard Williams, *Utilitariansim: For and Against* (Cambridge: Cambridge University Press, 1973).

10. Nicholas Rescher, "The Allocation of Exotic Medical Lifesaving Therapy," *Ethics* 79 (1969): 178.

11. James F. Childress, "Who Shall Live When Not All Can Live?" *Soundings* 43 (1970): 339–355; Paul Ramsey, *The Patient as Person* (New Haven, Conn.: Yale University Press, 1970), pp. 239–275.

12. Robert Sade, "Medical Care as a Right: A Refutation," *New England Journal of Medicine* 285 (December 2, 1971): 1288–1292. Sade has published his basic theory in other articles: e.g., "Is Health Care a Right? Negative Response," *Image* 7, no. 1 (1974): 11–19; "Medical Care: Not a Right," *Massachusetts Physician* 35, no. 6 (June 1976): 5–26.

13. Sade, "Medical Care as a Right," p. 1289.

14. Gene Outka, "Social Justice and Equal Access to Health Care," *The Journal of Religious Ethics* 2 (1974): 11–32. Page references will be made in the text to this journal, but the article has been published in many anthologies.

15. Robert M. Veatch, "What Is 'Just' Health Care Delivery?" in Veatch and Branson, *Ethics and Health Policy,* pp. 127–153.

16. Ibid., p. 142.

17. For opposition to the theory of equalitarian justice in health care and a proposal for the right to a decent minimum see the writings of Charles Fried: "Rights and Health Care: Beyond Equality and Efficiency," *New England Journal of Medicine* 293 (July 31, 1975): 241–245; "An Analysis of Equality and Rights in Medical Care," *The Hastings Center Report* 6, no. 1 (February 1976): 30–32.

18. *Ethics and Health Policy,* for example, does not discuss this theory. For one discussion which incorporates some of this theory see Joseph M. Boyle, "The Concept of Health and the Right to Health Care," *Social Thought* 3 (Summer 1977): 5–17.

19. Eberhard Welty, *A Handbook of Christian Social Ethics I: Man in Society* (New York: Herder and Herder, 1960), pp. 101–113.

20. Johannes Messner, *Social Ethics: Natural Law in the Western World*, 3rd ed. (St. Louis: B. Herder, 1965), p. 107.

21. Jacques Maritain, *The Person and the Common Good* (Notre Dame, Indiana: University of Notre Dame Press, 1966), p. 70.

22. Marcellino Zalba, *Theologiae moralis summa II: tractatus de mandatis dei et ecclesiae* (Madrid: Biblioteca de Autores Cristianos, 1953), pp. 425–432.

23. E.g., Messner, *Social Ethics*, pp. 326–330.

24. Josef Pieper, *The Four Cardinal Virtues* (Notre Dame, Indiana: University of Notre Dame Press, 1966), pp. 81–103. There is no need here to enter into the discussion about the meaning of social justice and its relationship to the other kinds of justice.

25. A. Vermeersch, *Quaestiones de justitia* (Bruges: Beyaert, 1901), pp. 49–69.

26. Paul Ramsey, *The Patient as Person*, pp. 240, 268.

27. John A. Ryan, *Distributive Justice* (New York: Macmillan, 1916), pp. 243–253.

28. Cited in Vermeersch, *Quaestiones de justitia*, p. 52.

29. E. Lio, *Morale e beni terreni: la destinazione universale dei beni terreni nella 'Gaudium et spes' e in alcuni fonti* (Rome: Città Nuova Editrice, 1976).

30. J. Diez-Alegria, "La lettura del magistero pontificio in materia sociale alla luce del suo sviluppo storico," in *Magistero et morale: atti del 3°congresso nazionale dei moralisti* (Bologna: Edizioni Dehoniane, 1970), pp. 211–256.

31. Thomas Aquinas, *Summa theologiae: Pars II^a II^{ae}* (Rome: Marietti, 1952), q. 66, a. 1 and 2. See also Odon Lottin, "La nature du devoir de l'aumône chez les prédécesseurs de Saint Thomas d'Aquin," *Ephemerides Theologicae Lovanienses* 15 (1938): 613–624; L. Bouvier, *Le precepte del l'aumône chez saint Thomas d'Aquin* (Montreal: Collegium Immaculatae Conceptionis, 1935).

32. Ryan, *Distributive Justice*, pp. 56–66.

33. Outka makes references to this throughout his article and refers to his earlier work, *Agape: An Ethical Analysis* (New Haven: Yale University Press, 1972). For a monograph from the perspective of Christian ethical warrants see Earl Edward Shelp, "An Inquiry into Christian Ethical Sanctions for the 'Right to Health Care' " (Ph.D. dissertation, Southern Baptist Theological Seminary [Ann Arbor, Michigan: University Microfilms, 1976, no. 76–23, 963]).

34. James F. Childress, "Priorities in the Allocation of Health Care Resources," in *No Rush to Judgement: Essays in Medical Ethics*, ed. David H. Smith (Bloomington, Indiana: The Poynter Center, 1977), pp. 135–144. For other references indicating the primacy of preventive health care see footnote 38.

35. Daniel C. Maguire, "Unequal but Fair," *The Commonweal* 104 (October 14, 1977): pp. 647–652.

36. *World Health Organization: Basic Documents,* 26th ed. (Geneva: World Health Organization, 1976), p. 1. This preamble was originally adopted in 1946.

37. Stanley Hauerwas "Medicine as a Tragic Profession," in *No Rush to Judgement: Essays on Medical Ethics,* pp. 93–128.

38. N. B. Belloc and L. Breslow, "The Relation of Physical Health Status and Health Practices," *Preventive Medicine* 1 (1972): 409–421; Belloc and Breslow, "Relationship of Health Practices and Mortality," *Preventive Medicine* 2 (1973): 67–81. See also Leon R. Kass, "Regarding the End of Medicine and the Pursuit of Health," *The Public Interest* 40 (Summer, 1975): 11–42; John H. Knowles, "The Responsibility of the Individual," *Daedalus* 106 (Winter, 1977): 59–80.

39. Rich J. Carlson, "Alternative Legislative Strategies for Licensure: Licensure and Health." This paper was presented at the Conference on Quality Assurance in Hospitals, Boston University, Program on Public Policy for Quality Health Care, November 21–22, 1975. Quoted by Walter J. McNerney, "The Quandary of Quality Assessment," *The New England Journal of Medicine* 295 (December 30, 1976): 1507.

40. Paul Starr, "The Politics of Therapeutic Nihilism," *The Hastings Center Report* 6, no. 5 (October, 1976): 24–30.

41. Veatch, "What Is 'Just' Health Care Delivery," pp. 142–150.

42. For overviews and comparisons of the major different legislative proposals see *Current History* 73, no. 428 (July/August 1977): 48–49; Veatch, "What Is 'Just' Health Care Delivery," pp. 142–152.

43. E.g., Ryan, *Distributive Justice,* pp. 102–117, 296–302.

44. For a discussion pro and con on a tax on smoking and other harmful behavior which would be paid to help meet health-care expenses under a system of national health-care insurance see Robert M. Veatch and Peter Steinfels, "Who Should Pay for Smokers' Medical Care?" *The Hastings Center Report* 4, no. 5 (November 1974): 8–10.

PART THREE

Medical Ethics

7: Roman Catholic Medical Ethics

By the middle of the twentieth century medical ethics flourished in the Roman Catholic tradition as a well-developed and firmly established discipline. Many books on medical ethics existed at that time in all the major European languages (e.g., Bonnar, Healy, Kelly, Kenny, Niedermeyer, O'Donnell, Payen, Paquin, Pujiula, Scremin).[1] In addition there were periodicals exclusively devoted to medical morality in many of the same countries, such as *Arzt und Christ, Cahiers Laënnec, Catholic Medical Quarterly, Linacre Quarterly* and *Saint-Luc medicale.* The existence at this time of a well-developed discipline of medical ethics in Roman Catholicism distinguishes this tradition from the rest of the Judaeo-Christian tradition and from the philosophical ethics of the time. This chapter will attempt to explain the general context, development, characteristics, principles, content questions and contemporary developments in Roman Catholic medical ethics.

I. The General Context

The Christian tradition rooted in both the Old Testament and New Testament and as exemplified in the story of the Good Samaritan has always encouraged the care for the sick. Sickness in the Christian perspective has a number of different dimensions. God is the author and giver of life and is also recognized as the healer who can give health. Sickness and death have been associated with the power of sin in the world, but sickness is also a sign of human weakness and fragility. Human beings can and should try to heal and overcome sickness if possible, but ultimately all will die. In the suffering connected with sickness the Christian tradition not only sees an evil to overcome if possible but also a mysterious sharing in the suffering, death and resurrection of Jesus.

Corresponding to the multiple understandings of sickness were the different aspects of the care of the sick fostered by the church. The spiritual care of the sick ultimately developed into the sacrament of anointing, one of the seven sacraments in the Roman Catholic Church. In the last few decades the church has recognized a false emphasis in restricting this sacrament to the moment of death (it had been generally known as the sacrament of extreme unction before the Second Vatican Council in the early 1960s) and has renewed the emphasis on the sacrament as the anointing of the sick. The sacrament celebrates the presence of Jesus in the community as the healer of sickness but also as the Lord who through his death and resurrection has transformed sin, sickness, suffering and death itself. Prayers for healing exist both in this sacrament and in the Christian life in general, but the believer knows that healing will not always come. The aspect of sickness as connected with sin appeared in the concept of demonic possession and gave rise to the rite of exorcism. However, the church, while acknowledging both the possibility of miraculous cures by God and of possession by the devil, has generally been quite cautious in these two areas. Obviously in both cases the dangers of illusion and deception are most prevalent. Also in this connection the church has been aware of the danger of magic and superstition in connection with healing. In other cultures healing was often associated with superstitious practices, but these were continually condemned in the Christian tradition.

The Christian tradition in general and the Catholic tradition in particular have emphasized that God usually works mediately through secondary causes and not immediately without the help of human causes. Chapter One explained that the acceptance of this principle of mediation characterizes much of Roman Catholic theology and ethical thought. In the area of healing, human means of curing illness have been encouraged, for in this way the doctor is cooperating in God's work, although ultimately sickness and death will triumph. To relieve suffering and strive for healing is viewed as working with God and in no way is an offense to divine providence, since the creature is called to take care responsibly of one's life and health. Thus the Christian tradition encouraged medicine as well as prayer and fought against superstition and magic as being opposed to both faith and reason.

The Christian church has fostered and sponsored the establishment of hospitals to care for the sick and the dying. The origin of hospitals, in fact, is due to the care and concern of the church. Catholic institutional involvement in hospitals and the care for the sick has continued to be a very vital aspect of the mission of the Catholic Church. Communities of religious men and women within the church have dedicated themselves to the apostolate of caring for the sick and the dying. In the first millennium of Christianity it was not uncommon for clerics also to be medical doctors. However, abuses crept in, especially in terms of clerics devoting all their time to medicine, so that prohibitions against clerics practicing medicine were introduced at the Fourth Lateran Council in 1215. The present Code of Canon Law (Canon 139 §2) continues to forbid clerics or priests to practice medicine or surgery without special permission, but such permission has customarily been given where there is necessity (e.g., missionary countries) or good reason. Religious women and men who are not clerics have been encouraged to serve as doctors and nurses. Likewise the church has held in high regard vocations in the health-care field for all its members.

In addition, as Chapter Three has indicated, the Catholic tradition has affirmed that in theory there can be no contradiction between faith and reason and has cultivated human reason, science and the arts. Obviously, there have been some tensions between medicine and the Catholic Church as exemplified in the older prohibition of using cadavers for medical research, but on the whole the Roman Catholic tradition has fostered and encouraged the practice of medicine.

II. Historical Development

There are many factors contributing to the existence of a comparatively large and well-defined discipline of medical ethics in the Roman Catholic tradition by the middle of the twentieth century. The Catholic tradition has constantly recognized that faith must be shown in works. In fact, Roman Catholicism has often been accused of an exaggerated emphasis on the importance of works in the Christian life. Intimately connected with this perspective has been a long-standing interest in the various duties of one's state in life. In this context it was only natural that discussion would arise about the duties and responsibilities of doctors.

Roman Catholicism acknowledges penance as one of the seven sacraments which celebrates the mercy and forgiveness of God for the repentant sinner. The sacrament of penance has taken many forms over the years, but from the sixth century onward the private confession of sins to the priest gradually became the accepted form of the sacrament of penance. One of the reforms of the Council of Trent in the sixteenth century repeated the obligation first proposed at the Fourth Lateran Council that called for Catholics to celebrate the sacrament of penance at least once a year. To carry out this reform of Trent it was necessary to educate the faithful and to train priests as ministers of the sacrament of penance, especially in the capacity of judging about the existence, number and gravity of sins. The individual penitent was instructed to confess sins according to their number and species. The tradition of moral theology in Roman Catholicism always had the practical aspect of guiding people in their daily life and especially preparing people for the sacrament of penance, but from the sixteenth century on training in moral theology in the Catholic tradition had as its almost exclusive purpose the preparation of confessors with a heavy emphasis on casuistry so that the confessor might know and judge the number and gravity of the sins of the penitent. Thus the actions of doctors and the actions of people concerning questions such as marriage and abortion received great attention.

Roman Catholic ecclesiology recognizes the visible aspect of the church and the importance of church structures, among others a hierarchical ordering in accord with certain God-given functions and offices in the church. Such an understanding of the church naturally led to the importance of church law and legislation, and there came into existence the discipline of canon law to deal with various matters of the life of the church, including the meaning and legalities of marriage. The interest in marriage and marriage legislation made it necessary to obtain the requisite medical knowledge in determining such questions as consummation and the meaning of impotency, which, as distinguished from sterility, made it impossible for the person to marry. There were many other moral and canonical questions connected with marriage and sexuality which required theologians and canonists to keep abreast of whatever medicine could say on these subjects.

Developments in embryology also were significant for Catholic theology and sacramentology. Catholic teaching maintained that baptism (either of water as in the sacrament, or of blood as in martyrdom, or of desire) was necessary for eternal salvation. Great stress was placed on providing for the eternal salvation of all, including the child in the womb who might face the danger of death without baptism. Also there arose the question about baptism in the case of beings that were doubtfully human.

There is another important factor that partially explains why other traditions and thinkers were not extensively involved in medical ethics before 1950. Until recently medicine was primarily concerned with the care of the individual patient. In this perspective there was general agreement between good morality and good medicine, since both justified any mutilation, loss of limbs, surgery or pain in terms of what was for the good of the individual. Problems arose wherever potential conflict situations existed, as in the case of abortion.

Roman Catholic medical ethics also saw conflicts in the area of sexuality. The Catholic tradition maintained that the sexual organs and functions existed not only for the good of the individual but also for the good of the species; consequently it was wrong to sacrifice the species' aspect of the sexual organs for the good of the individual.

More recent developments in medicine have brought with them new problems, since medicine now deals not only with the individual patient but also with others. Questions of experimentation, transplantation and genetic engineering all involve not only the particular individual here and now but also other individuals. In fact, in some of these cases the individual is harmed or exposed to risk in order to help the other. Modern developments raise the possibility not only of curing the individual but of producing better individuals and a better species. One can readily understand why the interest has grown in biomedical ethics in the last decade or so.

The historical development of medical ethics in the Roman Catholic tradition is closely connected with moral theology in general. Although the definitive history of Catholic moral theology has not been written, there are some rather generic overviews.[2] The first 600 years after Christ are usually referred to as the patristic age, since the major writers were the fathers of the church. At this time many of the specific moral teachings were first formulated and proposed. These writings generally had a more pastoral rather than academic perspective, although there existed somewhat systematic discussions of particular ethical questions.

The *Didaché,* or *Teaching of the Twelve Apostles,* one of the earliest documents of the Christian era, condemns slaying a child by abortion (2.2). In the course of the fourth century the distinction between a formed and nonformed fetus, which was probably based on a poor translation of Exodus 21:22, became the focus of analysis. This distinction refers to the time of ensoulment, and many maintained that at the beginning of life the fetus was not formed, or the human soul was not yet present. Although important figures such as St. Jerome and St. Augustine accepted the theory of delayed ensoulment, they still disapproved of abortion whether the fetus was formed or not.[3] The very acceptance and discussion of this particular distinction as early as the fourth century indicated that Catholic theology would be open to whatever biology and medical science could say about the beginning of human life.

Clement of Alexandria (d. 220), often called the founder of the first school of Christian theology, invoked the rule of procreative purpose to condemn artificial contraception. St. Augustine, recognized as the most outstanding figure of this period, wrote treatises on many moral topics such as lying, patience and chastity and also contributed very much to the Christian teaching on marriage.[4]

The period from the seventh to the twelfth centuries is generally recognized as not very fruitful in the area of moral theology, since most of the work merely involved collections or summaries of older writers. The most creative development concerned the *Libri poenitentiales*. At the beginning of this period private penance, involving confession of sins to the priest and his granting absolution to the individual penitent along with designating a penance to be performed, began to develop in Ireland and later came into Europe. The penitentials, which came into existence in the sixth century and flourished until the eleventh century, consisted of an arrangement of sins by subject matter together with the prescribed penance which the priest should give for every wrong act. In these penitentials one finds those actions which the church considered wrong and sinful. In the midst of many other wrong acts such as stealing, lying, cheating, adultery and so on, one also finds abortion, contraception and other questions connected with marriage and medical ethics.

The twelfth century set the stage for the development of modern canon law in the Roman Catholic Church.[5] Popes, various universal councils, particular councils and local bishops had issued laws and legislation for the church. About 1140 Gratian, traditionally identified as an Italian Camaldolese monk, collected and put in order many of the various laws and norms that had come into existence. He adopted a hermeneutic for determining what to do in case there were conflicting laws. This magnificent achievement was the work of a private individual and was entitled by him the *Concordia discordantium canonum* (Harmony of the Disharmonious Canons), which became known as the *Decretum,* or Decree of Gratian, and was later accepted as the basis for church law.

In 1234 Pope Gregory IX published an official collection of laws known as the *Decretales of Gregory IX,* which among other things speak about medical inspection to prove the existence of impotency and the nullity of the marriage (*De probationibus*).[6] These two sources plus four others later constituted the *Corpus iuris canonici,* which became the textbook in the schools of canon law and the generally accepted law book of the church along with additions made by subsequent councils, popes and other forms of legislation. Professors developed their teaching by writing commentaries on the various laws and collections. In 1331 Pope John XXII formed the church judges into a college of judges called the Roman Rota. In his decretal *Ratio iuris exigit* the pope speaks of medical skills and knowledge which help the work of the tribunal.[7] Thus from the early stages in the development of canon law the role and importance of the biological and medical sciences, especially in the area of marriage, are recognized.

The thirteenth century also witnessed the growth and development of a scholastic theology which achieved its high point in the work of Thomas Aquinas (d. 1274), who proposed a highly systematic theology in his famous *Summa theologiae.*[8] In the second part of this work Thomas treats the questions connected with the moral life of the Christian in the context of a threefold understanding—the human being related to God as ultimate end, the human being as an image of God insofar as one is capable of self-determination, the humanity of Christ as our way to God. The natural law theory proposed by Aquinas has become the characteristic approach of Roman Catholic moral theology. Thomas Aquinas was later declared a saint, a doctor of the church and the patron of Catholic theology and philosophy. According to the Code of Canon Law, which went into effect in 1918, philosophy and theology are to be taught according to the method, principles and doctrine of Thomas Aquinas (1366 §2).

For many different theoretical and practical reasons in the centuries after Aquinas moral theology developed as a distinct discipline in itself and generally became separated from systematic theology. In addition its concerns became more and more practical with a heavy emphasis on casuistry as it was connected with both canon law and the penitential practice of the church. The books concerned with penitential practices in the thirteenth century and especially in the fifteenth century took the form of *summae* which often discussed the whole Christian life in a very practical way. The most important *summa* is that of St. Antoninus, archbishop of Florence (d. 1459).[9] In the third tome of his four-volume work the archbishop of Florence considers the duties and obligations of different states in life—married people, virgins and widows, temporal rulers, soldiers, lawyers, doctors, merchants, judges, craft workers and many others. The discussion of the duties and obligations of doctors extends for five large pages and mentions the following duties and obligations— competence; diligence; care for the patient; the obligation to tell the dying patient of his condition, which is obligatory when the patient is not prepared for death but is counselled even if the patient is prepared for death; the possibility of accepting and caring for dying patients and receiving a fee from them; the proper fee or salary for the doctor, and the doctor's duty to care for the sick even though they cannot pay; the obligation not to prescribe things that might be against the moral law such as fornication; and the question of abortion. Antoninus became a most important and frequently cited source for later theologians. At the beginning of the sixteenth century the very influential *Summa Sylvestrina* of Sylvester Prieras (d. 1523)[10] treated in alphabetical order all the practical aspects of the Christian life. Under *medicus* (doctor) he had a six-page consideration touching on most of the topics treated by Antoninus.

Thomas Sanchez (d. 1610) published a very famous three-volume treatise on marriage considering all the legal and moral aspects of the question.[11] Sanchez, who was acknowledged as one of the great figures in the history of moral theology, especially in the area of marriage, often employs medical findings in dealing with questions such as sterilization, impotency and the expulsion of semen after rape. Sanchez illustrates how the moral theologian incorporated the contemporary medical and biological knowledge into his discussion of moral and canonical questions.

Beginning in 1621, Paolo Zacchia, a Roman doctor, published a multivolume work entitled *Quaestiones medico-legales*.[12] Here Zacchia treated many diverse subjects—age, birth, pregnancy, death, mental illness, poison, impotency, sterility, plagues, contagious diseases, virginity, rape, fasting, mutilation of parts of the body, conjugal relations. Zacchia's work was well known and often referred to by moral theologians and canon lawyers and was recognized as a standard reference until the nineteenth century.

After Zacchia there were a few works devoted to what might be called pastoral medicine or medical ethics. For example, Michael Boudewyns, a doctor in medicine and philosophy, published in Antwerp in 1666 *Ventilabrum medico-theologicum*[13] containing the questions and cases most often faced by doctors. The author describes his own work as necessary for theologians, confessors and especially doctors. In the seventeenth and eighteenth centuries there also appeared monographs on particular subjects. Theophilus Raynaudus in 1637 in his *De ortu infantium*[14] writes about the morality of caesarean sections in the various circumstances that might arise in birth. P. Florentinius in 1658 published his *De hominibus dubiis baptizandis*[15] in which he talked about the sacrament of baptism and the products of conception which were doubtfully human. F. E. Cangiamila in his *Sacra embryologia*[16] discusses questions connected with embryology such as the animation of the fetus and intrauterine baptism.

However, despite these significant developments in the seventeenth and eighteenth centuries, one still cannot speak of a well-developed and distinct discipline of pastoral medicine or medical ethics in Roman Catholic theology. In these same two centuries Catholic moral theology in general was characterized by the growth of the manuals known as the *institutiones theologiae moralis*. During this period acrimonious debate arose between laxists and rigorists which came to a solution in the sane middle course adopted in the work of St. Alphonsus Liguori (d. 1789),[17] who expounded a position of moderate probabilism. The work of Alphonsus was approved by subsequent popes. He was declared a saint and a doctor of the church, and in 1950 Pope Pius XII proclaimed Alphonsus Liguori the heavenly patron of all confessors and moral theologians. Alphonsus' approach to moral theology thus became the examplar in format, content and method for much of Catholic moral theology until the last decade or so. His discussion of moral theology under the general division of the ten commandments and the sacraments incorporated medical knowledge especially in his considerations of marriage, baptism, care for the sick and dying, and abortion.

In the nineteenth century pastoral medicine fully bloomed as a separate discipline in the Roman Catholic tradition. Obviously the newer developments in the biological and medical sciences and the need for theologians and confessors to be aware of this knowledge encouraged the growth of pastoral medicine. This name comes from the most important works on this topic, which were often titled pastoral medicine. Probably the most influential of these many works was written in 1877 by a German physician Carl Capellmann[18] and later translated into Latin and many modern languages. In his introduction Capellmann describes his purpose as one of providing the priest with the medical knowledge needed to carry out his ministry and of communicating to doctors the moral principles necessary to insure that they act in accord with Christian morals. The major areas covered by Capellmann are: the fifth commandment, including questions of abortion, medical operations and the use of medicine; the sixth commandment, including masturbation, pollution and marriage; the commandments of the church such as fasting and abstinence; the sacraments, particularly baptism, holy communion, extreme unction, and impotency in marriage; plus other topics of lesser importance. Other significant titles on pastoral medicine were published by Debreyne,[19] Eschbach[20] and Antonelli.[21] A good number of similar books were also published in various modern languages at the end of the nineteenth and the beginning of the twentieth century, so at this time one could recognize the existence of a developed discipline called pastoral medicine.

This trend continued and grew in the twentieth century. These problems were still considered in general treatises on moral theology, but books on pastoral medicine, medical deontology and medical ethics flourished in all modern European languages. In Germany Albert Niedermeyer published a multivolume work on pastoral medicine which included a complete and updated treatment of the topics covered in the older works as well as material dealing with psychiatry and psychotherapy.[22] In the United States there were many books written on medical ethics which often were textbooks for use in Catholic medical or nursing schools. Also the existence of Catholic hospitals following Catholic ethical codes stimulated the need for books and articles on these subjects.

In addition, as the twentieth century progressed, more and more monographs appeared on subjects in medical ethics, and journals published in different languages printed articles on this discipline. Topics in medical ethics became favorite subjects for doctoral dissertations in Catholic moral theology. Thus by the middle of the twentieth century there was a large body of literature and a distinct field in Roman Catholic theology generally known as medical ethics, although occasionally the more popular nineteenth-century term of pastoral medicine was still used.

III. Specific Characteristics

Catholic medical ethics, like all Catholic moral theology, is distinguished by three specific characteristics—natural law methodology, authoritative church teaching and its understanding of conscience.

Natural law is a complex term which has a number of different aspects. From the more theological perspective natural law theory recognizes that reason and human nature constitute a source of ethical wisdom and knowledge for the Christian. An important methodological question in Christian ethics concerns the source of ethical wisdom. Is ethical knowledge found only in Jesus Christ, in the scriptures and in revelation? Or on the basis of reason and human nature which Christians share with all other human beings can one arrive at ethical wisdom and knowledge? Catholic theology historically has recognized both faith and reason, scripture and the natural law. The twentieth-century textbooks in medical ethics rightly recognize that their teaching was primarily based on natural law and not on the scriptures.

The philosophical aspect of the question of natural law concerns the precise meaning of human reason, human nature and natural law itself. Here the Catholic textbooks in medical ethics, like all the Catholic ethical treatments in the first part of the twentieth century, appealed to the teaching of Thomas Aquinas and often summarized his teaching in the beginning of their discussions. According to Thomistic theory the eternal law is the plan of divine wisdom insofar as it directs all activity toward a final end. The eternal law is ultimately grounded in the very being of God.

The natural law is the participation of the rational creature in the eternal law. God directs all creatures to their end in accord with their own natures. There are laws by which the physical universe is governed such as the law of gravity. However, human beings are governed according to their rational nature. The human being is an image of God precisely insofar as endowed with reason, free will and the power of self-determination. Through reason the rational creature directs one's own activity toward one's proper end and thus is not merely passively directed by God to the end. Right reason is able to recognize the threefold natural inclinations within human nature—the inclinations we share with all living things, the inclinations we share with animals, and the inclinations we have as rational beings. Thus the natural law is understood as human reason directing the individual to one's own end in accord with one's nature.

The natural law in the best of the Catholic tradition was recognized as an unwritten or unformulated law—the very law of one's being as a rational creature. However, on the basis of the ontological structures of rational human nature reason is able to arrive at universally valid principles or prescriptions of the natural law. The first principles of the natural law are known intuitively by human reason—good is to be done, evil is to be avoided, act according to right reason. Human reason on the basis of these first principles can then deduce the secondary principles of the natural law, such as adultery is wrong and stealing is forbidden.

In the 1950s Catholic medical ethicists often recognized that other thinkers favored a greater relativity in ethics. Catholic medical ethicists responded that there could always be possible changes in the application of principles in particular cases. There could even be a growth in our knowledge of the implications of the principles and even in a clearer formulation of the principles, but there can be no substantial change in the statement of the principles. According to one respected medical moral text what is true of the secondary principles is also true of some of the particular applications. There can be no question of notable change in what is said about direct abortion, direct attacks on fetal life, contraception, contraceptive sterilization, immoral fertility tests and so forth. In these points the application of the general principle is so immediate and logical that a change in the morality of the procedure is inconceivable. Some of these condemnations are nothing more than restatements of the general principles. Changes are not only possible but are desirable in applications which are justified on the principle of sufficient reason. Certain drastic measures such as castration in the treatment of carcinoma or lobotomy in treating mental illnesses can be justified on the basis of proportionate reason at the present time, but it is hoped that less drastic remedies will be found in the future.[23]

A second distinctive characteristic of Roman Catholic medical ethics involves the authoritative teaching office of the church. Acceptance of the gospel message calls for faith and works. The Christian must live the new life received in Christ Jesus. The church as continuing in time and space the word and work of Jesus the risen Lord has a God-given duty and function to point out how the followers of Jesus should act. The teaching function of the church even in matters of morality is acknowledged by most Christians. The Roman Catholic Church also recognizes a special God-given teaching office and function belonging to the pope and the bishops as well as to general councils of the church. This hierarchical teaching office is a source of authoritative teaching.

It is important to recognize the various grades or degrees of the hierarchical magisterium, or teaching authority, in the Roman Catholic Church. In the nineteenth century the distinction became formalized between the infallible church teaching to which one owed the assent of faith and the authoritative or authentic, noninfallible teaching to which the faithful owed the religious assent of intellect and will. It is generally acknowledged that teaching in the area of medical ethics ordinarily does not fall under the category of infallible teaching, which in reality is very limited.

The noninfallible papal teaching office also admits of gradations in the way in which it is exercised, thus to give greater or lesser importance and authority to the teaching proposed. In papal encyclicals the pope usually addresses in a somewhat solemn way all the bishops and the faithful of the world. A less formal type of teaching is found in papal allocutions or addresses given to particular groups. The congregations, or bureaus, of the Roman Curia—the central administrative arm of the pope—also issue their own decrees and rulings. For example, the Congregation for the Docrine of the Faith, formerly called the Congregation of the Holy Office, issues authentic decrees and declarations on matters of faith and morals. It was acknowledged in the encyclical *Humani generis* by Pope Pius XII in 1950 that whenever the pope goes out of his way to speak on a controverted subject it is no longer a matter for free debate among theologians.[24] The God-given hierarchical teaching office in the church does not dispense the pope, bishops and councils from using every means available to investigate and study the particular matter under discussion. Generally speaking, in the 1950s any such Roman pronouncement or decree both theoretically and practically ended debate about the specific question, but it must be pointed out that the pope usually would not intervene when Catholic theologians were divided on a particular point.

These two specific characteristics of Catholic moral theology in general and medical ethics in particular at first sight might seem to contradict one another, since the natural law as based on human reason is accessible to all human beings. Why then is it necessary for a special teaching authority to exist in the Roman Catholic Church to interpret the natural law? Absolutely speaking, the natural law can be known clearly by any person with a sufficiently developed reason without any external help. However, in the present order of things, given human weakness and sinfulness, human beings need the help of divine revelation and of the teaching office of the church in order to have a clear and adequate knowledge of the natural law.[25]

Early councils in the church as well as letters of popes and other bishops spoke about specific moral questions such as abortion and marriage. Mention has already been made of authoritative collections of canon law beginning in the twelfth century. Significant interventions in moral matters by the papal teaching office, especially by the Congregation of the Holy Office, occurred in the seventeenth and eighteenth centuries. Here the papal teaching office wisely intervened a number of times in the controversy between laxists and rigorists to condemn the extreme opinions. There can be no doubt that the intervention of the papal teaching office increased significantly in the nineteenth and twentieth centuries with an ever-greater emphasis on the authoritative teaching function of the papal office. The existence of papal encyclicals addressed to all the bishops and faithful of the world and speaking on specific areas of faith or morals really only became prominent in the nineteenth century.

The growth and development of medical ethics in the

nineteenth and twentieth centuries corresponded with the greater emphasis on the papal teaching office in the Roman Catholic Church. Between 1884 and 1902, for example, the Holy Office responded to a number of inquiries about abortion and eliminated some of the exceptions which had not been expressly condemned. The Holy Office declared that one could not safely perform a craniotomy or directly kill the fetus to save the life of the mother nor could one extract an ectopic pregnancy.[26] Encyclicals on marriage by Pope Pius XI (*Casti connubii* in 1930)[27] and by Pope Paul VI (*Humanae vitae* in 1968)[28] strongly reiterated the condemnation of artificial contraception.

Perhaps the most significant development in the matter of authoritative church teachings was the number of allocutions and addresses given by Pope Pius XII very often dealing with questions of medical ethics. This corpus of papal teaching shows a wide ranging interest in the problems of medical ethics as well as a penetrating knowledge of medicine and its problems. To various medical groups Pope Pius XII spoke on such subjects as the duties of the medical profession, blood donors, artificial insemination, contraception, sterilization, abortion, the moral limits of medical research in experimentation, genetics, painless childbirth, transplants, death, the means necessary to preserve life. Obviously the interest and concern of Pope Pius XII also sparked the growth and development of the discipline of medical ethics. Subsequent popes did not retain Pius XII's great interest in medical questions, but the Congregation for the Doctrine of the Faith has continued to respond to inquiries and to issue decrees and declarations concerned with various medicomoral questions. For example, in March 1975 the congregation responded to the American bishops that direct sterilization is always wrong, and the fact that some theologians dissent from this teaching cannot be used to justify a decision in favor of direct sterilization.[29] Recent developments in the understanding of natural law and of the hierarchical magisterium will be treated later.

A third specific characteristic of Catholic moral theology and medical ethics is the understanding of conscience. Conscience is the subjective norm of morality, whereas law, basically the eternal law with all its parts, is the objective norm of morality. Conscience is a dictate of practical reason declaring that a particular action is right or wrong.

A true conscience is had when the judgment of conscience conforms to the objective moral norm, that is, human nature or the natural law; otherwise the conscience is erroneous. An erroneous conscience can be vincibly or invincibly erroneous, depending on whether or not one is morally responsible for the lack of conformity with the objective moral norm. The individual must always follow one's conscience, but there is guilt in following a vincibly erroneous conscience.

A certain conscience is a moral judgment made without fear of error based on evidence which is sound. A doubtful conscience exists when the intellect suspends judgment because of insufficient evidence. A certain conscience must always be obeyed and is also a necessary requirement for moral action. A doubtful conscience must somehow or other become certain in practice before one can act.

The controversy about probabilism in the seventeenth and eighteenth centuries involved the question of how one goes from a doubtful conscience in theory to a certain conscience in practice. The theory of moderate probabilism, which was ultimately accepted, appeals to the basic understanding that the human will is free and moral obligation can be known only through reason. If moral necessity is not certainly proposed by reason, the freedom of the will remains. In practice one can follow a truly probable opinion in favor of freedom from the law or obligation even though the opinion in favor of the obligation may be more probable. However, there are some instances such as danger to the life of another in which probabilism cannot be used. The practical question is often asked whether or not a particular opinion is probable? Probability is determined by the intrinsic force of the argument but in practice is often reduced to the fact that a number of theologians or recognized authorities hold such a particular position. It was generally assumed that a teaching of the papal magisterium either directly from the pope or through a

Roman congregation such as the Holy Office did not allow for dissent in theory or in practice.

IV. Moral Principles

Since the method of natural law talked about establishing the principles of natural law and then applying these principles to particular cases, it is evident that Catholic medical ethics did speak about a number of important principles. In fact, the textbooks in the 1950s often began their discussion with a very brief summary of the more important principles governing medical ethics.

The Right to Life

Human beings are made by God, who is the author of life and has dominion over all life. The human being as creature does not have absolute power or full dominion over one's own life or body, for the individual is a steward or administrator over one's life. A right enables the person who possesses it to achieve one's end. The right to life is a natural right since it flows from the natural law itself. The right to life is inalienable, that is, one which cannot be renounced. The right to life is also inviolable; otherwise it would not truly be a right.

However, the Roman Catholic ethical tradition recognized that there are cases where the life of another may be taken, for example, killing another as a necessary way of defending one's life. Just war was acknowledged as a moral possibility. Capital punishment was generally accepted in the Catholic tradition, but many contemporary ethicists argue against capital punishment. Accidental killing was also recognized as a possibility. The most precise formulation of the principle was that the direct killing of an innocent person on one's authority is always wrong.

Right of Use or Stewardship

Much in the area of medical ethics follows from the moral

principle that the individual possesses the right of use, limited by natural finality, of the faculties and powers of one's human nature. Since the individual is a user and not a proprietor, one does not have unlimited power to destroy or mutilate one's body or its functions (Pope Pius XII, Address to the First International Congress on the Histopathology of the Nervous System, September 14, 1952).[30] The principle of stewardship is the basis for the care one should have over one's own body as well as the justification in general for surgery, operations and other procedures.

Principle of Totality

One of the principles governing mutilation of the body was called by Pope Pius XII the principle of totality. Thomas Aquinas pointed out that a member of the body existed for the good of the whole body and could be disposed of according as it would benefit the whole. A diseased member may be removed if this is for the good of the whole. In the address cited above, Pope Pius XII described the principle of totality which maintains the good of the whole is the determining factor in regard to the part, and one can dispose of the part in the interest of the whole.[31]

The popes and Catholic moralists were very aware of the abuses of totalitarian governments in sacrificing individuals for the good of the state, so they carefully spelled out the meaning and limits of the principle of totality. The part must have its whole finality and meaning in terms of the whole. Since the individual person does not exist totally for the good of the state, the individual cannot be totally subordinated to the state. The obvious example where the principle of totality applies is to the individual organs and functions of the total bodily organism. However, in 1958 Pope Pius XII (Address to the International College of Neuro-Psychopharmacology) commented that to the subordination of the particular organ to the organism and its own finality one must add the subordination of the organism to the spiritual finality of the person.[32] Each single organ is subordinated not only to the good of the body but to the good of the person. The principle of totality applies to many medical procedures, operations and treatments which may often suppress or sacrifice a part for the good of the whole.

Human Sexuality and Procreation

The faculties and powers of human beings must be used according to the purpose for which they were evidently made by God and intended by nature; for example, the finality of speech is perverted if used to communicate to another as one's own judgment what is directly contrary to one's thought. The sexual function and organs have a twofold purpose — procreation and the love union of husband and wife. (An older terminology referred to procreation as the primary purpose of marriage and sexuality.) The human being thus can never go against the God-intended procreative purpose of human sexuality. Any use of human sexual powers is immoral when it directly impedes the very purpose for which God created these powers. As a result contraception and contraceptive sterilization are wrong. The individual person may not positively interfere to thwart the sexual act or faculty of its God-given purpose and finality.

Note how the sexual organs and functions differ from other organs. The sexual organs exist not only for the good of the individual but also for the good of the species. Since their whole meaning and finality does not exist totally for the individual, the species' aspect of human sexuality can never directly be subordinated to the good of the individual. The principle of totality cannot be used to sacrifice the species' aspect of the sexual organs and functions for the good of the individual.[33]

The Principle of Double Effect

Catholic moral theology has recognized the existence of conflict situations. What is the morality of actions which have two or more effects including a bad effect? The principle of double effect was employed by all medicomoral textbooks to solve these dilemmas. According to Kenny, who merely records the traditional criteria, one can perform an act with two effects, one good and one bad, if the following conditions are present: 1. The act must be good in itself or at least indifferent. 2. The good effect must follow as immediately from the cause as the evil effect. 3. The intention of the individual must be good. 4. There must be a proportionately grave cause for placing the action.[34] This principle was used at times to justify the possibility of indirect killing, indirect abortion, indirect sterilization, indirect cooperation.

Cooperation and Scandal

Especially in terms of the work of doctors and nurses questions arose about cooperation and scandal. Cooperation was generally defined as participation in the wrong or sinful act of another. Formal cooperation, described as intending the evil act, is always wrong. Immediate material cooperation, defined as participation in actually performing the wrong act and sometimes also called formal cooperation, is likewise always wrong. Mediate material cooperation, which presupposes there is no intention to do evil and involves placing an act which is good or indifferent, may be permitted if there is a sufficient reason for so doing. In this case the individual person neither intends nor does an immoral act. The morality of mediate material cooperation according to O'Donnell is to be sought in the principle of the double effect with special attention to the proportion between the cooperation (proximate or remote, how necessary or unnecessary, to the wrong act of the other) and the gravity of the crime in connection with which another will make use of one's cooperation.[35] On the basis of these principles a casuistry was developed concerning mediate material cooperation. A doctor, for example, can never do an immoral operation, since this involves at least immediate material cooperation. A nurse's cooperation in such an operation is usually only mediate material cooperation and might be justified, especially if it were not that proximate, by a number of reasons such as the other good that such a person can do in the hospital in which one is employed.

Scandal is a sinful or seemingly sinful word, action or omission which tends to incite or tempt another to sin. Direct scandal in which the sin of the other is intended is always wrong. Indirect scandal in which the sin of the other is not intended but only permitted may be allowed under two conditions—if the act giving scandal is in itself not morally wrong and if there is a sufficient reason for placing such an act.

V. Specific Questions

Obligations of Physicians and Rights of Patients

Under this heading the textbooks of medical ethics in the 1950s considered many of the questions originally posed by Antoninus of Florence more than 500 years ago—professional competence, the obligation to attend patients, selection of remedies, correction of errors, fees, and newer additions such as ghost surgery and fee splitting. Special emphasis was often given to a number of important questions such as the obligations of secrecy and of truthfulness, especially informing the patient about death.

The professional secret is a committed secret binding in justice, wherein the contract of secrecy is not explicitly put into words but is implied by reason of the professional position (e.g., doctor, lawyer) of the one who receives the secret knowledge. Professional secrecy obliges the doctor to keep the secret of the patient as long as the patient retains the right to the secret. A professional secret may be divulged when common necessity calls for it; for example, the law can ask doctors to report all gunshot wounds to the proper authorities. The professional secret may be divulged but need not be when the patient has now become an unjust aggressor and is threatening harm to an innocent third party under the cover of professional secrecy.

All human beings are obliged to tell the truth, but there are some special applications to the doctor-patient relationship, especially in terms of informing the patient about one's condition. Patients in general have a right to know about the nature of their ailment and illness. However, the physician must also take into account the medical, psychological, spiritual and material interest of the patient. The doctor like others can at times use broad mental reservations. Healy suggests some practical ways in which the doctor might avoid directly answering the question posed by the patient without lying if there are certain reasons why the patient should not be told at this particular time.[36] Very important is the obligation to inform the patient about impending death. Directive eight of the Religious and Ethical Directives for Catholic Health Facilities states: "Everyone has the right and duty to prepare for the solemn moment of death. Unless it is clear, therefore, that a dying patient is already prepared for death as regards both spiritual and temporal affairs, it is the physician's duty to inform him of his critical condition or to have some other responsible person impart this information."[37]

Sexuality and the Transmission of Life

The finality of the sexual organs and faculties and the limited stewardship that individuals have over these constitute the basis for the condemnation of contraception and contraceptive or direct sterilization. Human beings cannot positively interfere in the sexual act or the sexual faculty to deprive them of their God-given purpose.

However, Roman Catholic teaching has accepted the basic principle of responsible parenthood — while always being open to the gift of life, couples should have the number of children they can properly care for and educate as good Christians and human beings. This acceptance of responsible parenthood gradually appeared in Roman Catholicism. Pope Pius XII in 1951 in his Address to Midwives recognized that there were medical, eugenic, economic and social indications justifying the limitation of the number of children.[38] The Pastoral Constitution on the Church in the Modern World of the Second Vatican Council (no. 50) likewise endorses the concept of responsible parenthood. However, contraception and contraceptive sterilization are always wrong. Rhythm, or the use of the infertile periods, is permitted because there is no positive interference against the God-given purpose of the sexual faculty or act. There are various forms of the use of the infertile period. The form most recently advanced is the so-called natural family planning, or Billings, method which has been acknowledged to be a very effective means of family limitation.

The Catholic tradition has not emphasized procreation to the extent that it gives no importance to all other realities. Catholic teaching has opposed masturbation as a means of obtaining semen for fertility tests and thereby hoping to facilitate procreation. Pope Pius XII in May 1956, in an address to the Second World Conference of Fertility and Sterility, explicitly condemned masturbation as a means of obtaining semen for semen analysis because it is an unnatural act.[39] The pope was merely giving the long-standing teaching of Catholic moralists based on the understanding that the purpose and finality of the sexual act justified it only in the context of marriage and the act must be both procreative and expressive of the love union.[40]

On three different occasions Pope Pius XII spoke about and condemned artificial insemination, but again the condemnation is in keeping with the Catholic understanding of the nature, finality and purpose of the sexual act. AID (artificial insemination from a donor) was condemned because the child must be the fruit of the bodily gift of the parents. AIH (artificial insemination from the husband) is wrong because it goes against the nature of the sexual act. Emphasis was also given to the technological and mechanistic aspects of artificial insemination as opposed to the personal love union of husband and wife in the sexual act.[41]

The Beginning of Life and Birth

Catholic theology acknowledges a possible theoretical doubt about when human life begins, but in practice all must act as if human life is present from the first moment of conception. Since the fetus in the womb is defenseless, Catholic theology all the more feels the need to speak out in its defense. Direct abortion is always wrong. Indirect abortion is permitted for sufficient reasons. The two most often-proposed examples of indirect abortion are the removal of the cancerous uterus when the woman is pregnant and the removal of the Fallopian tube containing an ectopic pregnancy. Chapter Eight will study the abortion question in greater depth. Caesarean sections were also still discussed in the textbooks of medical ethics. Premature delivery of a viable fetus is morally acceptable if there is a proportionate reason justifying the danger to the fetus involved in such a procedure. Induction of labor follows the same general principle.

Care for Health, Surgery and Other Operations

The basic obligation to care for health comes from the stewardship we rational creatures exercise over our lives and bodies. The patient has a right to use all moral means possible to overcome pain even though in some way all will know the meaning of suffering in human existence. However, the Catholic tradition recognizes the right of the person freely to accept pain as a form of participation in the redemptive suffering and death of Jesus. The danger of habit-forming drugs is often discussed in this context of using drugs to relieve pain.

Surgery and other procedures suppressing bodily organs and functions other than the sexual organs and functions are permitted by the principle of totality provided they are for the proportionate good of the individual. Alleviative surgery (to alleviate pain) as well as preventive and corrective surgery is permitted if the good of the person proportionately justifies the harm done. Cosmetic surgery can also be justified, but if the operation involves any danger, it is much harder to justify. The textbooks of medical ethics also discuss the question of lobotomy, which had first been done in 1935. Before the use and availability of drugs, lobotomy was proposed as a way to alleviate problems connected with mental illness. However, such an operation also produces significant effects on the personality. Catholic moralists, invoking the principle of totality, generally justified lobotomies only as a last resort and with the assurance of postoperative care and treatment.

Organ transplants especially raised a problem when the organ was taken from another living donor. Here the one person is mutilated not for one's own good but for the good of another. Pope Pius XII in his Address to a Group of Eye Specialists, May 14, 1956, pointed out that the principle of totality cannot justify such transplants because the mutilation is not for the good of the individual who is harmed.[42] Some Catholic moralists, therefore, considered organ transplants among the living as immoral operations, but others justified them on the basis of the principle of fraternal charity. However, even those allowing such transplants cautioned that the donor cannot gravely endanger one's life or seriously impair one's functional integrity even for the sake of helping the neighbor.

Death and Dying

On the basis of the teaching that the individual exercises, not full dominion, but only stewardship, over life, Catholic moral teaching consistently opposed suicide and euthanasia. In addition to natural law arguments references were frequently made to scriptural arguments and to the evil consequences that would flow from euthanasia. However, pain killers could be given to the dying person even though an indirect effect of these drugs might be the hastening of the death of the patient.

Clearly distinct from euthanasia is the teaching (called by some non-Catholics passive euthanasia) that one does not have to use extraordinary means to preserve human life. The teaching arose in the context of the positive obligation to care for health. Positive obligations do not oblige in the face of moral impossibility. By the sixteenth century there was much discussion in the moral literature about the means necessary to preserve life, which was developed in the seventeenth century by Cardinal de Lugo, who referred to ordinary and extraordinary means. The principle is long established that generally speaking an individual has no obligation to use extraordinary means to preserve life. A well-accepted contemporary description views extraordinary means as all medicines, treatments and operations which cannot be obtained or used without excessive expense, pain or other inconvenience or which, if used, would not offer a reasonable hope of benefit.[43] From this ethical perspective there is no difference between not using an artificial respirator to sustain life for a few hours or even days or shutting off the respirator which is already in use.

Even before recent discussions about changing the understanding of the moment of death Catholic medical ethics discussed this question. The traditional theological definition of death as the separation of the soul from the body lacks precision. Exactly when death occurs is beyond the competency of the church or theology and belongs to the competency of medical science. Such a position was taken by Pope Pius XII in his Address to an International Congress of Anesthesiologists on November 24, 1957.[44]

Other Questions

Under the heading of the spiritual care of the patient questions concerning informing the patient about death and especially the celebration of the sacraments of baptism and anointing of the sick (extreme unction) were considered. On the question of medical experimentation the textbooks generally followed the teaching of Pope Pius XII (Address to the Eighth Congress of the World Medical Association, September 30, 1954) in distinguishing between experimentation for the good of the individual and experimentation in the strict sense for the good of others.[45] For the good of the individual, experimentation is allowed provided no certainly effective remedy is available, the dubious treatment most likely to help the patient is chosen and the consent of the patient can be at least reasonably presumed. Experimentation for the good of others (experimentation in the strict sense as opposed to therapy) may be permitted for the proportionate good of others and of science if the subject freely consents, if no experiment which directly inflicts grave injury or death is used, and if all reasonable precautions are taken to avoid even the indirect causing of grave injury or death. Later, theologians and ethicists would go into these criteria more deeply and apply them to the cases of children, prisoners and others whose ability to consent was in some way or other lessened or not present.

VI. Recent Developments

Significant developments have occurred in Roman Catholic moral theology and in medical ethics since 1960. These new developments affected especially two of the distinctive characteristics of Catholic moral theology and medical ethics — natural law and the teaching authority of the church. Chapter Two has considered the effect of theological reaction to *Humanae vitae* on these two characteristic aspects of moral theology.

A number of criticisms are directed against the concept of natural law as proposed in the manuals of moral theology and of medical ethics. Called for is a more historically conscious approach which gives greater emphasis to growth, development and change and likewise emphasizes the individual, the particular and the contingent more than had been done in the older natural law theory. In this context a more inductive, and not a totally deductive, methodology is seen as needed. Newer approaches put more emphasis on the personal and less on the natural and call for a greater stress on the subject. Morality according to some cannot be based only on the finality and purpose of the faculty seen in itself apart from the total person. Above all many contemporary Catholic moral theologians disagree with the physicalism of the older approach, according to which the moral aspect of the human act is identified with the physical aspect of the act. The distinction is often proposed between physical, or premoral, evil on the one hand and moral evil on the other. Physical, or premoral, evil can be justified for a proportionate reason.

Methodological difficulties with natural law led to the adoption of newer and different methodological approaches to moral theology and thus to medical ethics. Various types of approaches such as pragmatism, phenomenology, linguistic analysis, transcendental Thomism and others have recently been used by Roman Catholic ethicists. No longer can one speak of a monolithic natural law theory in Roman Catholic moral theology or medical ethics. There exists even now a pluralism of methodological approaches, but most of these are only in the incipient stages and need to be developed and explored systematically. On the other hand, there are some Catholic ethicists still using the natural law approach either in a revised form or as it has been handed down in the manuals of medical ethics.

Recent developments have also affected the understanding of the authoritative teaching of the church in moral matters. Reaction to the encyclical *Humanae vitae*, as discussed in Chapter Two, brought to the fore the possibility of dissent within the Roman Catholic Church. Appeal was made to the official documents of the church and to the historical tradition to justify the possibility of dissent from specific moral teachings of the hierarchical magisterium. The Constitution on the Church of the Second Vatican Council (n. 25) called for Catholics to give a religious submission of intellect and will to the authoritative teaching of the Roman pontiff even when he is not speaking infallibly. In the discussion over papal infallibility in the nineteenth century a distinction was made between infallible teaching to which one owes the assent of faith and authoritative or authentic, noninfallible teaching to which one owes the religious assent of intellect and will. The response to infallible teaching is certain, while theologians admitted that the response to noninfallible teaching is conditional and the possibility of error exists. This theological explanation found only in the small print of some theology manuals never entered into the mainstream of Catholic life, but it was recognized in certain responses of the doctrinal commission of the Second Vatican Council. In addition, some national conferences of Catholic bishops (e.g., West German, Canadian, Belgian) explicitly recognized the possibility of dissent in pastoral letters after the council, especially in connection with the encyclical *Humanae vitae.*[46]

Chapter Two has shown how newer developments in Catholic theology also lead to the possibility of dissent. Contemporary ecclesiology (the theology of the church) has emphasized in all matters the attitudes of collegiality and shared responsibility in the church. In particular, the teaching office of the church is not totally identified with the God-given hierarchical teaching office, so that some tension can and will exist. Newer methodological approaches stress that on specific moral questions the church can never have the degree of certitude which excludes the possibility of error. On the other hand, there are theologians who strongly argue against these recent developments, which are condemned as forms of subjectivism, relativism or utilitarianism. In practice these theologians do not allow dissent (e.g., Thomas Dubay).[47]

These newer developments have been applied to many of the particular questions in medical ethics. The understanding of morality as based on the finality and purpose of the sexual faculty and act has been challenged by a good number of Catholic moral theologians who now accept contraception, sterilization, masturbation for seminal analysis, AIH and, for some, even AID where there are sufficient or proportionate reasons. In addition, many theologians reject the principle of double effect as it has been proposed in the textbooks, especially because of the condition which emphasizes the physical causality of the act by saying that the good effect must be as equally immediate as the evil effect. The following chapter will show there has been some dissent on the question of when human life begins and how it affects the question of abortion. Also a few theologians (e.g., Daniel Maguire) argue for the possibility of active euthanasia in some circumstances.[48] However, on all these questions the official position of the hierarchical teaching office has not changed, and some theologians also vigorously defend these teachings. Now there are beginning to appear books on medical ethics which incorporate some of these new developments (e.g., Häring, Dedek, Curran),[49] but at the same time newer editions and new books (O'Donnell, McFadden, May) have been published in which the teaching of the hierarchical magisterium and the methodology proposed in the textbooks of the 1950s have been upheld.[50]

NOTES

1. Alphonsus Bonnar, *The Catholic Doctor*, 2nd ed. (London: Burns, Oates, 1939); Edwin F. Healy, *Medical Ethics* (Chicago: Loyola University Press, 1956); Gerald Kelly, *Medico-Moral Problems* (St. Louis: Catholic Hospital Association, 1958); John P. Kenny, *Principles of Medical Ethics* (Westminster, Maryland: Newman, 1952; 2nd ed., 1962); Albert Niedermeyer, *Pastoralmedizinische Propädeutik* (Salzburg: Pustet, 1935); Thomas J. O'Donnell, *Morals in Medicine* (Westminster, Maryland: Newman, 1956); P. G. Payen, *Déontologie médicale d'après le droit naturel* (Zi-Ka-Wei: T'ou-se-we, 1935); Jacobus Pujiula, *De medicina pastorali*, 2nd ed. (Turrin: Marietti, 1953); Luigi Scremin, *Dizionario di morale professionale per i medici*, 5th ed. (Rome: Editrice Studium, 1953).
2. Bernard Häring, *The Law of Christ*, 3 vols., trans. Edwin G. Kaiser (Westminster, Maryland: Newman, 1961), 1:3–31.
3. John T. Noonan, Jr., "An Almost Absolute Value in History," in *The Morality of Abortion: Historical and Legal Perspectives*, ed. J. T. Noonan (Cambridge: Harvard University Press, 1970), pp. 3–22.
4. John T. Noonan, Jr., *Contraception: A History of Its Treatment by the Catholic Theologians and Canonists* (Cambridge: Harvard University Press, 1965), pp. 56–138.
5. For this history see John A. Abbo and Jerome D. Hannan, *The Sacred Canons*, 2nd ed. (St. Louis: B. Herder Book Co., 1960), 1: xiii–xx.
6. *Decretals of Gregory IX*, II, 19 (Friedberg, ed., *Corpus iuris canonici*, II, 1959).

7. *Decretales de Joannes XXII,* XIV, *Magnum bullarium,* Tomus Primus (Luxemburgi: Andrae Chevalier, 1727), pp. 205–208.

8. 4 vols. (Turrin: Marietti, 1952).

9. *Summa summarum,* 4 vols. (Lyons: Vincentius de Portonariis, 1542).

10. 2 vols. (Venice: H. and N. Polum, 1602).

11. *De sancto matrimonii sacramento,* 3 vols. (Venice: Pezzana, 1712).

12. 3 vols. (Lyons: Posuel, 1701).

13. Antwerp: Cornelius Woons, 1666.

14. Lyons: G. Boissat, 1637.

15. Lyons: 1658.

16. Monarchii: J. F. X. Gratz, 1764.

17. *Theologia moralis,* 4 vols., ed. L. Gaudé (Rome: Typographia Vaticana, 1905–1912).

18. *Medicina pastoralis,* 7th ed. (Aquisgrani: R. Barth, 1879).

19. Pierre Debreyne, *La théologie morale et les sciences médicales,* 6th ed., ed. A. Ferrard (Paris: Poussielgue Frères, 1884).

20. André Eschbach, *Disputationes physiologico-theologicae* (Paris: Vict. Palme, 1884).

21. Joseph Antonelli, *Medicina Pastoralis,* 2 vols. (Rome: Pustet, 1905).

22. *Handbuch der Speziellen Pastoral-Medizin,* 6 vols. (Vienna: Herder, 1948–1952).

23. Kelly, *Medico-Moral Problems,* pp. 19–20.

24. *AAS* 42 (1950): 568.

25. Kelly, *Medico-Moral Problems,* p. 2.

26. T. Lincoln Bouscaren, *Ethics of Ectopic Operations,* 2nd ed. (Milwaukee: Bruce, 1944), pp. 3–24.

27. *AAS* 22 (1930): 539–592.

28. *AAS* 60 (1968): 481–503.

29. Official church documents since 1908 have been promulgated in *Acta Apostolica Sedis* (*AAS*). English translations of important papal declarations can be found in *The Pope Speaks,* which began publication in 1954. Textbooks in medical ethics often in the index (e.g., Kenny, *Principles of Medical Ethics,* 2nd ed., p. 272) give references to the major addresses of Pope Pius XII on these subjects.

30. *AAS* 44 (1952): 779–789.

31. Ibid., p. 787.

32. *AAS* 50 (1958): 693–694.

33. Healy, *Medical Ethics,* pp. 11, 156–161, 171–184.

34. Kenny, *Principles of Medical Ethics,* pp. 5,6.

35. Thomas J. O'Donnell, *Medicine and Christian Morality* (Staten Island, New York: Alba House, 1976), p. 47.

36. Healy, *Medical Ethics,* p. 43.

37. These directives can be obtained from the Publications Office

of the United States Catholic Conference, 1312 Massachusetts Avenue NW, Washington, D.C. 20005.

38. *AAS* 43 (1951): 844–846.

39. *AAS* 48 (1956): 472–473.

40. Kelly, *Medico-Moral Problems*, p. 219.

41. Kenny, *Principles of Medical Ethics,* pp. 90–96.

42. *AAS* 48 (1956): 461–462.

43. Kelly, *Medico-Moral Problems*, p. 129.

44. *AAS* 49 (1957): 1031 and 1033.

45. *AAS*, 46 (1954): 593–594.

46. Charles E. Curran et al, *Dissent in and for the Church* (New York: Sheed and Ward, 1969); Joseph A. Komonchak, "Ordinary Papal Magisterium and Religious Assent," in *Contraception: Authority and Dissent,* ed. Charles E. Curran (New York: Herder and Herder, 1969), pp. 101–126.

47. Thomas Dubay, "The State of Moral Theology: A Critical Appraisal," *Theological Studies* 35 (1974): 482–506.

48. Daniel C. Maguire, *Death By Choice* (New York: Doubleday, 1974).

49. Bernard Häring, *Medical Ethics* (Notre Dame, Indiana: Fides, 1973); John F. Dedek, *Contemporary Medical Ethics* (New York: Sheed and Ward, 1975): Charles E. Curran, *Issues in Sexual and Medical Ethics* (Notre Dame, Indiana: University of Notre Dame Press, 1978).

50. Thomas J. O'Donnell, *Medicine and Christian Morality* (Staten Island, New York: Alba House, 1976). For all practical purposes this is merely a somewhat updated version of his older book. Charles J. McFadden, *The Dignity of Life: Moral Values in a Changing Society* (Huntington, Indiana: Our Sunday Visitor Press, 1976). This book is completely new, although it follows the positions proposed in the author's earlier text on medical ethics. William E. May, *Human Existence, Medicine and Ethics: Reflections on Human Life* (Chicago: Franciscan Herald Press, 1977).

8: Abortion: Ethical Aspects

Since 1950 there has been an ongoing debate about abortion. Various reasons or indications have been proposed for justifying abortion: to protect the life of the mother, to safeguard the physical and mental health of the mother, to act as a remedy against injustices due to rape or incest, to prevent the birth of defective children, to vindicate the right of the woman to determine her own reproductive capacities and to have control over her body, to protect the reputation of the woman and to alleviate economic, sociological and demographic pressures. These reasons all enjoy some validity, but they must be seen in a larger context, including the zygote-embryo-fetus and its value or rights.

Most commentators recognize that the heart of the problem about abortion is the difficult question of the beginning of human life, since human beings as persons are treated differently from all other beings. A terminological problem exists in even framing the question, for some authors make a distinction between human life and personal life, between human being and human person, between biological existence and fully human existence. To avoid confusion the term 'truly human being' or 'truly human life' will be used and understood as that human life deserving the value, rights and protection due to the human person as such.

I. When Does Truly Human Life Begin?

Opinions about the beginning of truly human life may be conveniently approached in two ways. First, it can be done in terms of the conclusions about the beginning of truly human life, which range from the moment of conception to various stages in fetal development, viability, birth and for some time after birth. Second, the criteria employed for determining the beginning of human life may be examined. The following types of criteria best categorize and summarize the abundant literature on the subject—individual-biological, relational, multiple and the conferral of rights by society. There is no absolute correlation between the criterion employed and the conclusion about the beginning of truly human life, but the following tendencies exist: the individual-biological criterion tends to place the beginning of human life at conception or at early stages of development; the relational and conferral of rights criteria usually accept a later time for the beginning of human life; the multiple approach often results in an intermediary position.

One preliminary point is most important. Biological, genetic or scientific data alone will not be able to solve the problem of when truly human life begins. The ultimate judgment remains a philosophical or human judgment, which gives meaning and interpretation to the biological and other data involved. Such a conclusion is based on the recognition that human existence involves more than the biological and genetic and cannot be simply identified with only one aspect. However, it must also be pointed out that at times the human and the physical or biological are the same. Our personal existence as human beings is ultimately connected with our physical-biological existence. Human beings do not exist without or apart from their bodies. Human personal death is described in accord with individual-biological categories—the cessation of brain activity accompanied by other signs, if one accepts the more recent understandings of the criterion of human death, or the cessation of breathing or of heart activity.[1]

Individual-Biological Criterion

The individual-biological approach generally sees the criterion of truly human existence in terms of some physical, biological or genetic aspects of the individual. Exponents of the theory placing human life at an early stage based on the individual-biological criterion usually begin with the assumption that all humans accept the born child as a truly human being. The first serious question is raised about birth as the beginning of human life. But the fetus one day before birth and the child one day after birth are not that significantly or qualitatively different in any respect. Even outside the womb the newborn child is not independent but remains greatly dependent on the mother and others. Birth in fact does not really tell much about the individual as such but only where the individual is — either outside the womb or still inside the womb. Viability has often been proposed as the beginning of human life, but from the perspective of the individual-biological criterion viability again indicates more about where the fetus can live than what it is. The fetus immediately before viability is not that qualitatively different from the viable fetus. In addition viability is a very inexact criterion because it is intimately connected with medical and scientific advances. In the future it might very well be possible for the fetus to live in an artificial womb or even with an artificial placenta from a very early stage in fetal development.[2]

There are two other stages in the development of the fetus that have been pointed out as marking the beginning of truly human life. Joseph Donceel has based a delayed hominization, or delayed animation, theory on the Thomistic concept of hylomorphism, according to which there is a complementarity between the material and formal aspects of being. The form, which in this case is the soul, is received only into matter capable of receiving it. Thomas Aquinas and many other medieval theologians and philosophers accepted a theory of delayed animation. According to Donceel the insistence on immediate animation in Catholic circles in the last few cen-

turies is based on the erroneous biological theory of preforma-
tion and was influenced by a Cartesian dualism. The unity of
the human person demands that the bodily or material element be more highly organized in order to receive the truly
human form or soul. The fertilized ovum, the morula, the
blastula and the early embryo cannot be animated by an
intellectual soul. Donceel concludes that the least that must be
present before admitting a human soul is the availability of
these organs: senses, the nervous system, the brain and especially the cortex. Since these organs are not ready during early
pregnancy, there is no human person present until several
weeks have elapsed.[3] Others might want to insist on the
incipient presence of the major organs as the determining
point for the existence of truly human life.

Some (e.g., Grisez) reply that Thomas Aquinas' own position was determined more by poor biological knowledge,
according to which the seed was the primary active element in
human generation, the ovum was not known, and the seed had
to die before new life could come into existence in the womb of
the mother.[4] Whether Aquinas' position is based on faulty biological knowledge which is corrected in the light of modern
biology and genetics or is based on his philosophical theory will
continue to be debated. However, it seems difficult to maintain
that such early development of these organs constitutes the
qualitative difference between truly human life and no human
life. Self-awareness and reason are not truly present at this
time, and much more growth and development are necessary.
The rudimentary presence of these organs appears to mark
just another stage in the ongoing development—a stage directed by an inner teleology already present in the embryo or
fetus.

A somewhat similar theory (Ruff, and proposed but not
accepted in practice by Häring) places the beginning of human
life at the time of the formation of the cortex of the brain.
Electrical brain activity is detectable at the eighth week. Personal life is characterized by consciousness and self-reflection
which have their indispensable substratum in the cerebral
cortex. Today many accept brain death—a flat EEG—together

with other signs of no responses as a criterion of death. Is it not logical to insist on the same criterion for determining when human life begins?[5]

Within the individual-biological criterion it does not seem that the early formation of the cortex constitutes a qualitative threshhold distinguishing truly human life from nonlife. There is validity in the plea for consistency in dealing with the beginning and end of life, but consistency does not necessarily call for the same material test at the beginning as at the end of life. The test really measures whether there is any immediate potentiality for spontaneous life functioning. At the beginning of life this can be present before electrical brain activity can be detected and measured.

Many proponents of the individual-biological criterion by emphasizing a continual, progressive development of the fetus without any obviously qualitatively different thresholds conclude that the only logical place to mark the beginning of truly human life is conception. John T. Noonan has accepted as the conclusion of his analysis of the Catholic tradition that whatever is conceived of human beings is human and buttresses his conclusion with three different reasons—the presence of characteristics in the embryo and adult which are similar; an argument based on probabilities which indicates the great difference between the sperm or ovum and the fertilized ovum or zygote; and a critique of alternative proposals. Modern genetics, according to Noonan, supports this position by showing that the zygote is a dynamic blueprint which if it receives proper nourishment and suitable environment grows and develops from the inside.[6]

Germain Grisez develops a two-stage argument for his opinion that truly human beings come into existence at conception. The first stage is factual. The fertilized ovum is a single reality derived from two sources. The facts of genetics indicate that a new being comes into existence with conception, for the fertilized ovum is continuous with that which develops from it, while the duality of sperm and ovum are continuous with the duality of the two parents. This factual question leads to the moral question—is this new individual to be regarded as a person? Anyone who recognizes the importance of the body and does not adopt a dualistic understanding of the person must acknowledge that development is a continual process from the time of fertilization, so that the conceptus must be considered a truly human being.[7]

Lately, some authors (Chiavacci, Curran and Ramsey) have proposed on the basis of the individual-biological criterion that an individual is not present until sometime between the second and third week after conception.[8] Biological information heavily influences this judgment, but the ultimate reason rests on the recognition that individuality, which is a most fundamental characteristic of the truly human being, is not achieved before this time, up to which twinning and recombination can occur. Before this time there is no organizer which directs the differentiation of the pluripotential cells, and without this organizer hominization cannot occur. Also this theory contends that the large number (perhaps as many as 50 percent) of fertilized ova which are spontaneously aborted without the mother being aware of having conceived are not truly human beings. Rebuttal arguments downplay the fact of twinning and recombination, which are comparatively rare and can be explained in other ways such as the direct infusion of a new soul in the case of twinning.

The reasons proposed thus far have been of a philosophical nature and not based on any particular religious or theological perspective. Paul Ramsey invokes the religious understanding that the value and sanctity of human life are not something intrinsic in the human being but result from the gift of God. The sanctity of life is an alien dignity conferred by God, so that even a small zygote can have that dignity and value.[9] Interestingly, Roman Catholic ethics which has often insisted on an early beginning of human life does not usually employ such arguments, for God's gracious gift of life should become effectively present in the human being and can be observed by other human beings in truly human ways. This again illustrates the Catholic insistence on mediation which was explained in Chapter One.

The following arguments have been raised against the individual-biological criterion, especially the conclusion of an early beginning of human life. It goes against common experience, which does not consider the embryo or early fetus to be a human being; it absolutizes the biological and genetic and does not give enough importance to a broader understanding of the human; it fails to recognize that in addition to genetic factors environmental aspects are also necessary for human growth; it overemphasizes potentiality and does not give enough importance to development. Counter arguments can be proposed. Common human experience must always be subject to reflection, scrutiny and critique; granted that the human is more than just biological, nevertheless at times the human and the biological can be identified. The only human beings we know in this world are human beings in their physical and biological nature. Granted that environmental factors are important for human development, these factors also continue to be of great importance after birth. Potentiality based on something intrinsic in the being itself is a better criterion than a developmental approach that could open the door to differing value attributed to different human lives depending on their developed potential.

Relational Criterion

A relational criterion for the beginning of human life generally sees truly human life coming into existence late in the development of the fetus — usually at the time of viability or even birth. The starting point of the relational school emphasizes the common experience denying that the embryo or early fetus is a truly human being and insists that the human cannot be identical with merely the genetic or the biological aspect of human existence. In fact it is futile to look for a biological moment when fully human life begins even if it were possible to determine such a moment. The acceptance of brain waves as a test for death indicates that lower biological life can continue to exist even when truly human life is ended. These approaches frequently distinguish between human life and human person, between biological life and personal life, between human life and humanized life.

According to some French Catholic moral theologians fully

personal and humanized life must be seen in terms of relationships. An older objectivist epistemology sees the fruit of conception as a human being in itself, but contemporary epistemology shows the participation of culture and of a knowing or recognizing element in the very constitution of the object of discourse. There are economic, psychological, cultural and even faith aspects of human life in addition to the biological. The mere fact of biological procreation does not constitute a fully human personal life, especially if the parents were not intending such a result and were trying to prevent it. The fetus must be accepted by the parents and also to some extent by the society into which it will be born.[10]

One of the arguments frequently raised against the relational criterion is that the employment of such a criterion logically leads to infanticide and the killing of adult human beings who are no longer capable of entering into such human relationships. This problem raises the question about what are the constitutive elements of the human and how can one draw a line between allowing abortion and prohibiting infanticide. It should be pointed out that some authors, such as Michael Tooley and Joseph Fletcher,[11] are also willing to admit infanticide and/or the killing of some biological adults who do not fulfill the criterion of the human, but most defenders of abortion based on a relational criterion of the beginning of human life do not want to admit such killing and make a distinctive effort to show that acceptance of abortion does not logically entail acceptance of these other forms of killing.

However, it seems that truly human relationships cannot exist until after birth because full human relationships require a reciprocity of giving and taking in a human way that cannot be had until both partners have the requisite self-consciousness to enter into such a relationship. In a true sense fully personal life is not present at birth or even immediately thereafter. The infant does not possess the characteristics of rationality or self-consciousness that are generally proposed as definitive of the human person. Lederberg maintains that the infant becomes a human person only after the first year or so of life.[12]

H. T. Engelhardt has addressed this particular question and

proposed a second concept of person in addition to the strict concept used to identify actually self-conscious moral agents—a social category of person based on a social role or function which claims the intrinsic value of actual persons. The newborn infant, although not yet a full person, has such a potential personhood that it can play the role or function of a person within family and society. The mother-child relationship is a social relationship which depends upon the mother's agency and involves the child's being treated as if it were a person. The mother-child relationship is a social and willed structure of interaction and a cultural enterprise as contrasted with the mother-fetus relationship, which is a biological and imposed structure and a physiological enterprise. The biological reality of viability now becomes understood in broader social terms as indicating when the social role of a person can begin. This theory is thus based on two concepts of human life—biological and personal—and on a strict and social concept of person but insists that the social concept of person has exactly the same consequences as the strict concept of person.[13]

Does the relational criterion avoid the danger of exposing infants and other adult human beings to being judged less than fully human persons and therefore killed or sacrificed for others? As a matter of fact it can be pointed out that many people, countries and cultures which accept abortion do not endorse any form of infanticide or killing of the weak, the retarded and the defenseless. In theory most authors proposing a relational criterion oppose any extension to those who are already born, but there remains a grave doubt about the logic involved in such a criterion. Truly human relationships are not present immediately after birth, and often adult human beings seem to fall below the line of full human relationships. If one admits a distinction between a strict and a social concept of a person, it becomes very easy to say that a strict concept of a person results in more rights or more values than a social concept of a person, thus to deny the basic realization that all persons have equal rights and equal values in terms of the fundamental question of life itself.

A Multiple Criterion

A third type of criterion tries to avoid some of the problems associated with both the individual-biological and the relational by calling for a criterion based on multiple indications. Daniel Callahan in a well-documented monograph on abortion argues for a consensus approach to the question which will do justice to all the values involved and proposes a criterion for the beginning of human life based on biological, psychological and cultural factors. Callahan maintains that even a zygote is individual human life, but full value should not be assigned at once to the life thus begun. Interestingly, he never explicitly develops or describes in great detail when truly human life which is to be valued as such does occur, but he seems to indicate the existence of brain activity as the distinguishing mark. Callahan's criterion enables him to do three things: to allow for the possibility of decisions in which the woman would want an abortion; to avoid the unilateral approach of the biological; and to avoid some of the dangers of the relational criterion, which if used alone could endanger the rights of the newborn and other marginal people in society.[14]

There are many aspects of Callahan's mediating approach which are appealing, but in the last analysis doubts remain, perhaps increased somewhat by his apparent reluctance to discuss in greater detail precisely when human life is to be fully valued as such. The danger in an approach calling for the threefold criterion of biological, psychological and cultural considerations is that the psychological and cultural aspects are really not all that present at the time of birth and might also cease to exist for some adults after birth. Callahan himself implies a comparatively early point at which full value is achieved (brain activity), but one could really question if enough cultural and psychological development have truly taken place to mark this as the beginning of fully valued human life. Any developmental theory also is going to open the door to the recognition that such a criterion can be employed even after birth to distinguish the values involved in different human lives depending upon their devleopment in accord with psychological and cultural aspects.

Conferred Rights Criterion

Metaphysical considerations, the recognition that human beings must ultimately make the decision about when human life begins, and the difficulties involved with other criteria are some of the reasons proposed for a fourth type of criterion for the beginning of human life — the social conferral of rights. In the earlier years of the abortion debate after 1950 Glanville Williams and Garrett Hardin advocated such approaches. Williams believes that life is a continuum and the fundamental problem is to discover when human life begins. The basic criterion becomes what answer will have the best social consequences. Williams leans to viability as the dividing line.[15] Hardin also acknowledges that whether or not the fetus is human is a matter of definition and not of fact.[16]

More nuanced philosophical understandings of the same type of criterion have been advanced. R. B. Brandt proposes a contractual understanding of morality based on the criterion that what is right is fixed by what would be permitted in a moral code which rational, impartial persons, with no personal gain, living now or in the future, would prefer. The important condition emphasizes that these individuals would be totally impartial and would in no way know how they themselves as individuals might profit or suffer from their decision. It is prima facie wrong to kill a being that wants to live, Brandt contends, but the fetus is not sentient and cannot choose. Even if these people were altruistic, the fetus would not be an object of their sympathy. Nor can a human person ever truly put oneself in the place of a fetus, for the precise reason that the human person is not a fetus. On this basis Brandt concludes that abortion is not prima facie wrong.[17]

Ronald Green has proposed a similar approach of a rational theory of rights as a way of bypassing the thorny and seemingly insoluble problem of when human life begins. Understanding morality as a noncoercive means of settling disputes, Green identifies a class of agents who must have fundamentally equal rights—all those agents with whom we can possibly come into dispute, who display an elementary rational ability and who are capable of understanding and respecting moral rules. Such a broad understanding includes almost all human beings, but there are some who do not have these capacities, so that rights in these cases are conferred at the behest of rational agents who are concerned about behavior with respect to third parties that have ultimate effects on their own lives. A threefold criterion is proposed for conferring rights on others; on the basis of the effect on our capacity for sympathy, on the effect on the possible interests of particular agents and finally on the effect on the character or moral worth of rational agents generally. This threefold criterion would confer rights on the newborn but not on the eight-week-old fetus, although they would place some value on that life.[18] Somewhat similar standards are proposed by Sissela Bok as the reasons for protecting human life, most of which are absent in the case of prenatal life but some of which are clearly present with respect to newborn life, although not as fully as in the case of adult human beings.[19]

Various reasons have been proposed against the criterion of conferred rights. Biological data is given little or no importance at all, even though biology can never determine by itself when human life begins. It seems one cannot avoid the question of when human life begins, for our sympathy and our concern depend primarily on what we believe the fetus to be. Proponents of this criterion are very conscious of the charge of arbitrariness which would allow many people to be excluded from human rights. One way to avoid the charge is to include as many as possible within the class of moral agents who confer the rights, thus to include all races, colors and creeds. Another approach appeals to the neutral observer who behind the veil of ignorance does not know what one's own position is. However, if agents put themselves in the place of the fetus which all of them at one time were, it seems that they would be quite prone to protect the life of the fetus. One cannot exclude the rational agent from taking that position unless one first decides that the fetus is not a person. There always remains the philosophical problem that human rights must exist prior to any conferral of rights by the state or by individuals representing society.

II. Value and Rights of the Fetus

The question of the value and rights of the fetus is intimately connected with the question of when human life begins. For those who see the fetus as a truly human being, then the fetus has all the rights and values of every other human being. An opposite approach is taken by those who view the embryo or fetus as only tissue in the mother and give the mother the right to control her body as her personal property. If women are to be truly free and liberated, they must ultimately have full freedom to control their own reproductive capacities. The woman, according to Rachel Wahlberg, cannot truly experience the fetus as anything but a part of her own flesh.[20] Such reasoning is often proposed in some feminist literature, but it is seldom developed at great philosophical depth. This position seems refuted by the biological evidence that the embryo and the fetus constitute independent human beings even if one does not want to see them as full human beings.

The developmental school as exemplified in Callahan and others views the fetus from conception as individual human life, but development counts in assigning value to the fetus. On the basis of this there should be a strong bias against abortion, but the body life of the conceptus is not of the same value as the person life of the pregnant woman, so that many considerations would justify abortion. Relational approaches could give some value to the fetus as biological life, but fully human life becomes present only when the requisite relationship is present. Since the relational criterion does not generally give that much importance to biological life, the fetus before the time of becoming fully human would not seem to be of great overriding value. The conferred rights approach could also assign different meaning and value to the fetus, but, generally speaking, since such an approach gives little significance to the biological aspects, the fetus does not have that much value in such a generic approach.

R. M. Hare in dealing with the issue of abortion wants to avoid both rights talk and the question of when human life begins. The proper question is whether there is anything about the fetus which says we should not kill it. The primary moral question results from the fact that the fetus has the potentiality of becoming a person in the full, ordinary sense of that word. The potentiality principle in the case of the fetus asserts a presumption against the permissibility of abortion which is fairly easily rebutted if there are good indications, such as interests of the mother.[21] The above serve as illustrations of the various ways in which the value or rights of the fetus have been understood in the contemporary debate about abortion.

III. The Solution of Conflict Situations

Various reasons have been proposed to justify abortion — medical, psychological, sociological, economic, humanitarian, fetal, feminist, and demographic. The moral decision involves a proper balancing of the reasons or indications proposed in relationship to the rights, value or importance of the fetus. The position which regards the fetus as just tissue in the mother would then accept practically any reason which the woman proposed based on her right to the control of her body and reproductive capacities. The vast majority of commentators would see abortion as somewhat different from artificial contraception, but reasons of family planning or population control would be a sufficient reason to justify abortion for some. The balancing and weighing of the various reasons ultimately depends upon the value which one attributes to the fetus. The greater the value given to the fetus, the greater the reason needed to justify abortion. Generally speaking, the solution to such conflicts is based on the proportion existing between the value given to the fetus and the indications or reasons proposed for the abortion.

The question most discussed in the literature is the solution to conflict situations if the fetus is looked upon as a truly human being with all the rights of human beings. This is the problem that has been traditionally discussed within Christian ethics and especially within Roman Catholic ethics down to the present. Recently some philosophers have given attention to the same question, often with the intention of showing that the abortion question is not morally closed once one accepts or asserts, without necessarily conceding, that the fetus has the rights of a truly human being.

Roman Catholic theology in its historical tradition has acknowledged that conflict situations arise in which human lives can be taken, for example, war, killing in self-defense, capital punishment. In the question of abortion the hierarchical magisterium in the Roman Catholic Church taught that the fetus cannot be considered as an unjust aggressor, since the fetus in the womb is just doing what is necessary to preserve its own life—hence the mother cannot kill the fetus in self-defense. Conflict situations involving abortion, as mentioned in the last chapter, were dealt with in terms of the principle of the double effect which justified an action producing evil effects as well as good effects if the following four conditions were fulfilled: 1) The action itself is good or indifferent. 2) The good effect and not the evil effect is the one sincerely intended by the agent. 3) The good effect is not produced by means of the evil effect. If the evil effect is not at least equally immediate causally with the good effect, then it becomes a means to the good effect and intended as such. 4) There is a proportionate reason for permitting the foreseen evil effect to occur.[22]

The decisive criterion is the third—the causality of the act cannot be such that the good effect comes about by means of the evil effect. When applied to the question of abortion, this means that abortion cannot be the means by which the good effect is accomplished—for example, one cannot abort to save the life of the mother which might be endangered because her heart cannot take the pregnancy. The two most famous illustrations of indirect abortion are the removal of the cancerous uterus when the woman is pregnant and the removal of a fallopian tube or part of it which is threatened with infection from an ectopic pregnancy in the tube.[23]

The accepted Catholic teaching allows less conflict situations for the fetus in the womb than for human life outside the womb, because outside the womb the possibility of killing in defense against an unjust aggressor is recognized. One can argue that the older teaching on unjust aggression was referring, not to the subjective will of the aggressor or even to an objectively unjust act, but to the reality of a conflict situation. In this perspective it is easier to see that the right of defense even to the killing of the fetus might be extended to the mother, for truly conflict situations can arise even though the fetus is just attempting to provide what is necessary for its own growth and continued existence.

The theory of double effect has come in for closer scrutiny in the last few years. Some Catholic scholars continue to uphold it, but many contemporary Catholic authors reject some applications of the theory with its third condition based on the causal structure of the act itself.[24] Historical scholarship indicates, with some dissenting voices, that the third condition for the double effect was not found in Thomas Aquinas.[25] Chapter Two explained the tendency among many Catholic theologians to reject the identification of the moral aspect of the act with the causal and physical structure of the act. In my judgment there are at times some important moral differences between direct and indirect understood in terms of the physical causality of the act, but in the abortion case where there is some conflict existing between the fetus and the mother the physical causality of the act alone does not determine the immorality of the act. The human values involved must be carefully considered and weighed. Abortion can be justified for preserving the life of the mother and for other important values commensurate with life even though the action aims at abortion as a means to an end. The difficult problem concerns what values, if any, are commensurate with life. In the Catholic tradition killing an aggressor was justified not only in defense of one's life but even in defense of earthly goods of great value. Obviously there is the danger here of opening the door for reasons that are truly not of grave seriousness, but within the Catholic tradition other values have been proposed as commensurate in some situations with the value of human life.

Protestant authors generally do not accept the principle of double effect and usually employ some type of proportionate reasoning to solve conflict situations involving abortion. Paul Ramsey, an American Protestant ethician, originally praised the double effect theory, but lately he has in practice abandoned the all-important third condition of the double effect.[26] Some philosophers have lately discussed the principle of double effect in general and often reject the third condition, while they call for distinctions between positive and negative obligations, or between foreseen and unforeseen consequences. But even in philosophical circles there are some defenders of the principle of double effect (e.g., Finnis).[27]

Judith Jarvis Thompson sparked an interesting exchange by proposing that, granted only for the sake of argument that the fetus is a truly human being, it does not follow that abortion is always wrong. She draws an analogy with a person who unknowingly and unwillingly is plugged into a famous violinist who has a fatal kidney ailment which can be overcome only by using the kidneys of this other person. Does the person in this case have the right to unplug the violinist even though it will bring about the death of the famous musician? A minimally decent Samaritan or the normal human being is not required to make such huge sacrifices of being plugged into the violinist for nine months in order to sustain the life of another who has no right to demand this.[28]

Thompson has raised the very important question of conflict situations, but her analogy with the person plugged into the violinist for nine months decidedly limps. It seems that only in the case of rape one might hope to find a comparison between the two cases. A woman has to assume responsibility for her previous actions, and likewise there is a significant difference between an obligation to save the life of another and an obligation not to take the life of another.

There is another possible approach in conflict situations involving abortion which to some extent is also acceptable within the traditional approach of Roman Catholic theology. James Gustafson, a Protestant ethician from the University of Chicago, accepts the decision of a woman to have an abortion after she has brutally been raped by her former husband and acknowledges some financial and psychological problems in having the child.[29] Bernard Häring and even Gustafson himself recognize that from the viewpoint of Roman Catholic pastoral theology on the basis of an expanded notion of invincible ignorance, which prudently recognizes that one cannot ask another to do what is not possible, a counselor can accept the decision of the woman.[30] Others are continuing to debate if there are any real differences in the solutions originally proposed by Gustafson and Häring.

IV. A Survey of the Contemporary Debate

Protestant church teaching and Protestant ethicists until 1950 generally condemned abortion, but since that time many Protestant groups and theologians have come out in favor of abortion in certain circumstances and rejected the concept that the fetus from the moment of conception is a truly human being. However, it would be wrong to say that all Protestants are in favor of abortion.[31]

In Germany in 1973 a conference of German bishops (Catholic) and of the Evangelical Church (Protestant) issued a common statement on abortion which insisted that all decisions which involve human life can only be oriented to the service of life.[32] Generally speaking, more evangelical and conservative Protestant groups strenuously oppose abortion. Also a surprisingly large number of respected Protestant ethicians in the United States oppose abortion, although many others do not consider the conceptus from the time of fertilization to be a truly human being.

Developments have also occurred within Roman Catholicism. The hierarchical magisterium has continued to proclaim the accepted Catholic teaching. The Pastoral Constitution on the Church in the Modern World (n. 51) taught that from the moment of its conception life must be regarded with the greatest care, and abortion and infanticide are unspeakable crimes. Pope Paul VI in his encyclical *Humanae vitae* (n. 14) declared once again that the direct interruption of the generative process already begun and, above all, directly willed and procured abortion, even if for therapeutic reasons, are to be absolutely excluded as licit means of regulating birth. In the midst of debates in many countries about abortion and abortion laws the Sacred Congregation for the Doctrine of the Faith on November 18, 1974, issued a Declaration on Procured Abortion which in the light of faith and the light of reason reiterated the traditional teaching and recalled that Pope Paul VI on many occasions has not hesitated to declare that this teaching of the Church has not changed and is unchangeable (n. 7). National conferences of Catholic bishops throughout the world have continued to reiterate the same basic teaching.

The majority of Roman Catholic theologians still uphold the traditional teaching that from the moment of conception the conceptus is to be treated as a truly human being. There is, however, some dissent on this issue which has been most publicized in France, where a small, respected group of Catholic theologians has been proposing a relational criterion for determining when human life begins. An even greater number of Catholics have proposed that truly human life is not present until about the second or third week after conception. A comparatively large number of Catholic theologians from all countries reject the use of double effect to solve conflict situations involving the fetus.

A crucial and highly debated question within Roman Catholicism concerns whether the incipient dissent on when truly human life begins is legitimate and justified. In my judgment, as explained in Chapter Two, one can still be a loyal Roman Catholic and dissent on such a complex question because it is impossible to arrive at a certitude which excludes the possibility of error and because the question is somewhat distant from the core of faith. However, it must be pointed out that the vast majority of Roman Catholic authors accept the traditional teaching or disagree only to the slight extent that the beginning of truly human life is placed in the second or third week after conception.

Differences continue to exist within Judaism. The only authoritative text on therapeutic abortion in the Talmud recognizes that the fetus becomes fully human only if the greater part of it is already born. The controversy obviously centers on the value and importance of the fetus. All authors in the orthodox and conservative tradition accept the therapeutic abortion necessary for the life of the mother and, according to some, also for the mental health of the mother; but there is always a very strong emphasis in favor of the life of the fetus.[33] Within the reformed branch of Judaism there is a greater willingness to see the unborn fetus as prehuman, not a Nefesh or soul, with no independent human life. It is indistinguishable from the mother and may be destroyed for the mother's sake, just as a person may decide to sacrifice a bodily limb to cure a worse malady.[34]

One of the characteristics of the contemporary debate has been the interest shown by professional philosophers in the question of abortion. A few years ago philosophers tended to neglect content questions such as abortion, but changes in philosophy and the general interest and discussion within society on this question have occasioned a greater philosophical interest in abortion. In general there is no doubt that in the contemporary debate since 1950 many voices have been raised in favor of the position that the fetus is not a truly human being from the moment of conception and therefore abortion is morally acceptable for various reasons. Such sentiments obviously had an effect on public opinion and on the changing of abortion laws in a number of countries, even though there is not a strict correlation between questions of law and morality. However, it is interesting to note in the last few years some former advocates of abortion have expressed either a change of mind or doubt about the morality of abortion, at least to the extent that they want to caution against a too ready acceptance of abortion.[35] The general public, philosophers and theologians continue to be divided on this issue.

This chapter has summarized and evaluated the recent

debate about the morality of abortion. On the question of the beginning of human life I see great wisdom in the teaching of the hierarchical magisterium of the Catholic Church and modify it only to the extent of placing the beginning of truly individual human life at two to three weeks after conception. On the solution of conflict situations my position accepts a few more abortions than the official Catholic teaching on the double effect. The exposition of the question of abortion in this chapter reinforces the judgment made in Chapter Two that the possibility of dissent exists within the Catholic Church on this issue. The detailed study of abortion indicates both its complexity and its distance from the core of faith.

NOTES

1. "A Definition of Irreversible Coma," Report of the "Ad Hoc" Committee of the Harvard Medical School, under the chairmanship of Henry K. Beecher, M.D., to examine the definition of brain death, *Journal of the American Medical Association* 205, no. 6 (August 5, 1968): 85–88.

2. Paul Ramsey, "Reference Points in Deciding about Abortion," in *The Morality of Abortion: Legal and Historical Perspectives*, ed. John T. Noonan, Jr. (Cambridge: Harvard University Press, 1970), pp. 87–100.

3. Joseph F. Donceel, "Immediate Animation and Delayed Hominization," *Theological Studies* 31 (1970): 76–105.

4. Germain G. Grisez, *Abortion: The Myths, the Realities and the Arguments* (New York: Corpus Books, 1970), p. 283.

5. Wilfried Ruff, "Individualität und Personalität in embryonalen Werden," *Theologie und Philosophie* 45 (1970): 24–59; Bernard Häring, *Medical Ethics* (Notre Dame, Indiana: Fides Publishers, 1973), pp. 81–85.

6. John T. Noonan, Jr., "An Almost Absolute Value in History," in *The Morality of Abortion*, pp. 51–59.

7. Grisez, *Abortion*, pp. 273–287.

8. Enrico Chiavacci, "Le definizioni di aborto e i suoi problemi giuridicomorali," in L. Babbini et al., *Aborto: questione aperta* (Turrin: Gribaldi, 1973), pp. 254–274. Curran, *New Perspectives in Moral Theology*, pp. 188, 189; Ramsey, *The Morality of Abortion*, pp. 64–69.

9. Paul Ramsey, "The Morality of Abortion," in *Life or Death: Ethics and Options*, ed. Daniel Labby (Seattle: University of Washington Press, 1968), pp. 71–78.

10. *Avortement et respect de la vie humaine*, Colloque du Centre Catholique des medécins français (commission conjugale), especially the contributions by Ribes and Pohier. Also "Pour une réforme de la législation française relative à l'avortement," *Etudes* 338 (1973): 55–84; the entire issue of *Lumière et Vie* 21, no. 109 (Août-Octobre 1972) is devoted to abortion and includes some articles proposing the relational criterion.

11. Joseph Fletcher, "Medicine and the Nature of Man," in *The Teaching of Medical Ethics*, ed. Robert M. Veatch, Willard Gaylin and Councilman Morgan (Hastings-on-Hudson, New York: Hastings Center Publication, 1973), pp. 47–58; Michael Tooley, "Abortion and Infanticide," *Philosophy and Public Affairs* 2 (1972): 37–65.

12. Joshua Lederberg, "A Geneticist Looks at Contraception and Abortion," *Annals of Internal Medicine* 67 (September 1967), supplement 3, p. 26.

13. H. Tristram Engelhardt, Jr., "The Ontology of Abortion," *Ethics* 84 (1973–74): 217–234; idem, "Viability, Abortion and the Difference between a Fetus and an Infant," *American Journal of Obstetrics and Gynecology* 116 (1973): 429–433.

14. Daniel Callahan, *Abortion: Law, Choice and Morality* (New York: Macmillan, 1970), pp. 349–404, 493–501.

15. Glanville Williams, "Euthanasia and Abortion," *University of Colorado Law Review* 38 (1965–66): 178–201.

16. Garrett Hardin, "Abortion—Or Compulsory Pregnancy," *Journal of Marriage and the Family* 30 (1968): 246–251.

17. R. B. Brandt, "The Morality of Abortion," *The Monist* 56 (1972): 503–526.

18. Ronald M. Green, "Conferred Rights and the Fetus," *Journal of Religious Ethics* 2 (1974): 55–75.

19. Sissela Bok, "Ethical Problems of Abortion," *The Hastings Center Studies* 2 (January 1974): 33–52.

20. Rachel Conrad Wahlberg, "The Woman and the Fetus: 'One Flesh'?" *The Christian Century* 88 (1971): 1045–1048.

21. R. M. Hare, "Abortion and the Golden Rule," *Philosophy and Public Affairs* 4 (1975): 201–222.

22. For the historical development and a summary of Catholic teaching see Noonan, "An Almost Absolute Value," pp. 1–59.

23. T. Lincoln Bouscaren, *Ethics of Ectopic Operations*, 2nd ed. (Milwaukee: Bruce Publishing Co., 1944).

24. For rejections of the principle of the double effect by Catholic authors see Richard A. McCormick, *Ambiguity in Moral Choice* (Milwaukee: Marquette University, 1973); Leandro Rossi, "Il limite del

principio del duplice effeto," *Rivista di Teologia Morale* 13 (1972): 11–37; Bruno Schüller, *Die Begrundüng Sittlicher Urteile: Typen ethischer Argumentation in der katholischen Moraltheologie* (Düsseldorf: Patmos, 1973).

25. Vicente M. Alonso, *El principio del doble efecto en los comentadores de Santo Tomas de Aquino* (Rome: Gregorian University Press, 1937); J. Ghoos, "L'acte à double effect: étude de theologie positive," *Ephemerides Theologicae Lovanienses* 27 (1951): 30–52. For a dissenting voice see Joseph T. Mangan, "An Historical Analysis of the Principle of Double Effect," *Theological Studies* 10 (1949): 41–61.

26. Ramsey, "The Morality of Abortion," p. 78; idem, "Abortion: A Review Article," *The Thomist* 37 (1973): 210–226.

27. John Finnis, "The Rights and Wrongs of Abortion: A Reply to Judith Thompson," *Philosophy and Public Affairs* 2 (1973): 117–145.

28. Judith Jarvis Thompson, "A Defense of Abortion," *Philosophy and Public Affairs* 1 (1971): 47–66.

29. James M. Gustafson, "A Protestant Ethical Approach," in *The Morality of Abortion*, pp. 119–122.

30. Bernard Häring, "A Theological Evaluation," in *The Morality of Abortion*, pp. 112–115.

31. For a survey of Protestant opinion see "Abortion: A Paper for Study," a pamphlet from the National Council of Churches, 475 Riverside Drive, New York, New York.

32. Cited by Richard A. McCormick, "Notes on Moral Theology: The Abortion Dossier," *Theological Studies* 35 (1974): 328.

33. David Novak, *Law and Theology in Judaism* (New York: KTAV Publishing House, 1974), pp. 114–124.

34. Israel R. Margolies, "A Reform Rabbi's View," in *Abortion in a Changing World*, 2 vols., ed. Robert E. Hall (New York: Columbia University Press, 1970), 1: 30–33.

35. C. Eric Lincoln, "Why I Reversed My Stand on Laissez-Faire Abortion," *The Christian Century* 90 (1973): 477–479; B. N. Nathanson, "Deeper into Abortion," *New England Journal of Medicine* 291 (1974): 1189–1190.

9: Abortion: Legal and Public Funding Aspects

The last chapter evaluated the contemporary debate about the morality of abortion, but abortion has also been a controversial issue in other areas. There has been an ongoing political discussion in the United States about abortion and public policy for well over a decade. The debate now focuses on the question of payments for abortions for poor women.

The discussion originally concerned abortion and the law. In 1973 the Supreme Court ruled that existing state laws restricting abortion were unconstitutional and based its decision on the woman's right to privacy. In the first trimester the state can impose no restrictions on the woman who wants to have an abortion; in the second trimester the state can make restrictions only insofar as necessary to protect the health of the mother. In the third trimester the rights of the fetus enter into the picture. Here the state can regulate and even proscribe abortion except when it is necessary, in appropriate medical judgment, for the preservation of the life or the health of the mother.[1]

After this decision both the public debate and political activity continued. Right-to-life groups have organized and called for a constitutional amendment in an effort to overturn the decision of the Supreme Court. Proabortionists have tried to counter this political pressure and not lose what they have gained by the Supreme Court decision. There also developed a new area of dispute—the public funding of abortions. Prolife backers saw restrictions in this area as a way to gain some ground against the proabortion or prochoice position. On June 24, 1976, Representative Henry J. Hyde, Republican of Illinois, introduced an amendment on the 61.3-billion-dollar, one-year appropriation bill for the Department of Health, Education and Welfare and the Department of Labor. The original amendment stated none of the funds appropriated under this act shall be used to pay for abortions or to promote or encourage abortions. The wording was later changed to allow for therapeutic abortions. The House passed this amended version on September 16, 1976, by a vote of 256–114; the following day the Senate passed it 47–21. Congress thus barred federal funding for elective abortion for the fiscal year of October 1, 1976 to September 30, 1977.[2]

Court orders stayed the new abortion policy until the settlement of the constitutionality of issues about the payment of abortions for poor people under Medicaid which were already pending before the courts. On June 20, 1977, the Supreme Court ruled on three cases. In the first case (*Beal* v. *Doe*) the Court ruled that under Medicaid the state did not have to fund all abortions allowed by the law but could limit reimbursement to necessary, or therapeutic, abortions.[3] In the second case (*Maher* v. *Roe*) the Court ruled that a state participating in the Medicaid program did not have to pay for nontherapeutic abortions even though it paid for childbirth.[4] In the third case (*Poelker* v. *Doe*) the Court maintained that public hospitals do not have to perform elective abortions even though these hospitals provide care for childbirth.[5] The majority decision of the Court (6–3) in the Maher case written by Justice Powell argued that when an issue involves policy choices as sensitive as those implicated in the public funding of abortions, the appropriate forum for their resolution is the legislature. The legislature could pass laws allowing the funding of abortion in these cases, but it does not have to.[6]

Congress and the state legislatures thus have had to deal with the question. Congress debated all fall of 1977. The House of Representatives passed a rather stringent bill; the Senate passed a less restrictive bill. The final compromise restricts the cases in which Medicaid funds can be used to those in which the life of the mother is threatened, promptly reported incidents of rape and incest, and situations in which, in the judgment of two physicians, continuation of the pregnancy would result in severe and long-lasting physical damage to the mother.[7] Regulations for the implementation of this law have been issued by DHEW.[8] In the meantime state legislatures have been considering paying for abortions above and beyond what is covered in the Medicaid law.

Once again the recent judicial decisions and legislative enactments have only fueled the debate and the political activity. It seems likely that positions will probably not change, since they have become so hardened and since the same arguments which have failed to convince the other side in the past continue to be proposed. Unfortunately, the rhetoric of the debate is such that often more heat than light is produced. The purpose of this chapter is to examine the legal and funding questions from the ethical perspective, but sometimes it is impossible to explore the ethical reasons without considering other aspects, especially the legal.

There can be no doubt that the American people are deeply divided on the legal issue of abortion and the public funding of abortion. Both sides in the debate appeal to polls to prove that the public sides with them. Beverly Harrison, arguing against the 1977 Court rulings as too restrictive, speaks of the large number of polls that show that slightly over half of the public supports the Supreme Court's decision on the law of abortion.[9] James Burtchaell in responding to Harrison takes a different position on the polls, although both admit the question cannot be decided on the basis of opinion polls.[10]

It is difficult to know exactly what the polls themselves are saying about American public opinion, to say nothing about the accuracy of the polls in reflecting that opinion. Judith Blake, a respected scholar and a proabortionist, maintains on the basis of her studies, especially with the Gallup Poll, that public opinion is quite opposed to the position the Court took in 1973. In January 1973, after the Court's decision legalizing abortion in the first six months, Blake found that the majority of respondents believed that there should be a legal limit on abortion (or that abortion should not be performed under any circumstances) and that these limits should be within the first trimester of pregnancy. In responding in 1973 and in 1975 to questions about when human life begins, less than 10 percent of women and about 20 percent of men held life begins at birth. Most respondents claim that life begins at conception or quickening. In April 1975, as compared with January 1973, more women (60 percent rather than 50 percent) and more men (42 percent rather than 33 percent) believed that life begins at conception.[11] All should be able to agree on one point—the country remains sharply divided on the question of abortion and the public policy about abortion.

I. Overview of Two Opposing Positions

In the current debate on public-policy issues involving abortion two radically opposed positions seem to dominate the discussion—the prolife movement and the prochoice movement, to use the names which both sides seem to prefer to call themselves. Unfortunately, the arguments proposed by both sides seem unconvincing to the other. It appears that the two different positions on public policy and funding go back to two different presuppositions. I have some difficulties with both sides and would hope that the present impasse could be bridged, but I do not realistically think there exists any possibility of bridging some of the differences through a compromise measure.

The question of public funding of elective abortions for poor women is intimately linked to the question of the legal status of abortion and the ethical aspects of the question. Generally speaking, the prolife and prochoice groups strongly disagree on all these three questions, with the different ethical judgment on abortion being the ultimate reason for their disagreement about abortion law and public funding. Also there appears on both sides a great reluctance and unwillingness to understand what the other is really saying.

The prolife position begins with the understanding that

truly human life begins at conception or very early in pregnancy. As indicated in the last chapter, the prolife position relies heavily on biological and genetic data and accepts the reality of development on the basis of what is present from the very beginning. From the first moment of conception there exists the individual, never-to-be-repeated, genotype. Biologically, the zygote (the technical name to describe what is present for the first two weeks), the embryo (the technical name to describe the existence from the third to the eighth week) and the fetus (the term used after eight weeks) merely develop what is already present from the very beginning. It is obvious that what is present at conception is not a canine being or bovine being but a human being, and in this understanding a truly human being. This position strongly rejects quality of life arguments which suggest some human lives have more dignity or importance than others. Since truly human life is present from the beginning, it is morally wrong to take that life except to save the life of the mother, although there are some disagreements about the exact type of exceptions allowed.

The prolife position on the legal status of abortion follows from the ethical basis. The fetus is a truly human being and deserves the full protection of law. Since the fetus is helpless and defenseless, there is even more need to protect its rights.

The prolife position obviously opposes the public funding of abortion. Such a position claims to be in no way insensitive to the needs of the poor, but the right to life of the fetus must come first. No one would be willing to kill newborn children to help a poverty-stricken mother. The tax dollars of prolife supporters should not be used for what they believe the moral equivalent of murder.

The prochoice position starts from a different ethical position, which then guides the response to the other two questions. The fetus is not a truly human being or at least becomes a truly human being sometime in its development. The truly human being is more than the genetic package and biological reality present at conception. Only a very few people adopting a prochoice position would argue that the fetus is merely tissue in the mother. Since the fetus is a human being but not a truly human person, many maintain that decisions to abort the fetus are often tragic but can be morally acceptable. The mother should make this decision while she takes into account all the aspects of the situation.

The position on law stresses the freedom of the woman to make her own abortion decision. Since there is disagreement within our society, there should be no legal restrictions preventing the woman from acting in accord with her conscience. The freedom of conscience of all must prevail. The prochoice position strongly backs the conclusion of the 1973 Supreme Court decision.

On the level of public funding, failure of the government to provide funds for elective abortions for poor women interferes with their freedom of choice. It is unfair if middle class and rich people are able to have abortions but poor people are not able to have abortions. Such a practice goes against the right of the woman to free choice which was given her by the 1973 Court ruling.

As a result of these fundamental differences, the rhetoric of the two sides often misses the mark and leaves the opponents unconvinced. Prolife advocates accuse the prochoice adherents of denying the value of human life and of opening a wedge in an ultimate attack against the defenseless, the old and all those who are less than normal. This is true on their presupposition, but it is not true for the prochoice defenders. They believe themselves to be just as dedicated to life and the right to life as the prolife adherents, but the fetus is not truly human life deserving of such protection. Prochoice adherents claim that the prolife position is an absolutist one that wants to impose its conscientious beliefs on others and will not allow others the freedom to follow their own consciences. Prolife adherents respond that there are times when one must prevent people from acting in accord with their consciences, especially when the rights of other innocent people are involved. Would not most persons adopt the absolutist position and deny the right of Afrikaaners to practice apartheid? And so the arguments go—most often clarifying little and only heating up the discussion.

II. A Different Approach to Law by an Antiabortionist

I have difficulties and disagreements with both the prolife and the prochoice positions as outlined above.[12] This study will concentrate on the legal and public-funding aspects of the question. As explained in the last chapter, my approach to the morality of abortion is in general agreement with the prolife position. However, I have accepted the Supreme Court ruling of January 1973 and argued against attempts made especially within the Roman Catholic Church to work for a constitutional amendment to overturn the decision of the Court.[13] How is it logically possible to maintain a position that the fetus is truly human life and still accept a legal position which for all practical purposes allows the woman abortion on her request during the first six months of pregnancy? Such a position is open to the charge of inconsistency and of selling out the value of human life.

My position rests on the understanding of law and morality which is found in the Declaration on Religious Freedom of the Second Vatican Council and earlier proposed in the writings of John Courtney Murray.[14] The problem involves not only the question of the relationship between law and morality but also the question of how groups in society such as churches or individuals should relate their own moral convictions to the law of society. The basic principle is stated succinctly in the Declaration: "For the rest, the usages of society are to be the usages of freedom in their full range. These require that the freedom of man be respected as far as possible, and curtailed only when and in so far as necessary" (par. 7). The criterion governing the intervention of civil law is the public order which involves an order of justice, an order of peace and an order of public morality (not private morality).[15]

On the basis of this criterion it is possible for one to arrive at different opinions on abortion law. One could argue that the fetus is truly human life; justice demands that innocent human life be protected; therefore, there should be a law prohibiting abortion. However, one could give more importance to the existing pluralism in our society on this question and argue for certain indications allowing abortion or even for no law against abortion. Before the 1973 Supreme Court decision I advocated a compromise such as the approach proposed by the American Law Institute, or a limitation of abortion to the first twelve weeks after conception.

Although I did not originally favor the position taken by the Court, I am opposed to attempts to amend the Constitution to overturn the 1973 Court decision. I even now prefer a law that would allow the real possibility of free choice to the woman, including counseling and the necessary help for her in meeting all the costs of whatever decision she decides to make. However, I can understand how in our society one could accept the conclusions (not the reasoning) proposed by the Court. American jurisprudence accepts the same principle proposed earlier—as much freedom as possible and as little constraint as necessary. Whatever the exact figures, Americans are seriously divided on the question of abortion. In the light of this division the benefit of the doubt is given to the freedom of the woman. Theoretically I can thus accept the conclusion reached by the Court.

In addition to the theoretical aspect I have strong practical objections to attempting to amend the Constitution. There are two possible avenues of approach—a states' rights amendment or a federal amendment declaring the fetus to be a truly human being with all the protection of law. Any attempts for such amendments will be both divisive and futile. A states' rights approach will mean that many states will ultimately choose to allow some abortions as certain states did before the 1973 Court ruling. In addition, I fear that in advocating a states' rights approach I would be aligning myself with many people who over the years have obstructed the struggle for social justice in the United States. An amendment to the Constitution to protect the fetus will not be successful. Although many people, perhaps even a majority, may be opposed to the Court decision, it will be impossible for three-fourths (38) of the states to agree on the question of when truly human life begins. Some will argue for conception; some for segmentation; some for brain waves; some for twelve weeks after conception. In the light of the existing differences it will be impossible to find the political agreement necessary to support a constitutional amendment saying at what time the fetus is a truly human being.

There are weaknesses in my position. I accept the existing pluralism in our society, so that the prophetic, or teaching, aspect of law is greatly reduced. Some argue against my position by pointing to the past denial of civil rights to blacks. However, in abortion, as shown in the last chapter, there are serious reasons for recognizing some difficulties in proving the true humanity of the fetus, whereas in the case of blacks serious reasons did not exist for denying their humanity. Likewise the quantity and quality of the persons denying the true humanhood of the fetus must be acknowledged even if not accepted. A practical political argument can also be raised against my position. Perhaps a Constitutional amendment will not succeed, but this is one form of exerting pressure which will bear fruit in other areas such as the 1977 Court ruling on funding. In my judgment none of these reasons is strong enough to overturn my position.

It does not follow that the prolife adherents should do nothing in society to promote their position. The theory explained above, and developed in Chapter Four, recognizes an important difference between the state and society. The prolife adherents and the Roman Catholic Church could and should still try to influence society in the matter of abortion choice. I have advocated a nationally coordinated program voluntarily supported by Roman Catholics and others, if they wish, to publicize that the Catholic Church will guarantee for any pregnant woman the financial, psychological, medical and social help needed to carry her child to term and to care for that child after birth. Through its resources, both financial and especially in terms of persons willing to do volunteer work, the Catholic Church (and others) could establish a program that would both be effective in preventing some abortions and at the same time bear witness and be prophetic within society without causing the excessive divisiveness of futile efforts to amend the Constitution.

III. The Role of the Roman Catholic Bishops

The Roman Catholic Church in the United States through the leadership of its bishops has taken a different stance and is working for a constitutional amendment to overturn the 1973 Court decision. From the intra-Catholic perspective this is a legitimate decision for the bishops to take, even if one judges it is not the correct decision. I would only insist that the bishops recognize the right of other Catholics to disagree with this particular choice and adopt another.

The question must also be addressed from the perspective of the role of religion in American society: Do the Roman Catholic bishops have a right to try to influence and change public policy on the question of abortion? First of all, it must be pointed out that the prolife movement involves more than just Catholics, even though the Roman Catholic institutional presence is strong. Within a democratic society church groups have every right to try to influence the laws of society in accord with the criterion of public order proposed earlier. If anything, the history of the last few decades indicts the churches and their leaders for not speaking out more against what was happening in society. Recall, for example, the failure of the churches in Germany to speak out against Hitler, or the failure of the churches in the United States to condemn more clearly the use of the atomic bomb and the policy of unconditional surrender in World War II. In the 1960s one notes with some pride the leadership given by some churches in the area of civil rights and in peace, although at times the bishops of my own church were rightly criticized for not giving as strong a leadership as possible.

But do the bishops and other church people have a right to impose their morality on others? Remember prohibition. Or from the Catholic perspective remember the early attempts to prevent the use of federal funds for contraception.[16] Today advocates of both those legal positions would receive little or no support. But there is a difference here. In this case the prolife adherents believe human life is being lost. All admit that one of the primary purposes of law and government is to ensure an order of justice and protect innocent human lives. Just as people opposed the war in Vietnam because they believed lives were needlessly lost, so do people oppose abortion and call for a change in the present legal status of abortion. Although I disagree with the position taken by the Roman Catholic bishops because I give more importance to the pluralistic realities of our society and its existing disagreements, I strongly uphold their right to do what they are doing. People who conscientiously believe human lives are being taken in abortion have every right in our society to work to change the present situation.

Perhaps the Roman Catholic bishops and the Roman Catholic Church are vulnerable to the charge of being single-issue oriented. It is charged that abortion is the only issue on the basis of which political support for candidates is based. Again one might defend such a single-issue approach in the light of the belief that abortion involves killing the innocent. There are few, if any, issues as significant as that; consequently, abortion can rightly be the most important and perhaps at times even the single determining political issue. From my perspective, since I obviously disagree with the goal of a constitutional amendment, I also disagree with making this legal issue of abortion the only important issue in deciding about political candidates. The very issue itself is so complex that it really cannot be absolutized with such great certitude as the overriding political issue. Making abortion the only concern in the political arena or the only criterion for electing political candidates is wrong because it fails to recognize the need to consider many other significant issues.

Interestingly enough, there seems to be some ambivalence among the bishops themselves on making abortion the only political issue. There is no doubt that in the presidential election of 1976 the American bishops gave the public impression at least for a time that abortion was the only issue in the campaign and election choices should be based on that issue. The impression created by the bishops (and I purposely say bishops and not the press) was not in keeping with their own previous statements. On February 12, 1976, the Administrative Board of the United States Catholic Conference issued a statement entitled "Political Responsibility: Reflections on an Election Year." Eight issues involving some of the important matters which the bishops believe to be central to rational debate in that election year were proposed in alphabetical order—abortion, the economy, education, food policy, housing, human rights and foreign policy, mass media, and reduced military expenditures.[17] In later clarifications in the fall of 1976 the bishops again explained that they were interested in more than a single issue.[18]

Although the Catholic bishops themselves have rightly pointed out that abortion is not the only important political issue or the exclusive criterion on which elections should be judged, there does seem to be one area in which the bishops are open to that charge. In November 1975 the American bishops issued a "Pastoral Plan for Pro-Life Activities." The plan calls for three major efforts: public information and education programs, pastoral care and legislative, public-policy efforts. To achieve their goals, including a constitutional amendment, the bishops call for various prolife committees to be set up on many levels, including one organization in each congressional district. "Thus it is absolutely necessary to encourage the development in each congressional district of an identifiable, tightly knit, and well organized pro-life movement."[19] Here I maintain that the means used by the bishops is inappropriate in the light of the total context. Why is this the only issue on which they are calling for grass-roots political organizations in every congressional district? (Again they can respond that the nature of the issue is so significant that it justifies the extraordinary action and involvement.) In short, I disagree with the goal the bishops have in mind, but I defend their right to pursue the goal. I question one means they are employing and also want them to unequivocally maintain their position that abortion is not the only significant political issue and that voting in elections should not be determined only by positions taken on abortion.

IV. Critique of Prochoice Position

Thus far I have explained my differences with the prolife movement with which I share the same basic moral position on abortion. I disagree with the prochoice position on the fundamental moral question of abortion, but I agree at least on the conclusion of accepting the 1973 Supreme Court ruling and not trying to overturn it with a constitutional amendment.

My first disagreement with the prochoice adherents is basically the same as that with the prolife movement—the unwillingness to understand and perhaps try to accommodate the opposite position held by a great number of people in our society. Prolife people are appalled at the fact that there are more than 1.1 million abortions per year in the United States. Such a figure is of utmost concern to those who believe that truly human life is being taken in such numbers. The situation is frightening when in some areas there are more abortions than there are live births. I personally am dismayed at the number of abortions that are occurring in the United States. No one should lightly dismiss the very profound feelings of a great number of fellow citizens who hold that something akin to murder is taking place on such a vast scale in our society. Amidst the rhetoric and the political struggle neither side is really listening to the other.

Most prochoice adherents recognize that abortion is often a tragic decision. However, in practice we see little or no recognition of this tragic dimension. The vast majority of prochoice adherents admit that the fetus is not just tissue in the womb of the mother. Many hold to a developmental view according to which the fetus gradually comes to possess truly human life at some time in the womb. The failure even to mention this reality and to deal with it seems to indicate that the prochoice position does not take very seriously what many at least acknowledge in the beginning of their discussions.

Closely connected with this is the failure to recognize that many of the reasons for abortion might not be all that serious. One cannot deny that women can have very serious reasons for abortion, but also it seems all must admit the danger that abortion can become and to some degree has already become very commonplace—another form of birth control. These concerns, which are obviously of great importance to the prolife position but even seem to be implied in the position taken by most of the prochoice adherents, unfortunately do not find any concrete significance in their approach to this question.

The prochoice position frequently attacks the organized effort of the prolife group. Here I think fairness demands a recognition that both sides are comparatively well organized and well financed. Neither side really has a right to accuse the other side of being a well-organized, high-pressure lobby when both sides use the same means to accomplish their goals.

Another difficulty with the prochoice position points to the one-sided individualism of the approach. The entire question is decided by the woman with no relationship at all to the father or to others in society. Even here it would not be necessary to give a veto power to the father, the husband or others such as parents, but nonetheless there should be at least some form of consultation. This one-sided individualism stressing the rights of the woman seems to work against an understanding of familial relationships and bonds which are held in high esteem by many people in our society.[20]

V. The Public Funding of Abortion

What about the public funding of elective abortions for indigent pregnant women? The Supreme Court in June 1977 ruled that the government did not have to fund unnecessary, nontherapeutic abortions. The Congress passed a law in December 1977 saying that federal government funds can be used for abortions only when the mother's life is threatened, in promptly reported instances of rape and incest, and when two physicians judge that the continuation of the pregnancy would result in severe, long-lasting physical health damage to the mother. As a result of this action the question is now before the individual states: Should the state pay for elective abortions?

The Court ruled that states do not have to pay; the federal government will not pay for elective abortions this year.

There are some weaknesses and even contradictions in the reasoning of the majority opinion of the Court in the June 1977 cases. The Court claimed that on issues as sensitive as the public funding of nontherapeutic abortions the forum of the legislature and not the judiciary is the place for a proper resolution of the problem.[21] However, many opponents of the 1973 Supreme Court ruling on abortion laws attack the Court for exactly the same reason—the law should have been decided by the legislatures and not the judiciary.

The majority opinion in the funding cases uses an analogy with the famous Catholic school case in Oregon which was decided in 1925. The Court invalidated an Oregon law requiring a parent to send a child to a public school, thereby precluding the choice of a private school. The parents must be free to send their child to a private school if they so wish. The government, however, does not have to support the private school and is not infringing on the parental rights by financing the public school and thus favoring the choice of the public school. Likewise now the Court permits the state to make a policy choice favoring childbirth by paying for childbirth but not elective abortions. The woman still has the right to have an abortion, but she has to pay for it.[22] Many Catholics might be impressed by this analogy, but there is not an exact parallel. Even though private schools are not financed by the government, the child whose parents lack the money to send her/him to a private school still has the opportunity to attend a public school. In the case of abortion the poor woman without the funds cannot have an abortion.

The reasoning of the Court in the 1977 decision is basically simple. The failure to fund nontherapeutic abortions is illegal if it infringes upon a fundamental right of the woman. But it does not. The 1973 Court decision did not declare an unqualified constitutional right to an abortion. That decision affords constitutional protection against state or legal interference with certain aspects of an individual's personal privacy, including a woman's desire to terminate her pregnancy. A decision not to fund elective abortions places no obstacles or restrictions on access to abortion for the woman which were not already there. The indigency which may make abortion difficult and impossible was neither created nor affected by the Connecticut law withholding funding. The decision is totally in accord with the 1973 ruling. There is a basic difference between direct state interference with a protected activity and state encouragement of an alternative activity consonant with legislative policy (childbirth). Here the analogy is made with the obligation of the state to allow parents to send their children to private schools and the right of the state to fund only the public schools. The Court is not unsympathetic to the plight of an indigent woman who desires an abortion, but the Constitution does not provide judicial remedies for every social and economic ill.

There is some validity in this argument proposed by the Court. The concept of law and freedom in society explained earlier comes to a similar conclusion. The right is the right not to be interfered with legally in doing such an action. Such a right does not necessarily entitle one to be able to do this action in all circumstances. No legal obstacle may be put in the way. Everyone has a right to have cosmetic surgery if one so desires. No legal restraints may be put in the way. But the government does not have to fund cosmetic surgery for those who are not able to afford it. The right in this case is the right not to be interfered with and not the right of entitlement to be able to do whatever is involved.

Opponents of the 1977 Court decision argue that these decisions constitute a retreat from the earlier decision and show a distressing insensitivity to the plight of impoverished pregnant women. The basic ethical argument for those who disagree with the Court decision on funding rests on equalitarian justice. Justice demands that the poor should have the same rights as the middle class or the rich in this matter. There is inequity in denying to the poor what is available to the rich and the middle class.

This basic argument can be developed to show that in this case by omission the state is placing very significant obstacles or restrictions on the right of the pregnant woman to exercise her freedom. If financial help is given for childbirth, then freedom to abort is existentially missing if elective abortion is not also funded. Existentially the poor woman is restricted. The analogy with other rights such as the right to cosmetic surgery is not appropriate. Bearing an unwanted pregnancy is much more traumatic than not having cosmetic surgery and involves a more fundamental and basic matter for the woman. Since it affects her so intimately, she should have the existential right to an abortion.[23]

How should one react to the different arguments? Two preliminary considerations must be clear. Practically, the problem of poverty is not going to be solved by paying for abortions for poor women. Theoretically, an appeal to equalitarian justice fails to go to the heart of the matter. Distributive justice reminds us that all human beings have a right to that minimum of external goods which is necessary for decent human livelihood.

Also the problem should not be seen primarily in financial terms. Some might argue that providing abortions for all is too expensive and the money could be better used for other purposes. Others might argue that supporting unwanted children to be born in the future is more expensive, and therefore all abortions should now be funded. The ultimate rights and wrongs of the situation should not be settled primarily on the basis of finances.

Frankly, the problem of public funding for elective abortions places me in a dilemma which I think could be avoided. The very fact that we have to be faced with such a dilemma indicates the lack of rationality and willingness to compromise that has up to now characterized the public debate and political action over the very thorny question of abortion. The many people who believe abortion kills innocent human life have a strong argument on their side that their tax money should not support abortions. On the other hand, the poor people in our society are definitely disadvantaged by their poverty. I hope that ways can be found that abortions for indigent pregnant women can be financed without involving tax money of those who conscientiously believe that abortion is the taking of human life.

If the prolife side had accepted my earlier proposal to assure pregnant women the necessary medical, psychological, economic and social care necessary to bring the child to term and care for the child, then it would be appropriate to propose a similar program for the prochoice movement. Prochoice individuals and groups could organize to provide the necessary funding for elective abortions for all those who want them. Such a solution would be most equitable in our pluralistic society.

In theory it is also possible for a law to be proposed in such a way that the woman is truly free with the necessary counseling and financial help to make the decision either to bring the child to term or to abort. Another possibility might involve taxation of abortions to meet the cost of abortions for the poor.[24] Also a way might be found to allow conscientious objectors to make sure their tax monies are not used for abortions. There still seems to be room for creative political imagination to come up with some way of avoiding the dilemma mentioned above. I strongly hope such a possibility can become a reality.

As an antiabortionist and a believer in respecting as much as possible the existing pluralisms in our society I resent being faced with no other choice than the public funding of elective abortions. However, if this is the choice I am ultimately faced with, then reluctantly I would accept the public funding of abortions. The analysis of the arguments presented above tips me in this direction. In addition, I do not want to give an opportunity to others to weaken even more the rights of the poor. Opponents of public funding of abortion can point to a CBS News/*New York Times* poll indicating 63 percent of those polled do not believe the government should help a poor woman with her medical bills if she wants an abortion. But in the same poll only 64 percent thought the government should help a poor woman to pay her medical bills when she has a child. Such a strong minority opposed to funding childbirth indicates the strength of the opposition to the rights of poor people.

In summary, the need for public funding of elective abortions for the poor involving the tax monies of those opposed to abortions indicates a failure in creative political imagination in the midst of our pluralistic society. There should be a better and a different way to solve the problem. If I am faced with such a dilemma, I would reluctantly accept the public funding of elective abortions for the poor.

NOTES

1. Supreme Court of the United States, "Roe v. Wade," No. 70–18 (January 22, 1973), p. 49. (Slip opinion.)

2. *The New York Times* 125 (September 16, 1976), section A, pp. 1 and 30.

3. Supreme Court of the United States, "Beal v. Doe," No. 75–554 (June 20, 1977). (Slip opinion.)

4. Supreme Court of the United States, "Maher v. Roe," No. 75–1440 (June 20, 1977). (Slip opinion.)

5. Supreme Court of the United States, "Poelker v. Doe," No. 75–442 (June 20, 1977). (Slip opinion.) See also George J. Annas, "Let Them Eat Cake," *Hastings Center Report* 7, no. 4 (August 1977): 8–9.

6. "Maher v. Roe," p. 15.

7. P. L. 95–205, section 101.

8. *Federal Register* 43, no. 24 (February 3, 1978): 4832–4844.

9. Beverly Harrison, "How To Argue about Abortion: II," *Christianity and Crisis* 37 (December 26, 1977): 312–313.

10. James T. Burtchaell, "How To Argue about Abortion: II," *Christianity and Crisis* 37 (December 26, 1977): 314.

11. Judith Blake, "The Abortion Decisions: Judicial Review and Public Opinion," in *Abortion: New Directions For Policy Studies,* ed. Edward Manier, William T. Liu and David Solomon (Notre Dame, Indiana: University of Notre Dame Press, 1977), pp. 63–65.

12. In many ways this study is my response to a dispute which arose primarily among Christian ethicists in the fall of 1977 in reaction to the June 1977 Court decisions. The prochoice position is represented by "A Call to Concern" signed by over 200 ethicists which appeared in a number of places including *Christianity and Crisis* 37 (October 3, 1977): 222–224. This document recognizes that abortion, though serious and sometimes tragic, can be morally acceptable, strongly rejects the inflexibility of the absolutist position, calls for Medicaid

ABOUT THE AUTHOR

Charles E. Curran has been Ordinary Professor in the School of Theology, The Catholic University of America (Washington, D.C.) since 1971. Educated at St. Bernard's Seminary (Rochester, New York) and the Gregorian University (Rome, Italy), Father Curran has served as president of both the Catholic Theological Society of America (1969-1970) and the American Society of Christian Ethics (1971-1972). He was a senior research scholar at the Kennedy Center for Bioethics, Georgetown University (Washington, D.C.) in 1972.

His recent publications include *Catholic Moral Theology in Dialogue, New Perspectives in Moral Theology, Ongoing Revision in Moral Theology, Themes in Fundamental Moral Theology,* and *Issues in Sexual and Medical Ethics.*

Christianity and Crisis 37 (September 19, 1977): 202–207; (October 31, 1977): 253–255; (November 14, 1977): 264–266; (December 26, 1977): 311–318.

24. Peter Steinfels, "The Politics of Abortion," *The Commonweal* 104 (July 22, 1977): 456.

25. The results of this poll can be obtained from CBS News Information Services, 2020 M Street, N.W., Washington, D.C. 20036.

assistance for poor women seeking abortions and censures the heavy institutional involvement of the Roman Catholic bishops in seeking a Human Life Amendment. In response to "A Call to Concern" over twenty other Christian ethicists, including a high proportion of Roman Catholics but also others, issued "A Cause for Concern." Their position maintains that unborn children are truly human beings deserving the protection of the law, opposes abortion on request and defends attempts to enact legislation protecting the unborn child. I signed neither statement.

13. Here it is necessary to summarize positions I have developed at greater length elsewhere: see my *New Perspectives in Moral Theology* (Notre Dame, Indiana: University of Notre Dame Press, 1976), pp. 163–193; *Ongoing Revision in Moral Theology* (Notre Dame, Indiana: Fides/Claretian, 1975), pp. 107–143; *Issues in Sexual and Medical Ethics* (Notre Dame, Indiana: University of Notre Dame Press, 1978), pp. 198–226.

14. For a synthetic exposition of Murray's position see John Courtney Murray, *The Problem of Religious Freedom* (Westminster, Md.: Newman Press, 1965).

15. This criterion is developed in the Declaration on Religious Freedom, paragraph 7, *The Documents of Vatican II*, ed. Walter M. Abbott (New York: Guild Press, 1966), pp. 685–687. Footnote 20 on page 686 is not an official footnote of the document but a commentary written by Murray which clearly explains the criterion of public order and its threefold component parts. Footnote 21 is Murray's explanation of how this position dovetails with the American concept of jurisprudence.

16. Norman St. John-Stevas, *Birth Control and Public Policy* (Santa Barbara, California: Center for the Study of Democratic Institutions, 1960). St. John-Stevas, a Roman Catholic, here argues against efforts to prevent public spending for contraceptives.

17. Copies of this statement may be obtained from Publications Office, United States Catholic Conference, 1312 Massachusetts Avenue, N.W., Washington, D.C. 20005.

18. *Origins* 6 (September 30, 1976): 236.

19. "Pastoral Plan for Pro-Life Activities," p. 11. This document is also available from the United States Catholic Conference.

20. These criticisms refer to the prochoice position in general but also to "A Call to Concern."

21. "Maher v. Roe," p. 15.

22. "Maher v. Roe," pp. 12–13.

23. The negative position is developed in the dissenting opinion of Justice Brennan joined by Justices Marshall and Blackmun in "Maher v. Roe." The arguments for and against the 1977 funding rulings can be found in a symposium and in a continuing series of articles in

and tradition, xi, 13-5
Sanchez, Thomas, 181-2
Second Vatican Council, xi-xii,
  3, 8, 12, 13, 16, 43, 44, 50,
  64
sexual (conjugal, marital) act,
  31-5, 40, 193, 196-7, 203
sexual faculty, 33, 34, 35, 40,
  70, 193, 196-7, 203
sexuality, 32, 35, 39, 40, 41, 52,
  59, 71, 77-8, 177-8, 193,
  196
sin, sinfulness, 3, 4, 13, 31, 38,
  40-1, 61, 62-3, 66, 74-8,
  94, 124, 125, 128, 134, 154,
  161, 174, 176-7, 179, 188,
  194-5
situation ethics, 5
social ethics, xiii, 12, 50-1,
  Chapter 5
social mission of the church, 91,
  130-6
society and the right to health
  care, 147-150
  state, 44, 74-5, 88, 92, 107-9,
  117, 192, 230
  church and, 10, 44-5, 95,
  107-9, 131
sterilization, 7, 21, 33, 52, 54,
  182, 186, 189, 194, 196,
  197, 203
supernatural, 4, 65, 75, 86, 88,
  97, 99, 105, 112, 120,
  131-2
Syllabus of Errors, 11, 43

teaching office, 30, 103, 186-9,
  203
  and moral questions, 43-55
  see also magisterium, papal
  teachings
Thomas Aquinas, 5, 10, 11-2,
  62, 154-5, 180-1, 185,
  209-10, 222
Thomism, 4-5, 12, 185, 202,
  209
totality, principle of, 192-3,
  198-9
tradition, xi-xiv, 14, 154
  Catholic theological tradition,
  xii-xiv, 3, 8, 9, 13-5, 20, 22,
  38, 64, 72-3, 87, 129, 211,
  221
  Roman Catholic tradition and
  medical ethics, Chapter 7,
  esp. 173-84
  and scripture, xi, 13-5
transition, xi-xiv
transplantation, 178, 189
Trent, Council of, 176
Tübingen, 4

utilitarianism, 141, 203

values, 30, 32, 35, 39-43, 52,
  124, 135, 222-3
  abortion and the value of the
  fetus, 219-220
Veatch, Robert, 145-6, 164

Zacchia, Paolo, 182

natural law *(continued)*
  and religious liberty, 105,
    107–12
nature, 6, 14, 62, 65, 68, 74–5,
    87–8, 90, 97, 109–11, 120,
    128, 185, 192
  the natural, 4, 9, 106, 112,
    131
norms, 7, 30, 39–43, 52, 61, 179

Octogesima adveniens, 118
Outka, Gene, 143–6

Pacem in terris, 87, 102
papal teachings, xii, 10, 12, 29,
    30, 43, 44, 46, 103, 105,
    118, 187–9, 190
  see also magisterium, teaching
    office
paschal mystery, 40–1, 66
Pastoral Constitution on the
    Church in the Modern
    World, 64, 120, 197, 224
Paul VI, Pope, 29–30, 118, 189,
    225
person, 5, 6, 14, 31, 32, 39, 41–2,
    61, 93, 98, 101, 129,
    148–50, 151–3, 155, 162,
    164, 207, 212, 213–5, 217,
    220, 235
personalism, 94, 100–1, 134
physicalism, 30–7, 52, 202
Pius IX, Pope, 11, 43
Pius X, Pope, 106
Pius XI, Pope, 45, 94, 103–4,
    128, 189
Pius XII, Pope, 32, 33, 45, 49,
    60–1, 183, 187, 189, 192,
    196, 197, 199, 200
Plé, Albert, 61–2
pluralism, xi–xii, 7, 18, 21–2,
    50–2, 133–4, 162, 236, 238,
    240, 247

private property, 75, 77, 92–3,
    154–5
probabilism, 17, 183, 190
procreation, 31–2, 33, 41, 47,
    179, 193, 197
psychiatry, 24
  and homosexuality, 59, 69–70
  and moral theology, 24,
    59–68
psychoanalysis, 61–3
psychology, 61–4, 66, 67, 69

Quadragesimo anno, 94, 128

Rahner, Karl, 46
reason, 8–9, 13, 87–8, 89–90,
    111, 122, 123, 127, 129,
    185–6, 188, 190
  faith and, 9–10, 13, 64–5,
    175, 185
  and moral theology, 16,
    18–22, 25
redemption, 4, 9, 76, 87–8, 99,
    125–6
religious liberty
  see freedom, religious
Rerum novarum, 12, 88
resurrection destiny, 4, 76, 126
rhythm, 31, 32, 197
rights, 158
  abortion and the rights of the
    fetus, 219–20
  of patients, 195–6
  right to life, 191
Ryan, John A., 89–95, 101–4,
    109, 121, 134, 152, 155

sacraments, 6, 8, 14, 174, 176,
    177, 183, 200
sacred scripture, 6, 9, 10, 14,
    23, 69, 71, 87, 90, 99, 101,
    112, 121, 185

human life in the abortion
  discussion, 207
  its beginning, 7, 34–5, 198,
    203, 207–19, 225–7, 233,
    237
Human Sexuality, 39–42
Humanae vitae, v, 7, 18, 189, 225
  and moral theology, 29–55,
    201, 202–3
Humani generis, 187

in vitro fertilization, 164
incarnation, 4, 14, 76, 125
indissolubility of marriage
  see marriage, indissolubility

John XXIII, Pope, 45, 87, 102,
  104
justice, 49, 51, 88, 90, 92, 108,
    118, 121, 131, 133, 136,
    140, 142, 151, 155, 236
  see also distributive,
    commutative, equalitarian
    justice
Justice in the World, 131

Kenkel, Frederick P., 96–9
kingdom of God, 4, 5, 8, 75,
    90–1, 112, 120–1, 124–5

Leo XIII, Pope, 12, 44–5, 86–8,
    109, 118
liberation theology, 22, 23, 119,
    121, 135
liturgy, 6, 23, 51

McNeill, John, 72–3
magisterium
  hierarchical, xii, 7, 17–9, 33,
    43, 45, 47–8, 50–4, 70, 109,

    120, 187, 189, 202, 204,
    221, 224, 227
  of the laity, 48
  of theologians, 48
  see also papal teachings,
    teaching office
Maguire, Daniel, 48, 203
manuals of moral theology, xii,
    3, 6, 8, 15, 16, 19, 75, 201,
    202, 203
marital act
  see sexual act
marriage, 14, 42, 74, 93, 117,
    177, 179, 180, 182, 183,
    184, 188, 193
  indissolubility, 36–7
masturbation, 6, 35, 183, 197,
    203
Mater et magistra, 102
Maurin, Peter, 98–9
mediation, 8, 14–5, 87, 120–3,
    124, 125, 134, 174, 212
medical ethics, xii, 20, 22, 36
  Roman Catholic, Chapter 7
methodology, xi–xii, 6–7, 13,
    16, 18, 21–2, 30–43, 52, 55,
    64, 67, 88, 90–5, 97–8,
    99–101, 102–5, 106, 108–9,
    112, 118–20, 128, 133, 136,
    184–5, 201–4
models of moral theology, 4–5
  deontological, 4–5
  relationality-responsibility,
    4–5, 22
  teleological, 4–5
modernism, 11
Murray, John Courtney, 43–5,
    105–112, 236

natural family planning, 31, 197
natural law, 9, 37, 65, 74–5,
    87–8, 90–4, 97, 126, 127,
    147, 162, 180, 184–6, 188,
    189, 190, 191, 201–2

Day, Dorothy, 99–101
death, 49–50, 66, 174–5, 182, 189, 208, 213
and dying, 199–200
Declaration on Religious Freedom, 236
"Declaration on Sexual Ethics," 18, 40
dissent, v, xi, 7, 17, 29–31, 43, 46–7, 50, 112, 191, 202–3, 225
distributive justice, 91–2, 121–2, 151–6, 246
and health care, xiii, Chapter 6, esp. 156–67
divorce, 36, 52, 53
and remarriage, 7, 54–5
Doncel, Joseph, 209–10
double effect, principle of, 34, 52, 193–4, 203, 221–2

ecclesiology, 47–8, 51, 134–6, 177, 203
egalitarian justice, 142–7, 148, 159–61, 245–6
eschaton, 4, 75, 124
eschatological pull, xiv, 6, 77
eschatology, 38, 101, 123–6, 134
euthanasia, 36, 52, 199, 204
evil, 37–9, 40, 46–7, 72
moral, 37–8, 46, 77, 202
ontic, 37, 39, 46, 77–8
physical, 37, 46, 202
premoral, 37–9, 46, 61, 77–8, 202
experimentation, 178, 189, 200–1

faith, 9, 14, 16, 48, 52, 61, 63, 64, 65, 84–5, 120–1, 134, 176, 187, 225–7

family, 42, 74, 117–8, 185
finitude, 38, 75, 77–8
fornication, 35, 181
freedom, 10–1, 51, 59, 61, 84, 88, 101, 111, 122, 127, 131, 150, 152, 190, 235, 236–7, 246
religious freedom, 44, 84, 95, 105, 107–10, 150, 152
Freud, Sigmund, 24, 60–2, 64
Fuchs, Josef, 74–5
Furfey, Paul Hanly, 99, 105–6

genetics, 35, 66–7, 159, 163, 189, 211
genetic engineering, 178
German-American Catholics, 84, 95–8, 134
grace, 6, 65, 68, 88, 99
Greeley, Andrew, 30, 54
Grisez, Germain, 31, 210, 211

Häring, Bernard, 4–7, 9, 204, 210, 224
Harvey, John, 72–3
health care, 162–3
and distributive justice, Chapter 6
hermeneutic, 6, 43–4, 106, 121, 179
hierarchy of truths, 48
historical consciousness, 7, 38, 108–9, 120, 128, 162, 201
homosexuality, xii, 35, 38, 53, 63
and moral theology and psychiatry, 59, 68–78
and theory of compromise, 71–3, 76–8
human, the, 7, 9, 65, 66–8, 122–3, 177
and reason, 9–10, 13, 64, 175,

Index

abortion, xii, 21, 34–5, 52, 177, 178–9, 181, 183, 188–9, 194, 198, 203
  and the beginning of human life, 203, 207–19, 225–7, 233, 237
  constitutional amendment, 236–42
  ethical aspects, Chapter 8
  legal aspects (prolife and prochoice positions), 230–43
  public funding, 232, 243–8
  role of the bishops, 239–41
adultery, 35, 42, 186
American Catholics, xiii, 29–30
  and social ethics, Chapter 4, 131
Americanism, 86–7
analogy, 8–9
anthropology, 6
artificial contraception, v, xii, 7, 21, 29–34, 37–9, 43, 44–6, 50, 52, 54–5, 179, 186, 189, 196, 203, 239
artificial insemination, 6, 33, 189, 197, 203
  AID, 34, 197, 203

Capellmann, Carl, 193
Casti connubii, 45, 189
Catholic Worker Movement, 95, 98–101, 134, 135
Christian life and moral theology, 16, 20, 22–5
church and state, 10, 44–5, 95, 107–9, 131
common good, 148–50, 158, 162
commutative justice, 92, 151–2, 154
compromise theory, 73–8
  and homosexuality, 71–3, 76–8
Congar, Yves, 48
conjugal act
  see sexual act
conscience, 184, 189–90, 235
Constitution on the Church, 202
contraception
  see artificial contraception
conversion, 5, 76, 135
creation, 4, 9, 40, 75, 88, 92, 122, 125, 150, 154–5
  creator, 8–9
Cronin, John F., 102–5